THE EURASIAN CORE AND ITS EDGES

Dialogues with Wang Gungwu
on the History of the World

The **Institute of Southeast Asian Studies (ISEAS)** was established as an autonomous organization in 1968. It is a regional centre dedicated to the study of socio-political, security and economic trends and developments in Southeast Asia and its wider geostrategic and economic environment. The Institute's research programmes are the Regional Economic Studies (RES, including ASEAN and APEC), Regional Strategic and Political Studies (RSPS), and Regional Social and Cultural Studies (RSCS).

ISEAS Publishing, an established academic press, has issued more than 2,000 books and journals. It is the largest scholarly publisher of research about Southeast Asia from within the region. ISEAS Publishing works with many other academic and trade publishers and distributors to disseminate important research and analyses from and about Southeast Asia to the rest of the world.

THE EURASIAN CORE AND ITS EDGES

Dialogues with Wang Gungwu
on the History of the World

Ooi Kee Beng

INSTITUTE OF SOUTHEAST ASIAN STUDIES
Singapore

First published in Singapore in 2015 by ISEAS Publishing
Institute of Southeast Asian Studies
30 Heng Mui Keng Terrace
Pasir Panjang
Singapore 119614

E-mail: publish@iseas.edu.sg
Website: <http://bookshop.iseas.edu.sg>

All rights reserved. No part of this publication may be reproduced, stored in a retrieval system, or transmitted in any form or by any means, electronic, mechanical, photocopying, recording or otherwise, without the prior permission of the Institute of Southeast Asian Studies.

© 2015 Institute of Southeast Asian Studies, Singapore

The responsibility for facts and opinions in this publication rests exclusively with the author and his interpretations do not necessarily reflect the views or the policy of the publisher or its supporters.

ISEAS Library Cataloguing-in-Publication Data

Ooi, Kee Beng, 1955–
The Eurasian core and its edges : dialogues with Wang Gungwu on the history of the world.
1. World history.
2. Southeast Asia—Civilization—Foreign influences.
3. China—Civilization—Foreign influences.
I. Wang, Gungwu, 1930–
II. Title.
III. Title: Dialogues with Wang Gungwu on the History of the World.
D21.3 W24   2015

ISBN 978-981-4519-85-4 (soft cover)
ISBN 978-981-4519-86-1 (e-book, PDF)

Typeset by Superskill Graphics Pte Ltd
Printed in Singapore by Mainland Press Pte Ltd

CONTENTS

Prologue vii

Introduction xiii

Chapter One   Of Cores and Edges   1

Chapter Two   The Two-Ocean Mediterranean   57

Chapter Three   Southeast Asia and Foreign Empires   94

Chapter Four   China's Struggle with the Western Edge   141

Chapter Five   Combining Continental and Maritime Power   213

Epilogue   228

List of Publications by Wang Gungwu since 2008   238

Index   243

About the author   253

PROLOGUE

I should start by telling readers that they will not be enjoying reading this book as much as I have enjoyed producing it. The chance to talk undisturbed for hours with Professor Wang Gungwu in the quiet of his various offices at the National University of Singapore is not a gratification given many mortals.

Over the last decade living in Singapore and working at the Institute of Southeast Asian Studies (ISEAS) of which Professor Wang is the chairman, I have had opportunities — though never enough, I must quickly add — to listen to him talk on a wide variety of subjects and in many different contexts. Along with everyone else in the audiences, I have always been impressed by how someone like him who gives so many lectures always manages to stay entertaining and interesting, be it in strength of delivery or profundity of content. Often he seems to speak without prepared paper, and always he provides a big picture of the subject at hand, giving new angles his listeners had not thought of.

And so the idea came to me to write a book based on interviews with Professor Wang. Apart from the obvious goal of recording some of his thoughts that his busy schedule does not allow him to put in print, I hoped that listening to him as he formulates his ideas would offer me some crucial insight into how he thinks, thereby delving into the mechanics and the organics of how he connects his thoughts.

Using this approach of having the doyen of Asian and East Asian history talk at length to an amateur historian has certain advantages, the chief of which is that the listener, meaning me, can take on the role of conveying the expert's big picture to the common reader in a non-academic fashion. The major disadvantage also stems from that aspiration, though. An amateur lacks the deep understanding of world history that would allow him to probe certain issues more thoroughly, or to be more critical of what he hears. As it was, I was often overwhelmed by the tightness of Professor Wang's thoughts, and by his ability to present streams of thought in an impressively interwoven form.

But then, my aim is mainly about understanding this great scholar's insights on the historical forces that formed the world we know, and that are of salience to present scholarship about Southeast Asia, East Asia, South Asia, Asia at large — and, of course, the world as a whole. What this exciting project also makes me realize is that World History as a subject is only just emerging; and traditional attempts at describing humanity's past, fail for being too localized when not Eurocentric.

Also, there is another — a much more personal — side to this. My present job as deputy director at the Institute of Southeast Asian Studies loads me with the responsibility of constructing — with the director's help — the institute's areas of research as comprehensively as possible for the coming decade. To do that properly, I need all the inspiration I can get, and what more efficacious way is there than to get that from the institute's highly respected chairman, and through a series of concentrated interviews? And what better way to present that to the educated public than in dialogue form?

I would therefore advise the reader simply to sit back and enjoy the book as it is written, and treat it as a source of inspiration for further thought on the many aspects of world history, and how these influence how we think of the connectedness of humanity's many civilizations. Had a more academic version of these ideas been attempted by me based on what Professor Wang shared with me, I fear it might not have been completed and it would in any case have made the work less accessible to the general public.

What Professor Wang gave me — and for this I am eternally grateful to him — is an extensive understanding of world history. These interviews gave me nutritious food for thought that will sustain my curiosity on historical matters for quite a while. The tapestry that Professor Wang revealed to me is so multifaceted and yet so comprehensible that it has already enriched my own understanding of historical forces still at work in the world.

His generosity and kindness to me have been tremendous. I remember how often some old gentleman would proudly state to me in passing whenever the name Wang Gungwu was mentioned, "Oh, he was my lecturer at Universiti Malaya". Since I never went to any Malaysian university, and I would not have been wise enough to have chosen History as my subject in any case, that common boast always managed to unsettle me. I inevitably felt envious of those who actually did study under Professor Wang. These people do not boast in vain. That could be the real reason I thought up this project — I wouldn't put such slyness beyond me. At some deep level I must have seen a chance to be his private student for a while and to listen to him discuss brilliant ideas just for me — ideas that, by the way, once understood, seem so obvious.

We all have had that experience every now and then on hearing a novel idea, of wondering, "Why didn't I think of that?" Well, I had lots of these during the interviews with Professor Wang, and I am convinced any reader of this book will too. The implications of Professor Wang's rendition of world history are extensive indeed and I am very happy to have been instrumental in making it popularly available.

Professor Wang wished me already at the first interview to consider this book to be my book, not his. I gratefully accept that generosity and also full responsibility for the final product. This is my book then, I am proud to say. There are bound to be instances in this conversation where I missed some subtle point that Professor Wang was making, and which in the process of transcription and editing may have ended up as a misleading opinion. For these, I apologize and I am more than willing to take responsibility — it is a small sacrifice worth making for the purpose of achieving what I think is an exciting piece of work that will enthrall readers of all ages from any part of the world. That I dare say.

Given Professor Wang's illustrious career as an academician, the richness of this book's content should not surprise the reader. Famed for his groundbreaking work on the overseas Chinese and many other subjects, he has left a deep imprint on the intellectual world throughout the region — and the world. For the very few who do not know of him, let me provide a quick introduction. Born in 1930 in Surabaya in Indonesia, Professor Wang grew up in the town of Ipoh in the northern Malaysian state of Perak. He gained his Bachelor and Master's degrees in history at the University of Malaya in Singapore before obtaining his PhD in 1957 from the School of Oriental and African Studies at the University of London. In 1968 he moved to the Australian National University after several years teaching at the University of Malaya (in Singapore and Malaya), after which he became the vice-chancellor of the University of Hong Kong (1986–95). He has since been based in Singapore, holding key academic and administrative positions.

Deliberations on Chinese philosophy concerning politics, ethics and social cohesion are also included in this book. This is not strange, since both of us are of Chinese origin (brought up in Malaysia), and deeply interested in Chinese culture. This fact should act as a good reminder of the disruption to the internal dynamics of civilizations, polities and peoples that the sudden arrival of modernity — be it in the form of settlers, guns, germs or ideas — meant. *Cultural unsettlement* and *philosophical amnesia* are the unavoidable legacy for many throughout the world, no matter how well they have survived the intrusion of Western powers; and even with economic success, finding a natural place in the modern scheme of things remains a primary objective for them. China's case is poignant and illuminative. This unsettlement is certainly exacerbated by the ceaselessly changing nature of modern life, which affects everyone. But perhaps it is this climate of overwhelming change that will allow for old grievances and ancient quarrels to dissipate.

The five conversations on which the chapters of this book are based were each about three hours long. They took place in 2013, on the mornings of 7, 14 and 21 January, 25 March and 14 October, at the East Asia Institute and the Lee Kuan Yew School of Public Policy, both at the National University of Singapore. I would like to thank ISEAS Director Mr Tan Chin Tiong for the support he gave this project, Ms Li Shufen and Ms Ten Leu-Jiun for transcribing the interviews, and my lovely wife Ms Laotse Sacker for acting so graciously and ably as test reader for the final draft.

One final technical note: Chinese pinyin terms in this book are all written in italics except for those I subjectively feel have become common usage in the West. Those written in other transcription forms are not italicized.

INTRODUCTION

HUMAN HISTORY WAS CONTINENTAL HISTORY

To my mind, World History is an emergent subject made possible by the recent passing of the unipolar political world of colonial times and by the even more recent closing of the bipolarizing Cold War. The ideas found in this book should be taken as a cogent contribution towards the development of global perspectives that are at once inclusive of and sympathetic to the endless struggles of civilizations, against themselves and against each other.

Allow me here to simplify the content of this book, whose basic aim is to recognize and acknowledge a forgotten key actor in world history. With the traditional fetish for dividing the world into East and West — where for the West, the East started at its very doorstep; and for the East, the West was a much vaguer concept — the most important factor connecting these was often ignored, or was treated as a supplementary story. This is Central Asia.

The human dynamics exploding out of the Eurasian geographic core throughout the centuries did indeed configure the nature of the many civilizations settled around its edges. This is obvious to anyone knowledgeable about Chinese history, where the importance of Central Asia was testified to by the occasional successful conquest of imperial lands by nomadic groupings. For India, endless streams of conquerors would flow in from the north through the narrow passes of Afghanistan. It is undeniable that the history of Western civilization is strongly coloured by struggles against Eastern invaders, be they Persian troops, Arab horsemen, Turkish armies, or the hordes of the Huns and the Mongols.

The imperative for civilizations at the edges of the Euroasian landmass to resist military threats from within the depths of the continent has left dramatic legacies for modern man to observe. On physical landscapes, the elements, given enough time, clearly distinguish major terrestrial fault lines from minor ones. And so, rift valleys, volcanic cracks, grand canyons and growing mountain ranges reveal to us the persistent pressures that the Earth has to suffer. Human history does the same, conjuring over time political and cultural fault lines that express the tensions between peoples and reiterate the obstinacy of these conditions. The basic thrust of this book not only draws attention to major fault lines, but also reveals their related nature. In doing this, the rise of maritime powers in Europe and their ability to circumvent continental besiegement can be seen as the commencement of global politics and economics. As Professor Wang Gungwu reiterates ever so often, "The Global is Maritime".

One such major fault line cuts from east to west across the Mediterranean Sea, where battle after battle and war after war have over the centuries edged a deep divide between the Muslim lands in northern Africa and the Christian lands of Europe. The crusades, lasting from 1096 and 1291, did not decide things for good.[1] Far from it. In fact, the final fault lines between Europe and its historical nemesis to the east were decided through the fall of Byzantium in 1453, and in battles fought in the Mediterranean between the Roman Christians and the Ottoman Empire between 1521 and 1580.[2] The independence of Greece from the Ottoman Empire was achieved only in 1832, following a sea battle that saw combined British, French and Russian ships defeat the Ottoman-Egyptian navy.

On the other side of the continental landmass stands the formidable Great Wall of China. Its many sections may be standing in ruins today, but together they express most poignantly the fear of the marauding hordes of Central Asia, which dictated imperial policies for millennia, and in all probability historically reined in the maritime impulse of Chinese officialdom. The First Emperor, *Qinshihuang*, was already putting vast and ill-afforded resources into constructing walls to keep marauding horsemen out of his newly conquered agrarian lands; and we see the emperors of the *Ming* Dynasty sixteen centuries later doing the same, and with better technology. All was, however, to be in vain for the *Ming*, who fell in 1644 to the Manchus. Thus, the long-lived Chinese Empire entered modern times under the reign of invaders who originated from within the continental landmass.

At the northwestern end of the Indian subcontinent lies another region given to war and conflict. Through the passes here have flowed invaders from the north, such as the Mongols and the Moghuls, and from the west, Persian kings and Alexander the Great's Greek army.[3]

Other deep fault lines include the Palestinian corridor joining the Nile lands to the fertile fields of the Tigris and the Euphrates, and perhaps those within Europe, such as that between the Slavic and the Teutonic peoples, another between the Teutonic and the Latin peoples, and yet another between the British Isles and the continent.

For Europe, where the impetus for civilization and commerce had come from the Mediterranean lands, the loss of the southern coasts and the Holy Land signaled besiegement by a mortal foe and isolation from the riches of the rest of the world.

BREAKING THE SIEGE

With the advent of maritime technologies and skills that made global travel possible, the possibilities for commercial trade, resource extraction, military conquest and religious contest increased tremendously. The dynamics of global relations changed forever. Indeed, the global as we know it today is realized through maritime power.

The Spanish and the Portuguese took the lead, attaining huge tracts of real estate in the Americas and throughout the world within a few decades. All this took place sadly at the cost of indigenous peoples found in these lands. Their kingdoms were destroyed and their peoples killed, enslaved or infected with diseases by these invaders, who were in effect breaking continental besiegement and seeking religious freedom for themselves and supremacy for their religions. The discovery of the Americas brought new actors into the global fray.

In the meantime, powered by the rise of the middle class, a new force soon emerged in the form of Holland and Britain. Their impact on the political and demographic configuration of South and Southeast Asia has been enormous. In fact, the term "Southeast Asia" was coined for military purposes during the Japanese occupation of East Asia. It went on to serve in the Cold War as well, and now remains with us as a given geopolitical entity.

The Cold War, as argued by Professor Wang, was very much part of the traditional contest between continental power and maritime power; between the core and its edges. The United States of America, the dominant power of our times, is dominant through enjoying a secure continental base as well as unsurpassed maritime power. No other power can imagine attaining anything similar to this immutable advantage.

Today, a century after China was forced to become a republic, we see a new fault line appearing on the surface of the globe. As with the Mediterranean, this one is maritime, and runs across the East China Sea from north to south, extending into the South China Sea. Within the paradigm advanced in this book, this frontier, which some have recognized to be a maritime encirclement of China by Western powers, looks set to be the major fault line in the global age. The western edge of the Eurasian landmass, breaking out after centuries of besiegement, reached the eastern edge almost two hundred years ago. It took China, the great power on the latter edge, that long to reorientate itself away from its age-old fixation with continental strategy, to embrace modern techniques of public administration and economic production, and to realize that modern influence indeed requires maritime clout.

Japan managed that revolution much more effectively, no doubt. But it was Japanese expansion beyond their islands beginning just at the turn of the twentieth century that dug ever deeper the new boundary of conflict that had begun with the Opium Wars (1839–42; 1856–60). The Pacific War (1941–45) bonded the Americans to the eastern end of the Eurasian landmass, just as the war against Hitler in Europe (1939–45) had done at the western end. China turning communist in 1949 made East Asia a major arena for the Cold War. The Korean War (1950–53) and the Vietnam War (1954–75) that followed continued to etch a frontier of conflict along China's coast.[4]

In many ways, the rationale for this new fault line is better understood through reference to the powerful and persistent dynamics of war which centuries ago encouraged traditional coastal seafarers in Europe to escape religious besiegement and cross the oceans. These found more wealth, power and influence in faraway lands than in their wildest imagination, and globalized the world in the process. To be sure, this globalizing process disrupted the internal dynamics of all the civilizations of the world, bringing chaos to all. But those who survived this undermining onslaught have taken on new roles in the new maritime-conduced global order.

China's recent rise makes it the power most able to defy the United States in the near future. However, given the fact that its continental base is always vulnerable, the reach of its power is quite limited compared to that of the United States. But in breaking its historical besiegement, the Western world has also changed the game for the other continental edges. The game is no longer about the core and its edges, but about how edges are to get along most constructively. Strategic mindsets relevant to the old scenario are with all probability no longer effective in the new setting.

To me, the conversations I have had with Professor Wang have been extremely stimulating, and the implications of his ideas on how I should view world events of the past are great indeed. But most important of all is how his understanding of the historical dynamics that led to the modern international situation provides new options for how we are to solve — or at least diminish — present tensions between world powers. We are talking about the emergence of a paradigmatic shift in the study of international relations — and not only in the many disciplines more obviously affected by his way of thinking, such as history and area studies.

Notes

1. For an inspiring study of the Crusades and their profound and lasting effects on global politics and interfaith relations, see Karen Armstrong, *Holy War: The Crusades and their Impact on Today's World*. Incidentally, according to the *Oxford English Dictionary*, the term "crusade" came into use only retrospectively. It did not appear in English until as late as 1757, about a century after the French term *"croisade"* came to denote a series of military trips to the Holy Land.

2. See Roger Crowley, *Empires of the Sea: The Final Battles for the Mediterranean, 1521–1580* (London: Faber & Faber, 2008).
3. For a good history of this region, see Paddy Docherty, *The Khyber Pass: A History of Empire and Invasion* (London: Faber & Faber, 2007).
4. Incidentally, heightened American military engagement in the Middle East and in Afghanistan since the end of the twentieth century reveals further the persistent conflicts between maritime powers and continental ones that mark the last three thousand years of human history, which this book discusses.

Chapter 1

OF CORES AND EDGES

CHINESE ENTRY INTO THE GLOBAL AGE

OOI KEE BENG: Professor Wang, let's start with the idea of China as a nation state. China becoming a republic in 1911 must have been earth shattering for many Chinese. It certainly signified the crumbling of a world view that had lasted for millennia. Within forty years of that event, a form of communism would take over instead to dictate the national paradigm.

WANG GUNGWU: To be exact, that shift was precipitated by a nationalist paradigm more than a communist paradigm. China becoming a nation state was definitely very unfamiliar to most Chinese intellectuals, requiring as it did of them to shift away from their tradition of an Imperial China and from the ideals of Confucius and other historical thinkers, in order to adapt to what was a new and revolutionary idea. In that sense, the revolution in China was not a communist one to start with, but a nationalist one.

In moving from empire to nation state, they had to go through a period wherein they turned away from the past in order to look at China afresh, and to imagine a new kind of state. And

I must say that the early groups of scholars from the end of the nineteenth century down to 1949 were admirably adventurous in exploring other traditions. In other words, they took the West very seriously indeed. We tend to forget them now because they lost out after 1949, but the truth is a lot of them actually did a lot of studies on world history. They were looking particularly at Western history — why was the West so successful? They wanted an explanation, and quickly noticed how different Western history was from Chinese or East Asian history.

So what is the underlying difference? I think that when translating Plato, Aristotle, the Greeks and other European classics into Chinese, they already noticed that there was no world history as such. It was only European history *writ large* that they were reading, translating and reinterpreting for their Chinese audience. But they were also gaining a certain idea, a very important one in fact. They recognized that the West saw China as being on the fringes of civilization. Suddenly, the centre was *there* instead of *here*. And so, to what extent China could become part of that centre, or reengage as a new and opposing centre, was on their minds, and would remain on their minds for a long time to come. But the recognition that there was an ancient alternative civilizational centre that by the nineteenth century had proved to be more successful than China, inspired them to go in pursuit of something novel. All the social sciences were as yet new to them, even economics; and so they began to absorb some of these social science perspectives. But historians were the ones who impressed the Chinese audience most, because being able to place themselves in world history was important for them if they were to grasp where they were to go from here.

What they essentially recognized was that the successful centre they were dealing with was actually based around the Mediterranean Sea. They realized that the Western interpretation of history stemmed from Egypt, and from Babylonia. In that region, rival political and social systems had been evolving; and, eventually, it was Greek opposition to the Egyptian model, the Babylonian model and, most directly, the Persian model, which gave rise to the city states. Now, these city states were really quite different from what had gone before. They were miniature organizations, whereas the others were great states. Egypt controlled the whole of the Nile; Babylon ruled over the whole of the Tigris-Euphrates; and, ultimately, the expansive Persian Empire modeled itself on what went before. And so we have the great story of the Greeks resisting the Persians. The Chinese, on being introduced to Western history, could already see these two political systems fighting each other. In the end, the Athenian ideal lost out to the Spartans and to the Alexandrian Empire. Alexander was certainly imperialistic in the same way as the Persians, and Rome even more so. But, deep down, that different approach remained of "rule by miniaturizing political participation", which never took the ideal of imperial bureaucracy too seriously, and which would cause reversion to the city-state idea throughout the whole medieval period down to modern times. Deep down, the idea of the small political unit lived on.

OKB: All politics being basically local...

WGW: Yes. Small units collaborate as they will to form a larger system, but the root must be local. The Greek idea evolved towards a civil society idea. That is what is essentially still happening today.

Now, the Chinese read all that and realized that their case was very, very different. Recognizing that the centre of what they were up against came out of the Mediterranean, raised the question as to whether there was something moral, cosmological, philosophical, religious or spiritual, that sustains that centre and which is different from what sustains the Chinese. Whatever it is, it evolved from the Egyptians and the Babylonians down to the Roman Empire, and so into the rest of Europe. So what is this underlying something that is different?

The Chinese in their turn also did develop an empire, and their empire had many things in common with the Roman Empire. It had a bureaucracy, for example, although one could see that the nature of the two bureaucracies was different; one being based on warrior classes and the other on the literati. And this was a difference that moved the two in different directions.

Religious thought was also dissimilar. The religions of the Jews, the Christians and ultimately the Muslims all came with the idea of one god. In fact, the Egyptians already conceived of a monotheistic system, but it took a long time for the idea of one god overcoming all other gods to become dominant. It took over a thousand years, but the Jews did imbibe that idea. In fact, one should say that the Jews started in Egypt, and that the Moses story is an Egyptian one. Many other areas did not accept this one-god idea. Particularly in Central Asia and South Asia, there were other alternatives.

My understanding is that the Chinese realized that this one-god scheme was not something they could easily accommodate into their belief system, which has multiple gods. But the Chinese also have an underlying transcendental idea of *Tianxia* (All under heaven). Now, *Tian* may or may not signify god, and although there is oneness denoted, one still has to ask if *Tian* equates god. That's something that Christian missionaries in China have been struggling with for a long time. Chinese who convert to Christianity very often try to reconcile the difference and claim that *Tian* is in fact God. So you get *Tianzhu*. The Jesuits were very good at transcending such differences. They tried to combine the two — *Tianzhu* means Master of *Tian* — and this appealed to some Chinese. It got them away from the idea of multiple gods, which was both confusing and localized.

Chinese intellectuals educated in the Confucian and other traditions were not persuaded, however, and they continued to explore other ways. What they took in the end from the West, which was most appealing to them and which did not threaten their own insights, was *secularism* — secular science. It was eighteenth and nineteenth century post-Enlightenment secularism and science and all that followed from the scientific revolution which they found acceptable. The one-god faith and the idea of miniature political systems were difficult for them to embrace.

This explains to some extent why the Chinese intellectuals, when they gave up the Confucian state in the nineteenth century, turned to nationalism and republicanism. The model to copy for them was secular and scientific Europe. The spiritual and religious side was not for them. They did recognize that democracy and republicanism were part of the Greco-Roman tradition, and that that tradition did produce scientific thinking, logic, mathematics and so on. But the Judeo-Christian tradition they would not accept. They really started their understanding of the modern world from the French Revolution onwards. That revolution provided the model for them — secular, progressive, scientific; and dismissive of monotheistic reason, such as that propounded by the likes of Rene Descartes.

In the meantime, they had also to recognize that it was the conflict of ideas in the Mediterranean which produced a civilization that became incomparably powerful by marrying — if I may borrow the terms that Europeans would use today — the Judeo-Christian tradition to the Greco-Roman tradition. This conjunction eventually gave birth to the secular, modern and rational post-Enlightenment world. That's how these Chinese intellectuals would have seen it. No doubt, that point of view unacceptably pushed China to the fringes of world history. But, you see, that view is also somewhat narrow. For one thing, there are two fringes involved here — East Asia and South Asia. They are fringes in the sense that they have something distinctly their own.

THE CORE IN WORLD HISTORY

Now we come to the most interesting part, the part that I think puzzles the Chinese and others more than anything else — the role of nomadic Eurasia in history. For two to three thousand years an alternative existed there. If the nomadic Central Asian powers are acknowledged as a civilizational centre, then even the European Mediterranean is a fringe, just as China is a fringe. Giving recognition to Central Asia's central role in world history puts China on par with the rest. And in any case, threats from Central Asia had always been the major security concern for Chinese emperors.

Interestingly enough, the West has always had the same fixation. They experience similar problems with Scythians, Indo-Scythians, the various Huns down to the Tartars, the Mongols, the Turks — and Russia! Why, Russia has been absorbed into the Eurasian core to this day!

If we accept Eurasia as a civilizational centre, then it also becomes the core of world history, and all others become edges — East Asia, South Asia, Western Europe and the Mediterranean. Then, each edge studied for how it has been interacting with that core, gives China a valid chance to reinterpret history in a way that does not require it to be subordinated to other edges.

OKB: World history would have one core, and an integrated and balanced narrative would be possible.

WGW: Correct. Things now do make sense to the Chinese. The whole of Chinese history became continental because the driver of human history — Central Asia — always forced the Chinese to look inland. Their defences were always against that core; against the powerful horsemen who regularly came out of the Steppes to wage war against them. So the whole of Chinese civilization was built on differentiating the Chinese from those people. In that sense, even for the Chinese, the core was not China. The core was actually Eurasia, in differentiation from which the Chinese created a civilization to defend themselves.

More correctly perhaps, to them, the world had two centres — theirs and Eurasia's; and the engagement between these was in effect world history. South Asia and the Mediterranean were fringes, and quite irrelevant as far as they were concerned.

By resisting Eurasia, they evolved into a rich and powerful civilizational centre, creating an alternative to it and managing to defend their values against those of the nomads — again, again and again. Now, if that is a valid interpretation of history, then the European phase of maritime victory over the continental powers is just a moment in history. It is only three or four hundred years old, if you start with the rise of the Portuguese. It was really only in the eighteenth and nineteenth century that maritime power replaced continental power — and not entirely either. Even the Cold War was a contest between maritime and continental powers.

The Soviet Union collapsed in the early 1990s, but you see how even the United States now wants to be involved in Central Asia. It wants to have bases in Kyrgyzstan and Uzbekistan because the Americans recognize that they cannot think in maritime terms only. Maritime terms alone were fine for a small island country like Britain. The British Empire did set a particular pattern, but it was only a short-term one, lasting only one or two hundred years. But it has had to be replaced by this balancing between maritime and continental power.

This helps the Chinese understand their own history: The Continental Phase gave them their civilization; and then they lost out during the Maritime Phase. The latter destroyed their civilization, and for over a hundred years they have been trying to recover. But now that they are recovering, they must not miss out on developing a maritime power of their own. They feel that if they don't have a strong navy — and this is not for attacking anybody — they will be vulnerable, and they will never be able to represent this newly recognized force, this effective balance between maritime and continental power.

So they are like the United States in that sense — both are a maritime and continental power. If you take that broader perspective, the Chinese hope — it's still only a hope — is that they can offer another way of looking at the world, another political culture to stand up against the essentially naval and maritime Mediterranean culture that now encompasses the world. The Chinese have successfully turned their continental condition into a strength, while the Russians have failed so far. But the Russians can be useful to the Chinese, and if peace is kept, the two can work out a concord to ensure that intra-continental relations do not deteriorate. That way, the Chinese have a chance to establish themselves as a global presence even on the maritime side. They can offer an alternative, and at the least hope that they do not become simply subjects in a West-dominated world, but are partners who are equally relevant to world history, and who offer differences that the West ultimately has to respect.

I think this is their ultimate hope — that they do not become just another satellite of a dominant centre. This possibility excites them.

OKB: Before we go further along this exciting route, may I first ask you how you define the Eurasian core? What's a core and what's an edge, and what's the dynamic between these?

WGW: One of the stages in human evolution was the nomadic stage. This nomadic pastoral stage survived well in the heart of Eurasia, where agriculture was not the most profitable way of developing human societies. In time, some of these nomads began to settle down to agricultural life — along the Nile and the Tigris-Euphrates; the Indus and the Yellow River. And agrarian states began to evolve. These were in a way atypical. They had evolved out of something that still remained. The core remained — the original was still the nomadic. The nomads represent a more original human condition, and in Central Asia geography allowed them to prevail for a long, long while, right down to modern times in fact.[1]

They never lost their capacity to express their way of life — to live it and to impose it on others whenever possible. Many of them of course actually joined the agrarian civilizations when they moved into the Arabic world, into Russia, and into China. And northern India! After all, who were the Moghuls? The Moghuls were descendants of the Mongol Turks; they were the Islamized group who won that vital Talas Line against the *Tang* Empire. While those who remained Buddhist among the Mongols stayed relatively contained, the Islamized ones had a different mission, and they went on to take over North India. The Muslims ruled over the Indo-Gangetic plain for a very long time. The Sultanate of Delhi survived down to 1857, and thus had six to seven hundred years of history. They were Muslim rulers, and they didn't try to convert everybody; they didn't bother to as long as the Hindus played along. And with their many gods, the Hindus were very adaptable. What was one more god to them?

The core was continually pushing outwards and yet it always remained. It could not be transformed into agrarian societies, and was therefore sustained in that way. It was the agrarian societies instead which were subject to its pressure; and it could really put the pressure on. It was only in the twentieth century, finally, that the secular, modern, scientific and technological world finally overcame the core. What's happening to Mongolia today is absolutely tragic, and at the same time perfectly natural. What are Mongolians now doing? They work in coalmines, and they are trying to create a democracy. All the old is now destroyed. That's the end of it. A stage in human development is almost concluded.

The core is now totally undermined, and the edges are beginning to dominate the core as in the case of Soviet Russia. Places like Turkmenistan, Uzbekistan, Kyrgyzstan and Kazakhstan, are influenced by the Russian approach to such an extent that a vital part of the Islamic world is now secularized in a way that the Arab world has not been. The Arab world has resisted it, but it will lose out in the end. Look even at Turkey. Turkey was the most successful of the core states, but the West did Turkey in. The Russians did in the other Turks, and the Moghuls gradually became Indianized. So in the end the core is no longer stable, and is now threatened inwards.

The edges now have a say for the first time since the nineteenth century. What we now have is a rivalry between them. In this, we have to ask to what extent China is able to stand up to the most recent changes coming from the West, and can it offer something else, something that is not too greatly different from the secular and scientific perspective that the Anglo-American world stands for? This is why the Anglo-American world worries so much about China. It is obsessed with it at the moment because China is the only place left that can offer an alternative. Nobody else can. The rest are but extensions of the Anglo-American world; even India. Look at the way Indian intellectuals write. There is little difference between them and the Englishmen or the Americans. The Chinese, on the other hand, don't write like that. Why not?

The Japanese have been trying to be an alternative. They *are* different, but they don't seem strong enough. They talk of their exceptionalism, but that is exactly because they have not been powerful enough. China's problem now is to work out how not to arouse the fear of others, and how to persuade others that China is peaceful.

OKB: Given this scenario, I think of the recurrent Great Game in Afghanistan ... that would be where the edges concretely threaten the core.

WGW: Yes. I think so. The British started it long ago, but failed. They failed again and again. The Russians tried, and failed as well. Then came the Americans...

OKB: Are we in the twenty-first century not simply in a new phase of that core-edge pendulum process?

WGW: But I think the core can only hold out and defend itself for a little while longer. The days of the Eurasian core are ending because of modern science; communications technology; modern management methods; and the conquest of air, sea, and cyberspace. It has had its day. You can look at Mongolia and look at Kazakhstan and you see where they are going. They are now doomed to be extensions of urbanized territories.

OKB: The continental threat, for the Chinese, is certainly not as distracting as it had historically been.

WGW: It is now Russian and Islamic. And to the south, India represents the West pushing into Tibet.

Chinese history itself tells us quite a lot about the dynamics we are interested in here. Archeological findings show that during the *Xia* period (2100–1600 BC) and even before, cultures there were rather nomadic. As farming developed, the agriculturalists found that they could not really defend themselves as long as they remained small units. The peaceful ideal villages of yore imagined by Laotse (sixth century BC) simply could not have survived nomadic invasions. They would always have been overrun by these nomads. Agricultural peoples were easily victimized by mobile horsemen, and had to build walls and stockades to keep their enemies out. But the harassment did not stop. They could not get much beyond that until they developed the idea of the stable state, as opposed to the nomadic state that was really all about wandering around.

The nomads had no capital; they could move everywhere, and rapidly. You will have noticed that the ancient Chinese did not have capitals either. They also moved around. Rulers of the *Shang* Dynasty (1600–1050 BC) moved their abode many times. Even the *Zhou* Dynasty (1056–256 BC) moved a couple of times. It was during the *Zhou* though that the idea developed for the collaboration of all the feudal states under one *Tian Zi* (Son of Heaven) against the nomads. Already, they were building bits of walls up north to keep the nomads out. They fought among themselves, no doubt, but they eventually had to recognize one authority when it came to external defence. But all that took nearly a thousand years to develop — from the end of the *Shang* to Confucius in the *Chunqiu* (Spring and Autumn) period (770–475 BC), down to the *Zhanguo* (Warring States, 475–221 BC).

From thousands of different units to hundreds of petty states down to the seven of the Warring States Period, political units were continually being reduced in number. Each step of the way, they were trying to consolidate an agrarian state against the nomads. This is where I was very inspired by the historical geographer Owen Lattimore's *Inner Asian Frontiers*[2] in his use of the moving frontier. What he stimulated me to think about was that there was always a borderland between the really nomadic continental territories and the agrarian regions. And whoever controlled that borderland determined the history of the world.

All the time, between the *Zhou* and the *Qin* (221–206 BC) this borderland was the main issue. The nomads then were known as *Xiongnu*. Whoever they were we can't quite determine, but they were probably ancestors of the Turkic peoples. In between were borderlands over which agrarian peoples were spread. This was a movable frontier; a useful one that separated the two sides, allowing them to deal with each other. As one side became stronger it moved in, and as the other side became stronger it pushed back. I don't want to oversimplify things, but there was a kind of rhythm to this.

OKB: Trying to control the Silk Road was part of this strategic adjustment, was it not?

WGW: That's part of it. That does indicate recognition that there were other agrarian edges to this formidable Eurasian core, doesn't it? There were powerful states in Babylon and in the Indus Valley. The Silk Road allowed for contact with these other peoples. The nomads produced little, and at most one could perhaps trade furs and horses with them. But these others were making beautiful goods. So the Silk Road was to link up with other edges; but it was always with the permission of Eurasian powers. In other words, you had to make your peace with the Eurasian powers to keep the Silk Road open. After all, they were the ones who controlled it, not the fringes. And anytime they wished to, they could cut it.

But whenever they thought it was to their benefit, they let it stay open and they would just take their share. So they built little oases here and there, and instead of fighting and invading you, they just lived off your trade. You had to trade, but you also had to pass through their territory. It was quite a peaceful arrangement, and there were periods when the Eurasians were not fighting and were on the whole willing to protect the Silk Road for their own interests. The edges had to use the Silk Road, again reaffirming the centrality of this Eurasian land power, this nomadic power.

If this interpretation of global history holds sufficient validity, the Chinese then could perceive themselves as a balance to the other edge, which in any case had been dominant for only about two hundred years.

The British were not really dominant until the late eighteenth century, when they finally mastered the oceans. That was most apparent when people like Robert Clive and Warren Hastings moved into India.[3] Once the French and the Dutch were pushed out of the way, the British basically ruled the waves. What is most interesting here is that the British now offered an alternative power to the Eurasian power for the first time in history — and on a global scale. Since then, the British have no doubt lost out to the Americans. And why have they? Because the Americans have a continental base while the British didn't. You see, a purely maritime power can never be sustained for want of a continental base. You will always be peripheral because of that. You depend on the oceans; and penetrate inland only at your own peril. We talk about imperialism, but really, it was very, very difficult for the maritime British to penetrate into continental Asia.

In fact, British — and American — power is essentially about port systems. And Singapore is a living example of that. The Portuguese set the model, and simply controlled key ports and sea lanes. They could not move inland. The Spanish were the exception, though only to a small extent, succeeding only where there was no resistance. They succeeded in the Philippines because there was no agrarian state to resist them, except in the south, in Mindanao.

OKB: In Malaya, the British founded the port of Penang in 1786, and it took as long as another hundred years before they moved into Perak, on to the proximate peninsula itself.

WGW: For a long time they didn't even try. It was not in their interest to try. You don't want the responsibility of running huge territories; you just want an island! You see how clever they were — it was always islands they were interested in. They picked those that were easy to defend — Penang is a very good example of this in many ways. It started with the Portuguese taking places like Goa, Malacca, Macau, and a few Spice Islands. They never moved inland. They tried Nagasaki but the Japanese threw them out because the Jesuits were too successful converting the Japanese to Catholicism. The Dutch actually started that way as well. They didn't want the Indonesian archipelago. They didn't even want Java. They were happy with Batavia and Malacca.

The big difference came when the British entered India. And in many ways that was the tragedy; the end of the British Empire. That move did not fit their business model, which was coastal trade. But the East India Company was finally drawn into Indian internal squabbles, to take over Madras, and to take over Bengal. Internal fighting drew them in; they had to help one side against the other. So they thought: "OK, we will just expand our business!" In theory, yes, that may be so, but the Indian Mutiny of 1857 really sucked them in, and that basically undermined the

British Empire. They lost out everywhere else after that because they got too caught up in trying to rule India.

OKB: So they had to close the East India Company down in 1874.

WGW: A company can handle ports ... a string of ports even, but an empire? How could it do that? In fact the government started to move into the East India Company from the end of the eighteeenth century already. Whenever the government found that the Company couldn't manage, it put in more naval forces.

But they had first to defeat the French, who were their real rivals at sea. The French were pushed out of the Indian Ocean when they were crushed in the Mauritius Campaign of 1809–11. On sufferance, the town of Pondicherry in India was allowed to remain in French hands by the British because they now had their peace.

But after being drawn into Indian continental adventures after Hastings and down to the Indian Mutiny, they found themselves trapped. India — Queen Victoria's Jewel of the British Empire — was actually their Achilles Heel. They became overextended. Of course, it was really extraordinary brilliance on the part of a handful of people to devise ways of defending this vast empire, and to continually innovate. And that is America's heritage. The Americans studied British imperial history with great care to understand what it is they have inherited. Basically they're finishing the job for the British; and to finish the job, they need to be the only supreme superpower. After forty years opposing the Soviet Union, they achieved that — 1990 was the closing of an era. It was the complete subjugation of the continental; it marked the failure of the continental powers in the struggle against maritime power. Eastern Europe completely collapsed; and practically all the countries have been absorbed into the Western European system. Russia has had to retreat, from all directions. Thinkers at the Pentagon and European strategists say there is one last holdout — China.

OKB: They see the Chinese as purely continental then.

WGW: Yes, and they see the Chinese as wanting to develop beyond that, as the last gasp of continental power which the Anglo-American imperial system has to overcome. They know that the Chinese are starting to build up a naval presence, and are moving on to aerospace technology and cyberspace. All these are transformative technologies that are reshaping the world. The Chinese are learning very fast and are leapfrogging.

OKB: The latecomer's advantage...

WGW: Latecomers do have an advantage, but they are still dependent on the West, because all their technologies are learnt from the West. But basically they have to become a maritime power. Historically they had been very reluctant in doing that. They actually had their chance in the fifteenth century. In fact from the *Song* Dynasty (960–1279) down to the *Ming* (1368–1644), for about three hundred years, China was in fact a maritime power. They dominated the East and South China seas, and could sail all the way to the Indian Ocean. But they gave it up, because in a way, they were being traditional. They decided there was no real threat out there, so why waste resources? If people wanted to trade, they were welcome to come to China instead. The Portuguese had not turned up yet, you see.

The threat from the continent, however, was real — the Mongols and others had been invading incessantly. There you see the classic divide in Chinese history. It made sense to move all the resources from the coasts and put them into building the Great Wall, linking up all the separate bits. It took them a hundred years, and during that time all the resources went there. As we know, in the end they failed. The nomadic power was still too powerful for them. In the end it was a combination of Manchus and Mongols — with some Chinese help — that overcame the *Ming*. That made it worse, because now the Central Asian core had actually taken over the agrarian world. The *Qing* Dynasty was essentially a Manchu-Mongol partnership — with some *Han* participation — to overcome the agrarian society, and to utilize agrarian institutions to ensure their power. They adopted the Confucian system, not because they were Confucians, but because that was just one of the ways of making sure they could run these 300 million people. How do you keep so many under control otherwise?

But the Manchu-Mongols continued to be nomadic powers, to think like nomads. That was why they went into Tibet and Xinjiang. It was a very un-Chinese expansion. Only people like the Mongols and the Manchus would have done that. The Chinese would never have undertaken such a project.

OKB: The *Qing* had to be both agrarian and nomadic to achieve what they did.

WGW: The Manchus were both; and they were brilliant, I tell you! Look at the first three *Qing* emperors — *Kangxi*, *Yongzheng* and *Qianlong*. They were really fantastic emperors, the most powerful since the *Qin-Han*. The most dynamic period in ancient times was from *Qinshihuang* (reigned 221–210 BC) to *Hanwudi* (reigned 141–87 BC) — about a hundred and thirty years. But the hundred and thirty or so years (1661–1796) from *Kangxi* to the end of

Qianlong was the most powerful period in Chinese history. These emperors were continental and nomadic. Moving down from the north, they were part of the Eurasian core's project of taking over the agrarian state. They then pushed *Qing* borders westward to an extent that had never been done before by any dynasty.

RELIGION'S CAPTURE OF POLITICS

OKB: What about the *Tang* Dynasty (618–907) in this context?

WGW: The *Tang* basically ran the Silk Road. The *Tang* were like the Portuguese and English empires, controlling port cities but not much beyond that. The nomadic peoples managed to retain the core, while the *Tang* Chinese controlled oases and ran the garrisoned oases. But even then, that balance held only up to a point. The Chinese stayed within *Xinjiang*. They didn't go beyond that, and didn't control Ferghana and Samarkand, for example. These were all beyond their reach.

But the important element back then was the Arabs coming in; Islam coming in. In other words, another edge was also pushing into the core area. While the *Tang* had a defensive posture, others adopted a much more aggressive approach. In conquering Persia, the Arabs were left without a choice. They had inherited the Persian Empire, and the Persian Empire was Central Asian. For centuries, Persian culture was spread all over Central Asia, way before the arrival of the Arabs. During the time of the *Tang* in China, the Sunni–Shi'ite division was not yet important among the Muslims. They all belonged in the same Umayyad Empire (661–750).

Anyway, they went into Central Asia, and their greatest success was against the Indo-Scythians, who were Nestorians, Jews and Zoroastrians. These were won over; and even Indians, a lot of Hindus and Buddhists in what is now Pakistan, all became

Muslim. The Persian border was very porous — like Afghanistan still is today — and they met with virtually no resistance because there was no great state there. There were only oasis outposts. The Arabs seized them all, and at the other end they ran up against the *Tang*.

People talk about the Battle of Talas (AD 751) today as a historic conflict between the Chinese and the Arabs. For the Arab side, it was indeed important because it drew the line for Arab-Muslim influence. For the Chinese side, it was just a minor event. They lost a few garrisons and didn't think much of it. The *Tang* general who led the fighting was a Korean named *Gao Xianzhi*. The Chinese records do mention Talas, to be sure, but just as one of the little battles they lost.

If you look at the bigger picture, however, it was very significant. That was the battle that placed the Chinese on one side and the Arabs on the other. The Arabs did not penetrate much beyond that. Talas is actually on the border between *Xinjiang* and the Muslim states today. With the base that the Arabs won there, Islam was able to convert the nomads to the west of it.

The tribal groups in Eurasia were essentially all part of the culture of the Steppes. But from this point on, a divide came between those we know as Mongols and those we know as Turks. The division was religion. While Central Asian peoples became Muslim, those to the east remained Tibetan Buddhists. Turks may have more Arabic, Persian or European features, while Mongols tend to have Mongoloid features. But among the Turks, you find a lot of people with Mongoloid features, too. This was not even a cultural division. Their way of life as nomads remained very similar.

OKB: Even in Southeast Asia we see that clear line between Islam and Buddhism.

WGW: It's not accidental. Each represents a completely different world view. They reached a point where neither side had enough power to push further, and so came to an understanding and left things alone. But the fact that Islam could overcome the Hindu-Buddhist Malay Archipelago is remarkable! In fact, that was where the line could have been drawn, with all of Southeast Asia remaining Hindu-Buddhist and within the Indian tradition, as India did. Of course, the Sufis and others were able to put Islam in a form that was acceptable to Hindu-Buddhist peoples, and were successful in India because of that. They were also doing that in Sumatra — in Aceh and further south. So you can see that at some point, all the rulers found it in their interest to accept Arab and Indian-Muslim traders as partners in developing a large political and economic system that allowed different riverine and island states in Java, such as Majapahit, to continue — but now under Islam. Aceh and Malacca were Islamized in principle through the conversion of the ruler.

That was incidentally how Christianity spread amongst the Germans and the Scandinavians as well. You convert the king! That was also what the Jesuits tried to do in China as well.

So, it was a basic pattern. The monotheistic approach towards gaining control of the world was to convert rulers. There was no other way. If the ruler is against you, you cannot penetrate his kingdom. It started with the Roman Empire itself. What were the Christians then? They were slaves who were being fed to the lions! The women folk were transmitting the faith, with the men helping, no doubt. But men on the whole were the ones who had to do the fighting and who were being killed! But the women preserved the faith; and for three hundred years they converted just slaves.

That soon led to the conversion of kings, which then became a well-established method. After their success with Constantine the Great (272–337), who turned the Roman Empire into a Christian empire, wherever they went, be it to France or Britain, the Christians would target the leaders. There's a book called *How the Irish Saved Civilization*,[4] which shows that the monks who went to Ireland were the ones who eventually converted the Scandinavian and German kings.

Islam basically used the same formula. Here you see how the power of religion overcomes secular thought and all other political systems, that in the end are vulnerable to an ideational alternative that offers them something transcendental and spiritual — something no king can offer. But if a king can combine his physical force with religious faith, then he is unmatched. After all, rulers are politicians. They look for advantages and they look for legitimacy: I may have beaten the other guy in war, but then somebody will beat me in turn. But if I can establish that I am really related — and my descendants — to something greater than just battlefields, and that all my victories are sanctioned by something higher than me, then my legitimacy is assured. That gives me a fantastic advantage. Then I can say that my son, my grandson, and his son all have legitimacy.

That was how the Chinese state began too. What is the basis on which the *Zhou* state took over from the *Shang*? They won the decisive battle, no doubt. But how were they to justify the takeover? This is where *Geming* (revolution) comes in. It originated from the idea of rightful rebellion — it is rightful, therefore it is successful. And in its success, the *Zhou* totally transformed the system into a new one; and that is *Geming*. The word was first used in the *Shangshu* (Book of Documents) to describe the handover of power from the *Shang* state to the *Zhou* state. It was then read retrospectively and used as the basis on which the *Shang* state had also taken over from the *Xia* state. This reading backwards into history by the *Zhou* granted it legitimacy.

And why did it succeed? Because of *Tian* (Heaven)! *Tian* now functions politically, providing the legitimate basis for the *Zhou's* new rule being different from the earlier one. It is sanctioned by something greater than humans. This also leads us back to the question of whether or not the Chinese had a religion that legitimized the state. I think it had! I think that has now been well established, and one of the best books on this is a fairly recent one by Anthony C. Yu.[5] I found his book very persuasive in arguing that the *Shang* did have a religion. And *Tian* was actually not a *Zhou* idea — it was a *Shang* idea. The *Shang* in turn may have received it from earlier times, at the emergence of the agrarian society; the idea that there is some natural cosmic force whose wishes one can read.

OKB: This was the period when tortoise shells were used for predictions.

WGW: The tortoise shells were certainly a part of it — for reading the mind of *Tian*, what *Tian* means us to do, and what it wants us to do. You read it and you interpret it to justify what you are going to do. If you're intending to invade your enemy, you draw a symbol and interpret it to mean, "*Tian* approves". And if you win, then that confirms it — *Tian* did want it that way.

Although the *Shang* had developed that idea, they didn't institutionalize it in a monotheistic way because they didn't have a separate church. You see, in a way, the most revolutionary idea in the Middle East and the Mediterranean was the separation of church and state. The Christians came up with the bit about serving Caesar being different from serving God, as part of their adaptation to the Roman Empire. They had to devise a way of giving legitimacy to these rulers who had power over them, and who were not Christians — you give unto Caesar what is Caesar's, and you give unto God what is God's. That was a major innovation that had never happened before. The Egyptians never separated the two — God and the king were exactly the same. But the idea that Caesar and Jesus were separate was brilliant!

That is also why Christianity could lead back to secularism later in history; and that is why Islam still can't. Islam did not separate worldly rulers from Mohammed and Allah.

If we go back to our discussion about the beginning of modern progress in the West, the Chinese also understand that it really stemmed from the separation of Caesar and Jesus enabling the Christians to develop the sanctity of the Church, for example. Inside the Church, the king had no say. Now, that does not apply in any other religion. There was also this idea that the king could be excommunicated. God could punish him. How did they manage that trick? It's ingenious! It divided power, and in the process guaranteed the sanctity of monasteries. No ruler could enter without paying obeisance to God. These priests were very clever indeed!

Having done that successfully, the basis for universities was created — the idea that knowledge inside the Church is outside the realm of the state, and the Church controls that knowledge. Now when the Church could do that, then of course the next key question is, can you overcome the Church's dominance? It took them hundreds of years to answer that. But what enabled them to do that was that the universities could have knowledge that was protected by the Church. So as long as it was not opposed to the Church, it could go on and the state could not intervene. And the Church then enabled some of these scholars, from St. Thomas of Aquino (1225–74) all the way down to the Renaissance, to pursue the edges of knowledge.

The Europeans also discovered that the works of the Greek philosophers had all been translated into Arabic after the fall of

Constantinople in 1453, and that the Arabs had been developing the ideas found therein. Once these classical texts were released to the European world, these Church-based knowledge centres studied them. Needless to say, that utterly blew their minds. They had forgotten all about it. It was the Arabs who had preserved it — in Spain, in Damascus, and elsewhere.

THE SUCCESS OF LOCAL POLITICS IN EUROPE

OKB: The Byzantines must have remained familiar with Greek philosophy.

WGW: Apparently. Now, I find that very peculiar. The Byzantine state had more say in church affairs than on the Roman side; the reason being that the Holy Roman Empire assumed the Pope to have a transcendence that no earthly ruler could oppose. The Byzantines didn't hold that distinction. To them, their Emperor and their Church were basically in cahoots, exercising power together. That's my reading of it.

On the Roman side — and this brings us back to my earlier point about miniaturized political units — there was, underlying the Germanic tribal systems, a sanctioning of small units. The Germans were always suspicious of centralized units. Their tribal units, with their chiefs who claimed legitimacy through military prowess, bravery and courage, had their roots in miniaturized political units. This constrained the centralizing power of the Holy Roman Empire, and the small units remained. The city states remained; and the small agrarian states also remained. All the time, one always had to refer back to the Church and to get its blessings before doing anything.

That, I think, was paradoxically the secret of European success. It was at first a barrier to progress because this control of knowledge gave few opportunities for people to innovate. Everything had to conform to church doctrine. But eventually, because it also protected knowledge from governments, every now and then, within the system and pushing at the edges, would appear people who would test out new ideas. These were monks or priests, and their knowledge was allowed as long as it did not contradict the Bible. There was a limit of course. Wherever a contradiction did turn up, the hammer would come down.

The Reformation — really the Revolution — was enabled by the Renaissance, by the reintroduction of ideas that Plato, Aristotle and other Greek philosophers had discussed ages ago. Philosophically, these were very persuasive. Scientific curiosity about the stars, for example, and how they relate to the world's geography was a pursuit of knowledge that promised to make the Bible more credible. But, at some point, serious contradictions cropped up, especially concerning the movement of the planets and stars.

At that point, the whole structure was shaken, and the Protestant movement broke out. The case of Henry the VIII of England (1491–1547) was merely accidental. The real hero was Martin Luther (1483–1546), whose challenge was an intellectual one and not simply the whim of some powerful king seeking to serve his own selfish interests. Furthermore, Luther's challenge came from within. He was a well-educated monk, and for a long time a conformist to boot, until he finally could not stand it anymore. His breaking away also became a measure of the corruption of the system. If the Catholic Church had been really well run and had not been politicized by the Medicis and other big politicians who had gone into the Church to make use of it, the story would have been different. But the Church had become blatantly corrupt, and people could see that. Luther could not possibly have succeeded if it was not so obvious to people that the Church was rotten to the core.

OKB: The time was ripe...

WGW: The time was ripe! It was not Luther. The Germans did it, the Swiss, the Austrians, the Slavs, the French, and the British; they all suddenly had other ideas, producing people like Desiderius Erasmus (1466–1536) or Benedict Spinoza (1632–1677). Many of these were from small places no doubt, but they were there. Those who were not priests were educated by priests — every educated man back then was educated by the Church.

THE CONFUCIAN ORDER

OKB: Was it a similar case in Scotland?

WGW: Yes, but that happened much later. They had to wait till the eighteenth century. By that time, the Reformation was in full flood. The Scots were getting ideas from the Swiss Calvinists, but the changes were all out there on the edges of the Latin world. The French in the end retreated, throwing out their Protestants — who had to run to Holland, to England, and to Germany.

OKB: And over to America...

WGW: To America. So that was a major struggle indeed.

But all this is not directly of relevance to China. The idea there in modern times has been to identify something in Western development that the Chinese could understand, but have not themselves had. The Chinese did not have the separation of Church and state. This was not because of any great ideological rejection though, like in the case of Islam where it is ruled to be impossible by the Qur'an.

For China, it was just not necessary, and this is where the Confucians played a key role. I guess if the Confucians hadn't been so successful in the state, other things could have happened. If the Buddhists, for example, had taken over, the Chinese state would have been very different. But the way the Confucians managed to keep control provided for a stable political base, and made it unnecessary to separate Church and state because the Confucians were *in* the state. They can be said to represent a kind of socially conscious church that was not much worried about the next life. The way this worldly group of intellectuals were trained, the way they held together studying the same classics, completely absorbed in one set of books ... to that extent, they were a monastic order. Now, that order was necessary to the state. In fact, the state was practically a machinery that gave Confucian ideas public legitimacy in return for which Confucianism provided the intellectual ballast to support the military, the aristocrats, and so on. The two had married so well that the idea that Church and state should be separate never occurred to them. So it remains to this day.

China still has these roots. Mao was in his own way, without being conscious of it, creating a state in which the state machinery and the communist bureaucratic machinery interlocked. The intellectual store of scientific socialism and the resources of the state were one and the same, and therefore the separation of Church and state was again not needed. Having a group of intellectuals outside the state who could contribute towards enriching society was unnecessary.

The Chinese are not really going along the way that the West had gone, where secularization has come to the point where you actually have an intellectual class separate from the state, and is constructively critical of it, and keeps the state honest. That is missing from the other two traditions, although the Chinese are not as extreme as the Muslims. They are actually capable of moving either way. Mao Zedong actually pushed it one way, and pressed for the supremacy of a set of ideological concepts and doctrines to dominate the state. And the state used all these to be absolutely totalitarian. He pushed it very far, and the Chinese rejected it, finding it simply impossible to live in that kind of state.

They have now pulled back from it, but they are not prepared to go the other way either. In fact, they pulled back to be where they always used to be. It is not Confucianism per se that they seek; it is about finding a balance where a bunch of people can exist; who are educated, trained and have the welfare of the state and society at heart; and who are committed to ensuring that the state behaves itself and does all the right things. They haven't found that balance yet, but that is the new struggle.

My understanding is that the Confucians were quite modest about their intervention into the private affairs of people. They saw themselves as bearers of a tradition of respect for the family as a unit. That is not Confucius; that is more ancient than that. In the religion that we talked about earlier, already during the *Shang* period you can see an emphasis on the family, on heritage, bloodlines, ancestry and genealogy. Already, there was a sense of it. After a thousand odd years, Confucius simply re-embodied it, gave it an intellectual flavour and a moral justification, tying to it the social and political responsibilities that each educated person should have.

So it goes deep. It's very deep-rooted, and the Confucians reinforced it. They didn't fight it; they actually gave it legitimacy and a clearer definition, and forged a stable relationship in which the *Tian Zi* (the Emperor) respected the autonomy of all families and clans, and these in turn produced people who would serve the *Tian Zi*. Confucius himself did not spell it out as clearly as that, although he himself was an exemplar of it. He was there not to take over the state but to help the state be better, to help rulers be better. He saw himself in that role and he taught a whole generation of people to do the same — never to take over, but always to serve. And they failed, all of them failed.

Success came instead with the Legalists, who supported *Qinshihuang*, the First Emperor of China (259–210 BC). They said you must first have power, then you can do some good. Without power, all talk is useless nonsense. And the Warring States, of course, proved it. All of them were fighting each other, and the Confucians were nowhere to be found. They were complete failures. The Taoists, too. All of them were failures. In fact, we should really call those who succeeded Realists, not Legalists. They were not interested in the law; they just wanted power.

They understood that in the end you need to collect taxes and defend your frontiers. These come first; people have to live. What's the point of saying: Be nice to people, be good to people, have morals and so on, if you don't have the soldiers and you don't have the revenues to pay the soldiers. You can't even survive! Earlier groups were interested in administration, like *Shen Buhai* (died 337 BC). In a way, this was what we would call public administration today. *Shen Buhai* was not a Legalist per se; he came before them. Some would consider people like him to be *zonghengpai* — they were strategists. They did the same things as the Confucians did, but what they offered was not how to be a good ruler, how to be successful, or how to run the country. They went out with ideas about how to collect taxes, how to generate officials, how to recruit staff, and this and that. Out of this came the Legalists and the Confucians. Among the Confucians were people who also saw in the end that Confucius was a failure. They saw the need to come up with something else. These were people like *Shang Yang* (390–338 BC), *Xun Zi* (312–230 BC) and *Han Feizi* (280–223 BC).

Han Feizi was a follower of *Xun Zi* and started out as a Confucian. He recognized that the Confucians were going nowhere, and like *Shang Yang*, who came from the *Shen Buhai* tradition, thought that they needed to have one leader who could unite them all. All the fighting was destroying them — people perishing, fields untilled, resources limited, and the country impoverished. They must unite. So they concentrated their energy on the one ruler they thought could win, and this was *Qin Xiaowu*, the father of *Qinshihuang*. For eighty to a hundred years, these rulers built up the military state that ultimately won, and won not only by military means but through a bureaucratic structure. Every time they won, they extended their bureaucratic network until they covered the whole of the empire. In the course of doing that, they also built up a most powerful military system.

But having succeeded, they went on to conquer further afield, into territories that were not part of the Warring States at all. They extended their borders into Korea, into Mongolia, *Sichuan*, into the Yangtze Basin and all the way down to southern China. The *Qin* armies went right down to Vietnam. That was because they had a military system already in place, with nobody to oppose them. They just marched right down. It was not intentional. It was not an imperial system in the sense that they went out to seize territory, but they were so powerful that they simply moved on, like with the Roman Empire, and in a way as with the British Empire, too. All empires have the tendency to do that. When you meet no enemies, you push on until someone stops you.

But in this case, the *Qin* stopped simply because the First Emperor died. There followed a period of chaos, and the first *Han* emperors reviewed the fact that they now had control over huge territories. And having set up this bureaucratic system, who was to run it? At first they just used aristocrats. These were all educated in different schools. They were not only the Confucians;

they were also Taoists, Legalists, disciples of *Mo Zi*, the *Yin-Yang* school — all of them having some kind of religious background. It took another fifty to sixty years before *Han Wudi* (156–87 BC) decided that those most useful to him were the Confucians. He made that decision, and it was a personal one. He appreciated the Confucian *Dong Zhongshu* (179–104 BC) greatly, you see. He clicked well with him.

The Confucians had always been on the fringes, always offering advice with nobody paying much attention because they were too idealistic or too moralistic. But these guys were pretty good at administration. So *Han Wudi* brought them in and, by the end of his period, had basically entrusted the running of the state to them.

Their principles were as follows: never attempt to take power; always be of loyal service; be as educated as you can be; learn all about institutions and the best way of making use of them for the sake of the kingdom, for the emperor. This was all very objective on the whole and with no vested interest — and it was also secular. Confucius did say that the other world was not our business ... we don't know it at all, you see. Why discuss something of which we know nothing? Act on what we know, what we see.

They were very realistic, very practical, very pragmatic and very willing to compromise with the state. Now, that's very important. The Taoists, for example, were not willing to compromise. They had said basically that you could not trust the aristocrats, which was probably right. But Confucians said, well whether you trust them or not, you should help them. Make them better! You see, that's the difference. They all had ultimately the same goal. They all wanted peace and stability — *heping* and *tianxia wei gong* and *tianxia taiping*.[6] All said the same thing. But to achieve that, the Confucians thought you should work with the rulers, and actually provide them with the machinery to make things better. So when they found themselves faced with the fact that the Legalist state had already been established by the *Qin*, and the *Han* Dynasty had no alternative to it, they just retained what the *Qin* had built. Basically, what the *Han* did to begin with was to soften things — they brought in Taoism and played down Legalism. They made the laws less stringent, and applied them less rigidly. But that was not quite enough. In the end, somebody had got to run it. How do you secure the collection of taxes? After all, the two major functions of the state are collecting taxes and defending the frontiers. How do you make sure that's done properly? The Taoists, for example, were simply too vague and impractical to come up with an answer.

OKB: Was this when the *Wen* (civil) and *Wu* (martial) distinction developed?

WGW: I suppose it was already there before that. This distinction was there during the Warring States — *Wen* were the people going around giving advice, and *Wu* were the soldiers. In this context, the idea of *Shi* is very interesting. *Shi* originally applied to *Wu*, to the military. But it became a word to describe the more educated and intellectual part of the machinery of government during the *Han* Dynasty. *Shi* came to denote *Wen*, the civil, but its origins were martial, as in *qishi*, a cavalier, or even *shibin*, a soldier. *Shi* was used initially for anybody who used power to do things. The separation was not that firm, but the Confucians made it more and more rigid, because they thought that in order to be really free from suspicions of being ambitious for power, they must not have military power. You see, if you have any military power, the emperor can never trust you because you can always use your power against him. To be absolutely sure that the emperor would trust you, you must show that you have no power! So the basis of the denotative for Confucianism — *Ru* — is very interesting. Some say *Ru* originally meant weak. In a way, the Taoists would approve of that. Softness can transform things.

OKB: The element of water and the like...

WGW: Yes, the element of water. You must not, as it were, fight or resist; and so you serve. You have no power, and so you serve well. Now, to establish that sort of reputation, the Confucians elaborated on what Confucius had said, and Mencius in particular emphasized this more and more. By the time of the *Han* Dynasty, the concept of *Xiao*, of filial piety, was linked to the concept of *Zhong*, loyalty. Confucius never made that connection. He did talk about how important *Xiao* was, but *Zhong* meant something else then! It meant being true to yourself, being faithful to what you believe in, your ideals, the tenets and doctrines you believe in. But during the *Han* Dynasty, partly thanks to *Dong Zhongshu* and others who served *Han Wudi*, there came a re-interpretation of some of the Confucian texts. This was required to make these people even more trusted by the state. And *Xiao* and *Zhong* became inseparable. *Xiao* was no longer a family matter; it became a necessary part of educating children to be *Zhong*, to be loyal to the state.

The argument was, if you are not *Xiao* (filial), how can you be expected to be *Zhong* (loyal)? So, the way you serve your parents would be a good indication of your willingness to serve your ruler. All this came after Confucius.

It is very important to distinguish between Confucius and his immediate disciples on the one hand, and on the other, Confucianism as a body of thought derived from the original ideas of Confucius, which was independent of the state and had its own momentum and dynamics. And then there is State Confucianism. These three are really quite separate. State Confucianism was, of course, the derivative of the other two. It propounded a very focused and narrow set of ideals, and represented the part of Confucianism that the state was prepared to support and that it found most useful.

But if you had gone too much into what Confucius believed in, the state would not have approved either. For example, the complete autonomy of the ruler would have been challenged. Like the Christian Protestants who say, "I can talk to God myself", the Confucian can go back to Confucius and reinterpret things: "My understanding says that this is what Confucius meant, and you as emperor are not doing the right thing. I have the right, and the duty, to tell you that you are wrong." Now, that is Confucianism. It is not Confucius, but it is Confucianism.

State Confucianism and Confucianism conflict at some points, and if you want to be in the state, you have to accept the limits of State Confucianism. The Confucians who didn't want to join the state could stay out and accept the fact that their ability to influence events would be very limited. Many minor officers did spend their lives teaching and performing small services instead.

This is where the literati as a stable sociocultural force is so important to Chinese civilization. In a way, the state trusts them. They do not have power, and they will never organize themselves against the ruler. They have great autonomy because the emperor is not bothered with them; and as long as the emperor had his State Confucians working for him, the non-State Confucians could say what they liked!

So that's part of the tradition. The Confucians could bring this sense of stability and cultural unity to the whole nation because they were spread out everywhere. In every town and village in the country, there was somebody studying Confucian classics outside of state control. Nobody cared about them because they had no power, and they would never organize themselves against the state. They were not like the Taoists and the Buddhists who could do that because they had their own gods.

These non-State Confucians had no gods. Their only god — their divinity — was Confucius, and their texts taught them to be always loyal to the state. When things become absolutely impossible, then they would stand up and say what they must, and they would have their head cut off! And they did that. That is the tradition. So the state says, OK, we actually do not have to control everything! They know they can count on this body of literati who are found everywhere, to provide peace and stability in the villages and towns. These will provide leadership, have the respect of the people, and will never tell the people to rebel. On the contrary, they are always teaching the people how to be more loyal, and how to serve society better. And the state can afford to leave them alone, as long as it can recruit from those who pass the exams — and these don't necessarily have to be the best guys — to serve in the state system. So State Confucians are those who are part of the system. They are not actually collaborating though; they are more the backbone of the system. The state can trust them because they will not rebel.

The examination system was invented during the *Tang* (618–907), basically by *Wu Zetian* (625–705), to fight the aristocrats. The aristocrats had real power and some of them had military backgrounds. They were also very educated. So to balance them off, *Wu Zetian* allowed these exams to pick people from among the learned. They did not have to be Confucians; they could be Buddhists and Taoists, but they were all very literate. And you use that to test their ability to write, ability to think, ability to create, and so on. You then pick from among them, and you put them in public office as State Confucians to counteract aristocratic power. The aristocrats, too, were not necessarily Confucians — they could be Buddhists, Taoists or Confucians. But they could be very ambitious, and *Wu Zetian* found things rather frustrating because she was not a member of the imperial family. She was married into that family and was regarded very suspiciously for it; so she used the exams as a means of establishing a new balancing group.

And out of it gradually emerged the *Jinshi*. These were originally simply one of various groups, but by the end of the dynasty they were taken into the highest positions of the empire. By the time of the *Song* Dynasty (960–1279), they had become the system's core, and they reproduced themselves. They tried consciously to keep State Confucianism and Confucianism as closely linked as possible, but at the same time they knew that there was an invisible line between those who served their consciences and those who served the state. And since that was not easy to transcend, you don't draw it too sharply. The Confucians don't believe in drawing anything too sharply anyway. You let things merge and you can recruit back and forth.

It is like in modern societies, such as in America, where there is the ability to recruit from the universities. The universities provide the Confucians, and those among them willing to serve the state are like the State Confucians. Every branch of government in the United States is full of PhDs, or Masters at least. In other words, they've passed some examination that has made them loyal, and they are never going to rebel against the state. All these qualities are not too dissimilar from the Confucian case. They have the same kind of function, and when they finish, they go back to being a Confucian again, back to the university to do the social sciences, and so on. They'll never organize themselves against the state, and they will always be serving somebody. In the American case, you have a two-party system. You serve either one party or the other, but you're always loyal to one or the other.

So in a way, the gap between the western and eastern fringes of Eurasia is actually diminishing because the Chinese are also adapting themselves to the modern system. They have had the roots; the heritage was already there. Both State Confucianism and Confucianism can appeal to the Confucian texts. But on the whole, the texts are very modest. They are very broad and they can be interpreted in many different ways. That is fine though; that's actually the best kind of text. All the best texts are those that are not too sharply divided. So when the Confucians attack State Confucians, the latter also use the words of Confucius to defend themselves. The two have a balance in their relationship, a mutual respect because both can quote Confucius against one another, just like Europeans can quote the Bible against each other. Certainly, the Catholics and the Protestants quote the Bible against each other. The similarity is fascinating.

OKB: In our time, the concepts that grew out of other fringes are neglected because the western fringe is epistemologically so dominant.

WGW: No question about that. The West has been dominant for two hundred and fifty years. Some scholars in China today are going back to their tradition, but they are going back with fresh eyes because they have been through Marxism-Leninism. They have read the classics of the liberals, they have read the Greeks and the Romans, but they tend to return to Confucian things. Some were doing this from the beginning of the twentieth century already, but they remained peripheral; they were very few. And then they were caught in the political struggle between the nationalists and the communists, and never had any real influence. These people were completely ignored and neglected. But after Deng Xiaoping brought a new stability to the Maoist revolution, and gave it a new legitimacy, the system became a little more open-minded, and now allows Confucians to reappear.

There is an analogy there, perhaps not an exact one; but something that fascinates me also is how the Confucians historically survived the onslaught of Buddhism. Buddhism was a minor influence that appealed to a very small number of people when it first came to China. But by the fourth century, devotees like *Faxian* (337–422) were going to India to look for the texts, as did *Xuanzang* (602–664) in the seventh century. *Yijing* (635–713) as well. All these priests went to India to retrieve sacred texts. In the fifth and sixth century, every state, whether in northern China under Turkic rulers or in southern China under *Han* Chinese, was Buddhist. The ruler of the *Liang* Dynasty (502–557) actually thought he was going to be a kind of Buddha on Earth. This is not very different from the way Thai, Cambodian or Burmese kings in the past saw themselves — as Buddhas on Earth.

In all this, the Confucians were totally marginalized. They were barely surviving, and so they had to compromise. You see, they were taught to be loyal to the state. So if the state became Buddhist, they studied Buddhism. They continued to represent their Confucian ideas and tried to marry the two without giving up on their core convictions. Buddhism was not quite right, they felt, but they didn't know how to overcome it because the rulers were Buddhist. So you had to make yourself useful, to show that a Buddhist ruler may believe in all these other things, but when it came to running the country and the institutions of state, you could do it for him. The ruler may be Buddhist, but that did not stop you from doing your job capably. In any case, the ruler couldn't trust anybody else, because none of them were dedicated to that same principle of loyalty. Buddhist monks may not wish to topple the emperor, but then they could not be of service since what they wanted was to enter Nirvana. Confucians could tell the emperor, if you want to stay in power, if you want your son to succeed you, we'll help you. They continued to make themselves useful, even though they were not fully trusted. In the meantime, the rulers could pray and build Buddhist temples and worry about the next world and about immortality. The Confucians would worry about this world, and about getting the job done.

My own question here really is this: How did the Confucians survive the four hundred years between the *Han* and the *Tang* (220 to 618)? Great *Tang* emperors like *Tang Gaozu* (566–635) and *Tang Taizong* (598–649) were really Taoists and Buddhists, not Confucians. In fact, they were very much Taoists by then because they considered themselves descendants of Laotse since they had his surname — *Li*. That was of course ridiculous because the *Tang* emperors were actually of Turkic origin, descendants of the *Toba* Turks. Yet they claimed a connection and were therefore very accepting of Taoist practices. In fact, they used the Taoists as they used the Buddhists. If you look at descriptions from the courts, you see that the Taoists and the Buddhists were always present, in close proximity to the emperor. There were always superstitious practices going on, and the emperor was forever hoping to gain immortality. The Confucians were at the edges, offering to run the empire, to collect more taxes, and to make sure the military remained loyal.

The Buddhists didn't know how to do all that. They could teach you things, but that could make them ambitious to be emperors themselves, something the Confucians never did. Almost none of the top Confucians held important positions, except under Emperor *Xiaowen* (467–499) of Northern *Wei* (386–534). So what were these guys thinking in their own minds? They must have said, we'll just keep at it, show that we are loyal and not dissenters.

When *Mo Yan* won the Nobel Prize for Literature in 2012, the non-state literati made fun of him. They said the Swedes had sold out and were accepting *Mo Yan*, who belonged to the state literati. But really, *Mo Yan* represents a kind of independent and creative thinking, but is doing it without fighting the state. He just says, "Why should I join the rest of the world and ask for *Liu Xiaobo* [the incarcerated 2010 Nobel Peace Prize winner] to be released when I can do more by being in the state? And furthermore my works get read."

And his works are very creative. They are actually full of very fascinating ideas. *Mo Yan* feels, "I work in the system and I do what I can to open up people's minds and to open up the system. But if I do it as a dissident, I am just isolated, and even if I don't go to jail, I'd be marginalized." So it is a difficult dichotomous problem. The analogies are there, obviously.

"THE CHINESE ARE LEARNING EVERYTHING"

OKB: In Western societies today, the Confucian role we are defining here would analogously be played by the people active in NGOs, wouldn't it?

WGW: They are civil society — the public intellectuals who are not willing to collaborate. The ones who are willing to collaborate are often in the universities, with academic skills but without political ambitions. The government trusts them, but not those other guys — the NGOs and civil society — even though they are trained by the universities as well! So the universities play the role of training the Confucians and training the State Confucians also! So the analogies are not that far apart.

When you think about it, why is China seen as such a threat to the American way of life? China may have something that actually works a little bit better in some ways. It doesn't work very well in other ways, but it can be more stable. You don't get something like the American "fiscal cliff", where you are so polarized that the government is stymied and completely stuck! Now, should the Chinese become more successful in administering the state, people will begin to have doubts about the Anglo-American global system.

The Americans do feel the threat of an alternative modified system that actually denies some of the most central ideals that the West represents. This they find unacceptable. But in terms of trying to establish a stable society, which is peaceful in itself, and finding ways of getting things done — collecting taxes and defending the country, which is what the state is for — and accepting the most advanced knowledge of science and technology that the West has, the Chinese are very quick to learn. The only hesitation is over political ideals. But everything else they are learning from the West, very, very fast, including literary and cultural matters. No reluctance, no barriers! The Chinese are learning everything! The only thing they are not prepared to accept — and that's the one thing that the West is trying to hold against them — is the ideal of liberty. That is indeed what the Chinese are most fearful of, because they are not sure how to control it. If they can understand how to control it, if they think it possible to have liberty and still be in control, I think they'll accept it. In fact, the State Confucian group we were talking about is actually relatively free, as it is!

It's the other group — the Confucianists — that the state is watching. Their final text is still in doubt. Is it more about Confucius or about Marx? To be sure, Marx is just a symbol to represent the modern West, not the Christian West, but the modern secular West, including the science and technology. That's Marx in shorthand.

As I said, there had been three groupings in the past — Confucius and his disciples, Confucianism, and State Confucianism. It's still the same now, and this mix is still a struggle. You do find a number of Confucian scholars drawing upon Marxist texts, and a lot of Marxist ideologues quoting bits of Confucius. In other words, there's an attempt, as happened in the *Song* Dynasty concerning Buddhism and Confucianism, to syncretize. However, I think the conflict has been reduced, and they are now fighting about very specific things. These are over a few key words — liberty, rule of law, and individualism.

Freedom of expression and democracy are of course just extensions of liberty. The Chinese don't deny democracy, but their interpretation of it is different. In the West, the idea of democracy must include rule of law and freedom. The Chinese idea of democracy is that as long as we are doing it for the people and the people approve, you have democracy! It is why you call it *minben* — the people as the base. Even Confucius talked about it; Mencius as well. If you do it for the people, you are serving the people! *Wei renmin fuwu* (serve the people) was not coined by Mao Zedong. The notion was already there, even though they didn't have that phrase. It is clearly from Mencius — the people come first, the ruler comes last. He always said that, in the end, the determination of a ruler's righteousness is that people accept him. If they don't accept him, they overthrow him, and that would be the end of his Heavenly Mandate, his *Tianming*. When you give that a democratic interpretation, the Chinese don't find it too much of a conflict.

OKB: It is rule *for* the people, but not *by* the people.

WGW: Not by the people, because "by the people" brings in questions of rule of law and liberty ... and the individual. The individual is something that the Chinese are very ambivalent about. Confucius actually did place a great deal of emphasis on the individual, but that's the individual with a conscience, with education, a person at the top. In other words, your *shidafu*, your gentleman, is an individual, but your *laobaixing*, your common man, should be organized in family units. And their *Xiao*, their adherence to family values, is more important than themselves. So the collective is more important than the individual at that level. Now, the *Shi*, to have his conscience to serve, is still a member of that community; he still has *Xiao*, he still belongs to the community when it comes to family affairs, and he accepts a collective judgment. But, when he is serving the state, and to be loyal, to have *Zhong* to the state, he has to have a conscience that is drawn from Confucian ideals. For that, he must be free from his family, for fear of nepotism. He cannot help his family because that is not helping the state or the emperor. His loyalty to the emperor demands certain other things, including his conscience. What advice to give to the emperor about running the state and society is a separate duty done by the individual, and not by the collective mind.

OKB: How does *Li* come in here?

WGW: *Li* is a brilliant concept. In a way, it is the Chinese alternative to the rule of law. But it is not always a very satisfactory one because it is very difficult to institutionalize, except in terms of rituals. That's why it is translated as "ritual", which is very wrong, very misleading. But that's how it is institutionalized, in terms of behaviour. But underlining it all is a sense of right and wrong.

OKB: I find the *Li* and *Ren* connection to be a very central and interesting one.

WGW: You see, *Ren* is the highest Confucian ideal. It's quite untranslatable, really. It includes all kinds of love, caring, compassion, righteousness, and being proper. I am not able to find an adequate translation. I've not mentioned it so far only because I have just taken it as a given. It is the heart of Confucianism, and *Li* is the expression of it. How do you express *Ren* except through *Li*? In a way, this is to institutionalize it ... though not very strictly. After all, there was a lot of autonomy given to the literati's families. You can have your family *Li*, your *Jiafa*. In the thinking of *Zhu Xi* (1130–1200), it is called *Jiafa*. But there the *Jia*, the family, is again really an institutionalizing measure; it is working out in point form something that is not really definable. But you try to operationalize it, and you express it through either *Fa* or *Li*. Now *Fa* is very much associated with the Legalists; and Confucians on the whole avoid that. Their own word for it is *Li*. But whether they like it or not, it is still a kind of *Fa* — it is an alternative to the Western idea of law. If one follows all the *Li*, there should be no injustice. So justice itself is an expression of *Li*.

Of course, failing to institutionalize *Li* in the form of "laws" and "courts" saddled them with a weakness, which is why in the end they also accepted that some legislation, some *Fa*, was needed. The legalism underlying the Confucian system is very obvious because the Confucians never rejected it. They understood it to be an expression of *Li* in a very extreme form. What they tried to do was to reduce its extreme aspects and make it more acceptable to ordinary men, make it less frightening. Whenever possible, things should be left to the people to sort out through *Jiafa*. In other words, they decentralized it. It's up to the families to make sure that their children behave properly. You don't attack other people's families, and you don't bring the state in. The Confucians say that once the state comes in and you set up law courts and so on, you are just inviting people to be criminals. People will stop caring about their *Jiafa*, and instead take on the attitude that as long as the law doesn't prevent them from acting, they will do what they like.

What the state wants is for people to behave within their own unit, meaning the state can then stay out of it. But of course that has broken down now. Since the nineteenth century, nobody knows how to work the system anymore. They have the judiciary and legislature, but nothing works quite right because they haven't got the institutionalizing process quite right. This is a big struggle that is going on in China.

OKB: The Confucian attitude is something that grows over generations, isn't it?

WGW: It is a kind of secular religion, with a set of secular values which one has faith in. It is not based on logic. It is based on the faith that one grows up in, based on one's relationship with one's parents, brothers, sisters, cousins — the whole network.

Confucius and Mencius continually underlined the fact that this was the most natural thing to do; the most natural because you do grow up with your parents, your brothers and sisters, your grandparents, and your aunts and uncles. The Confucian idea is that if you get that right, the whole of society should develop in the right direction. If all the families are well run in themselves, why should there be any need for the state to intervene? In minimal things like collecting taxes and defending frontiers; yes, the state is needed because no single family can do that. Like Thomas Hobbes (1588–1679) says in his classic, *Leviathan*, you give something up to the sovereign, to the king, and you close a deal with him. Jean-Jacques Rousseau (1712–1778) as well — you give up certain things, enabling the king to do certain things, like collecting tax revenues, defending the empire or the civilization, etc. The rest he should not bother about; the rest can look after itself.

And that worked for a long time. That fascinated the Jesuits when they arrived in China. That was the one thing that caught their eye. They brought it back to Europe and it became very influential, particularly among the Germans and the French. The French took one side of it and developed a fantastic centralized bureaucracy; while the Germans took the more philosophical side of it, and tried to work out the ethics of it.

Now while the Catholics found the bureaucratic part highly interesting, many Western philosophers in the following centuries, mostly Protestants, were inspired by the idea of the autonomy of the people from the state; that the state and society had different functions and could maintain a relationship not based on religion or a church.

OKB: In the Chinese system, when things didn't work out, the punishment for the common man was quite different from that visited on the gentleman, the *Shi*. Shame played an important role.

WGW: That was a Confucian contribution. I am reminded of how hard we fight today for the idea of academic freedom. For example, what was the justification for academic tenure? The idea was that with it, a teacher would be able to teach what he thought he should teach, without being subject to the state. And your point has something like that, too. If the *Shi* is treated with respect and not like an ordinary person, it gives him autonomy and enough encouragement to give the best advice. The best advice comes from someone who is free to see where you are wrong. Because if he is not free, how can he be of use to you? If you are an emperor, a ruler, and he serves you by simply saying "Yes sir" all the time, then he is of no use to you. He just does what you say, which is not what he is supposed to do. You actually trust him to tell you what to do. You trust him, and you must give him some guarantee of protection so that when you don't like what he tells you, you don't automatically cut his head off, which was the case in some societies in premodern times. Or you sack him.

So you should say, "OK. I'm sorry. I don't like your advice. Forget it", and you then send him away. But he's still around. It's just that you don't take that particular advice. The respect involved here is a bit like your academic tenure. For your mistakes, you do not get sacked.

This was so during the *Tang* and *Song*, but by *Ming* times (1368–1644), every now and then you find that the emperors couldn't stand unwelcome advice. What had happened was that the system — the *Ming* coming after the Mongol *Yuan* Dynasty (1271–1368) — had been influenced by continental systems that had things like eunuchs, a private bureaucratic group that serves the emperor personally, and not the state.

Now, the Confucians serve the state, and the emperor is only a symbol of the state. It's nothing personal. I am not serving you as a person. I am serving the institution of the monarchy. You see the same thing in the West, where one talks about loyalty to the Constitution. An American is loyal to the president, but not to Mr Obama! It's the presidency he is loyal to. Even Nixon says it was the presidency that he wanted to protect. Now, that's the Confucian line as well. We protect the monarchy, not the monarch personally.

When a Confucian does something wrong, he just resigns, or goes home, or he just shuts up. That's fine! For example, in the *Song* Dynasty, in the struggles between the reformist *Wang*

Anshi (1021–1086) and the conservatives opposing him, nobody lost their jobs and nobody lost their heads. They may get pushed out of a particular job, but they moved on to something else. But they were fighting on principle!

Now, this is a point of some importance. The *Song* rulers were all invariably very well educated by the Confucians. Neo-Confucianism was very new then, and all of them more or less recognized its supremacy as a set of ideals. By *Ming* times, however, China had gone through a hundred years of Mongol rule. The Mongols were very different, and were loyal to Kublai Khan (1215–1294), not to the institution. So under their rule, the *Shidafu* were at first just pushed out altogether. They had no say. It took the Mongols sixty years to reinstitute the examination system. They had to do that because, in the end, they could not find anyone they could trust to work for them! That's why they brought back the Confucians.

Then came the *Ming* Dynasty (1368–1644). The founder, *Zhu Yuanzhang* (died 1398), came from a very different background. He was not of the literati class; in fact, he did not have much of an educational background. He was a poor peasant who was educated by monks in a Buddhist temple. He learned how to read and write, and joined a religious rebel group, precisely the kind that the Confucians were afraid of. They were sort of a *Falun Gong* equivalent.[7] All these peasant rebellions had Buddhist and Taoist roots, and *Zhu Yuanzhang* came from such a background. But these were acceptable to everybody then, including the literati, because they were trying to drive out the Mongols who had by that time degenerated into a terrible set of rulers. The Mongol system had been badly corrupted, so the literati backed these rebels, something they would normally not do. Zhu managed to recruit some of the literati against a common enemy.

Zhu became emperor, but with roots that were not at all Confucian. He respected the help he had received from the Confucians, and he was very distrustful of his own men because they were all like him. These were his military commanders, brilliant guys like *Xu Da*. He didn't trust any of them because they all had ambitions, like *Zhu* himself. So he had to trust the Confucians. But he would nevertheless observe them carefully, because they were now in the system, in the organization, and his commanders also had friends amongst the literati. So there developed the idea that the ruler didn't completely trust the Confucians. *Zhu* had to play the Confucians one against the other. About twenty years after he came to power, he used the case of *Hu Weiyong*, who had literati connections and who was close to the top military leaders, to wipe the whole lot out. He was like Mao. In fact, he was even more successful than Mao. Mao didn't succeed really; the communist party resumed and Deng Xiaoping did come back.

Zhu carried out an absolute massacre, a slaughter of the top leaders. Only a few remained with him, and he rebuilt the whole system in the last years of his life. A very busy man indeed! So it became part of *Ming* tradition to use the literati, but without the respect that they used to enjoy.

In a way, it's like the British system, which has a bit of the Chinese idea in there. The higher ranks of the civil service have men like the Confucian literati who have no political ambition, no plans to join the ruling party, and who just render loyal service to the state and the king. So you can always trust them. They may argue with you, but they will never turn against you. But when you start bringing senior civil servants into the inner circle of party politics, as is sometimes done in Singapore, America and Australia, you blur the line. In Australia, it began with Gough Whitlam (prime minister, 1972–75) and it became more common for leaders after him to do the same.

In the Chinese case, what happened after the *Hu Weiyong* executions in 1380 smudged that line, and the Confucians who supported the second emperor against his uncle were seen as political protagonists. When the uncle, son of *Zhu Yuanzhang*, won and became the *Yongle* Emperor, he surrounded himself with eunuchs. He couldn't trust the senior literati because they had supported his nephew. To summarize the situation, *Zhu Yuanzhang* had not passed his throne to his sons. He had given it instead to his grandson, the son of his eldest son. The uncle in Beijing couldn't accept that, and led a rebellion against the new emperor. Bound to be loyal to the emperor, the whole literati class sided with the young *Jianwen* against *Yongle*. So *Yongle* came to power without literati support. He basically only had eunuchs and soldiers behind him, and so he recruited a fresh young group of *Jinshi*. The old ones wouldn't accept him because they were good Confucians, and did not consider *Yongle* the legitimate emperor. So he tried to regain his legitimacy by killing some of them, and one of the leaders of the Confucians was executed with all the members of his clan. This should not have been done. But *Yongle* did it and the tradition of respect was broken. Although the Confucians tried very hard to repair it, it was never the same again. Once that trust was not one hundred per cent, it could never be the same again. There was always the possibility that the Confucians could actually side with another claimant.

No doubt a new bunch of Confucians was recruited by Emperor *Yongle*, but these acted like eunuchs. So you had a group of these inside the palace, and another outside the palace. All of them had to listen to the emperor though, and so they balanced each other out.

The eunuchs could be very cruel. Every time a Confucian displeased the emperor, and the emperor wished to get rid of him, the eunuchs would torture and execute him. The eunuchs had a spy system, a special branch at their service; and they had their own prison system. They were personally loyal to the emperor, but not to the state. This was the opposite of what should theoretically have been; but during the *Ming* this state of affairs became very obvious. One group was loyal to the emperor and the other group was not quite able to maintain their Confucian principles. So these had to be loyal to the emperor in the same way. If they were not, he would pit the other bunch against them.

OKB: Did that remain the system throughout the *Ming* after the *Yongle* period?

WGW: The system actually modified itself and it went back and forth, back and forth. The Confucians never quite succeeded in getting the balance back. So it's hard to say that it remained right to the end. For example, *Zhang Juzheng* was a very able member of the literati who was also highly political. He recruited some of the eunuchs over to his side, played politics and became a most powerful prime minister. But then, he also helped to undermine the system.

I think the fresh start came with the Manchus who founded the *Qing* (1644–1911). When the Manchus first came to power, there were no eunuchs. They didn't need them. They had the whole Manchu aristocracy to draw upon. So their aristocracy and their loyalty were based on something else, something not Chinese. Their loyalty oath was to the Steppes and to the nomadic system. This was a loyalty that was more personal. But once they married their ideals to the Chinese system, all these Manchurian aristocrats began studying Confucian classics to bolster the dynasty. Now, a whole generation of the literati who were loyal to the *Ming* had been slaughtered by the invaders, but now they were given a chance to serve the Manchus.

The Manchus were smart. Unlike the Mongols, they immediately put the examination system back into place. We mustn't forget that they were not new to this game! They were the descendants of the Jurchens who had ruled northern China earlier.[8] So they were already familiar with Chinese institutions. They were in fact already semi-*Han* by the time of the invasion, so they used *Han* Chinese to serve them and gave them their trust, at least up to a point. They could do that because they had loyal aristocrats on their side, so a balance could be kept. They didn't have to use eunuchs, and what they did was to educate themselves to become like the *Han*.

The argument was, the more Confucian a Manchu became, the more reason there was to put him on top of a *Han*, and to work in the government. And this was what happened. They created what John Fairbank called a diarchy, where you had a Manchu as well as a *Han* in the top positions.[9] The *Han* probably did the work while the Manchu wielded the political power. Whatever it was, the Manchu had precedence because he had a different line of communication with the emperor.

And today, what do we see in China? We actually have a similar system! You have your party secretary and your governor in every province. Of course these two are both party members, while during the *Qing* they would have been Confucians. And all of them at that level had to handle both Manchu and Chinese. It was a bilingual state. We forget that now. Even the Chinese have forgotten that it was always a bilingual state at the very top. While everything was done in Chinese, once you reached the very top, things became bilingual. So you could, for example, go to the *Junjichu*, which was like a military commission, a ministry really — old China had no concept of a cabinet. The *Junjichu* was like the American National Security Council, to which the emperor chose some aristocrats and some bureaucrats. There, the material was in both languages. They may discuss in either language, but it was all recorded in both languages. Now we are finding all these; they are in the archives. After the fall of the *Qing* these were neglected because they had all been taken to Manchuria, when the Japanese set up Manchukuo there. The Chinese just brushed them out of their mind.

Scholars are now getting back into it and are reading them. Foreign scholars in the nineteenth century did study them. German and French scholars back then could read Manchu because they had to know Manchu to have access to the top echelons of power. But after 1912, the Chinese threw it all out — the Manchus were losing their language anyway. But people are now relearning it in order to read the archives; and you find Chinese and Manchu records parallel at the top level, but not at the bottom. At the bottom, all was done in *Han* Chinese. At the top, the most crucial decisions were recorded in both languages and, interestingly, the two were not quite the same. There were always some additional things in the Manchu version, which were for the Manchus to read. Very interesting.

So what we have here was a dual system. In a way, even in the distant past, the Chinese had a bit of it: There was the man given a job of running the province, the governor, and then there was an imperial censor who went around checking on him, and who reported directly to the emperor. While the governor reported to the central civil service, the *Liubo*, the censor, the *Yushi*, reported to the emperor. Now, why most of the Chinese literati in the final stages found it easy to turn against the *Qing* was because the Empress Dowager *Cixi* (1835–1908) had turned more and more towards the Manchu aristocracy. She didn't trust the *Han*. So they said: "Well, this system has gone awry", and supported the revolution instead.

OKB: *Kang Youwei* (1858–1927) came along at the end in an effort to change things.

WGW: In a way. He messed it up because the Empress Dowager never forgave the *Han* Chinese for attempting the Hundred Days' Reform.[10] "They're ruining my empire! They cannot be trusted!" She was not very smart; she was very old fashioned and very much focused on the preservation of Manchu privilege. That was her heritage, you see, and she couldn't see beyond that. So, do you save the *Qing*, or do you save China? That was the question.

Sun Yatsen (1866–1925) in a way represented a new force, and the Manchu response reinforced Sun Yatsen's message that they could not have Manchu rulers anymore.[11] If the last imperial house had been Chinese, they could have done what the Japanese did. But with the Manchus, there was no way that could happen! Who was to replace the emperor? Who to replace the *Man* rulers? Who has the right to be *Tian Zi*? There was nothing for it but to declare China a republic.

Notes

1. For a quick introduction to Central Asian political history, see Peter B. Golden, *Central Asia in World History* (New York: Oxford University Press, 2011).
2. Owen Lattimore, *Inner Asian Frontiers of China* (Capitol, 1951).
3. Robert Clive (1725–74), also known as "Clive of India", is credited with establishing the English East India Company's political and military supremacy in Bengal. Warren Hastings (1732–1818) was the first Governor-General of Bengal (1772–85). These two together played key roles in the creation of British India.
4. Thomas Cahill, *How the Irish Saved Civilization* (Rosetta, 2004).
5. Anthony C. Yu, *State and Religion in China: Historical and Textual Perspectives* (Chicago: Open Court, 2006).
6. Respectively, these mean "Peace", "All under Heaven is Common Property", and "Great Peace in All under Heaven".
7. *Falun Gong* is a modern-day Buddhist *qigong* sect that was founded

in 1992 by *Li Hongzhi*, and grew enormously in membership during the 1990s. It was banned in China in 1999.
8. The Jurchens ran the *Jin* Dynasty from 1115 to 1234 in northern China, covering the area that would be Manchuria as well as large parts of the Yellow River basin.
9. John King Fairbank, "The Manchu-Chinese Dyarchy in the 1840's and '50's". *Far Eastern Quarterly* 12, no. 3 (1953): 265–78.
10. This vain last-minute attempt at reforming dynastic rule was done with the emperor's consent, and lasted from 11 June to 21 September 1898.
11. Sun is widely considered the "Father of the Republic of China".

Chapter 2

THE TWO-OCEAN MEDITERRANEAN

SOUTHEAST ASIA ON THE PERIPHERY

OKB: Let's talk about Southeast Asia as a phenomenon. Modern nation building in the region can to an extent be seen as a defence strategy inherited by the region's peoples as a postcolonial contingency. ASEAN, the Association of Southeast Asian Nations founded in 1967, would then be understood as a collective attempt in that direction. Elsewhere, you have drawn some parallels between the Mediterranean and archipelagic Southeast Asia.[1] Can we continue our discussion in that direction?

WGW: One must acknowledge that Southeast Asia was very much peripheral to the main action in world history for a long, long time. And one of the reasons for this was because the main action was between powers that were essentially continental ones, land powers.

To what extent the peculiar features of the Mediterranean acted as a trigger for civilization is arguable. Egypt's civilization or the Babylonian civilization didn't actually depend on the

Mediterranean. They were riverine civilizations, and the urban conditions that rose out of the two great river systems of the Nile and the Tigris-Euphrates didn't have much directly to do with the Mediterranean, although they — the Egyptian one particularly — had an impact on the Mediterranean development later on. The entire struggle to define themselves as peoples, as economies, ultimately as states, was done mainly on land, except for the Mediterranean.

The Mediterranean story is fascinating to me because that was the only place in ancient times where they fought at sea. Everywhere else the fighting was on land. In the Indian Ocean there was virtually no fighting at sea. No naval warfare, or at least no record of such. And on the China side, very little as well; just some minor conflicts along the coast with Japan and Korea, but all quite negligible. So the only real fighting on water was in the Mediterranean, and it has a special resonance for me because the creation of modern civilization really came out of the fact that land and water conditions were combined for a particular system of political governance. The truly continental one — the Eurasian one — developed on its own. It had a nomadic pastoral base, and it remained very dominant for thousands and thousands of years, because the geographical conditions did not really favour anything else. Throughout, it stayed nomadic and pastoral, mobile and dynamic, and its peoples remained a threat to all the settled communities nearby. The settled ones built cities and towns, and their power was largely land-based, except around the Mediterranean. There, they had to have ships, and so you had the Phoenicians and the Greeks fighting at sea.

One of the decisive battles of history was the Greek defeat of the Persian fleet in the Mediterranean.[2] That was to my knowledge the first major and really significant naval defeat that was ever recorded. I know of no earlier references.

OKB: Would you class northern European culture as being part of the Eurasian?

WGW: The Scandinavians were just as much on the fringe as the Chinese and the Southeast Asians were. They were not part of the major power bases of the earliest civilizations, states or nomadic confederations. These were continental-based, and when they expanded, they always expanded overland. None of them really expanded overseas. The first to do so were the Greeks — and then the Romans. You see, even the Egyptians didn't do that. And all the peoples who attacked Egypt came by land. The ones who came from the Tigris-Euphrates or from the Syria area came through the Palestinian area. That's an entrance into Egypt. They basically fought over that. They are still fighting over that today.

Riverine civilization developed what we know as urbanity. They also developed powerful land armies bent on conquest. The Greeks developed an urban civilization as well, but their land was limited and they had little economic surplus to expand, except during the time of the Macedonian king, Alexander (356–323 BC). The Macedonians led the other Greeks overland to build an empire. They marched right up to the borders of Afghanistan, of India. That was absolutely remarkable. The Greeks of that period were definitely being drawn into playing the continental game.

OKB: I am reminded of a history of the Byzantine Empire, which I read recently.[3] We tend to put the two terms "Greek" and "Roman" together today, but the Eastern Roman Empire that remained for hundreds of years after the Western Roman Empire fell is more accurately described as "Greek" rather than "Roman".

WGW: Yes, that's right. The Greco-Roman term is a balance. We normally think of the Greeks in terms of the Athenian Greeks, but that phenomenon actually died out.[4] It was the Hellenistic Empire of Alexander which produced the Byzantine Empire, and which produced the Greek Empire in Egypt along the coast of the Mediterranean. The Macedonians who went overland to India were not the original Greeks we associate with Socrates, Plato, Aristotle, Athens, Pericles, the Peloponnesian wars, and all the rest of it.

The Greek world was drawn back into the continental system. You see, when Western Europeans talk about the Greco-Romans, they are referring to the Mediterranean Greeks and Romans, not to the Byzantines. The Byzantines were the Greeks who went the other way. They are regarded as the East, as opposed to the West. The Russians and all the Orthodox Christians are all regarded as the East.

OKB: Yes. Byzantine culture and its considerable influence are somewhat disregarded.

WGW: Yes, because our view is dominated by the Holy Roman Empire that became important from the Renaissance onwards. What happened there was that Western Europe came to manage the balance well between land and sea; and took things out to the sea, as it were! And this finally led to the Portuguese, the Dutch, and the British grabbing the advantage. All these countries border the Atlantic.

The Mediterranean's dynamics switched over to the Atlantic. That became the counterpoint to the continental past. The British in a way are exemplars there because when they say, "Fog in Channel, Continent Cut Off", you realize that there is a certain mentality being expressed. It's the continent that's cut off, not Britain.

That is the basis of the modern world. The globalized, maritime world of naval power may be a British perspective, but it was started really by the Portuguese, the Spaniards and the Dutch. However, they didn't give it the shape that it took by the late eighteenth century when the British destroyed all the other navies, especially when they smashed the French in the Indian Ocean and cleared the way for their total dominance.[5] They imposed a completely different alternative to the continental system. And I call it the Mediterranean system because it refers to the Greco-Roman heritage. By ignoring the East, Greco-Roman means Athenian democracy, Roman Empire, British Empire. A lineage is exhorted. The emphasis is on the naval empire of the Greeks and the Romans, which was the basis of the British Empire.

OKB: The British see themselves as inheritors of this ancient resistance to continental power then.

WGW: Oh yes! Look at the way the British elites educated themselves in the nineteenth century. At Rugby, Marlborough, Eton, Harrow, etc., they studied Greco-Roman history in those terms. The Byzantines never came into it at all. They might have touched on Alexander because Alexander's story then justified British India. In any case, Alexander is a heroic figure in his own right. The Greco-Roman tradition they really identify with is the Mediterranean one. And that, of course, is what their Christianity is — Mediterranean Christianity. There were other Christians, certainly — the Christians of Ethiopia, the Nestorians and so on. But these were of no real interest to them. It was the Roman Empire's Christianity that they associated themselves with. And so it is that we talk about the Judeo-Christian and the Roman Christian, not the Greek Christian. The Greek Christian was on the other side, on the continental side. You can see the bias there. This was a heritage that incorporated the whole Mediterranean world in which the balance between continental and naval power was understood for the first time.

The Scandinavians came much later. They had a naval focus, but they did not have the civilization to back it up. The German-Viking tradition was carried on by the Dutch and the British. It was they who managed to link it up with the state and with their civilization.

Southeast Asia, if you see it in that context, was peripheral to continental dynamics. So it enjoyed a relatively beautiful and peaceful time. The Austronesian-speaking people, the Malayo-Polynesians, if you like, were left alone to do whatever they wanted to do in the south.

To the north, as the Chinese pushed southwards, tribes moved down from Yunnan and Guangxi into Southeast Asia, mixing with the Mon-Khmer base and the Austro-Asiatic language speakers. The Vietnamese, the Khmers, the Mons, all intermingled. They were much more continental though, because they were resisting a continental power. Interestingly enough, none of them developed a naval tradition.

You see, again, the idea of power expressed through the sea was never developed, even in Southeast Asia. It was never the basis of a very powerful state, except for Java perhaps. Even Java in the early stages was never quite powerful enough. None of the other Malay Archipelago peoples managed this. Java was the only one because — and this is controversial — they had an understanding of a great Indian political tradition. The Sanskritic idea of kingship and divinity gave them a sense of something greater than being a small riverine kingdom — a sense of ruling in the name of some higher transcendental power.

OKB: ... As with the Thais, perhaps.

WGW: Yes, yes, but the Thais, don't forget, were actually latecomers. The Thais and the Burmans all came from Yunnan.

The original people were really Mon-Khmers, who were eventually completely overcome in Myanmar by the Burmans and in the Menam Valley by the Thais, and only in what is today's Cambodia, did they survive. Only the Khmers survived — the Mons have basically disappeared now. You see how hard it has been for the Khmers to survive against the Vietnamese coming on one side, and the Thais coming on the other ... till this day!

If you read King Sihanouk's works, there is an obsession with Angkor. After all, Angkor fell to attacks from the Thais.[6] The threat from the Thais and the Vietnamese continues to this day! That is why the Khmers are, in a way, grateful to the French, because at the final stage, when they could have been wiped out by the Thais or the Vietnamese like the Mons, or been divided among them, the French stepped in and recognized the Kingdom of Cambodia. And that is why Sihanouk always refers to the idea that they were actually saved. The Khmers were declining, and now they try to rewrite history from the time of Angkor to Sihanouk's time. But a lot of it is merely a defensive exercise.

At the same time, the Vietnamese were obsessed with fighting China, and so didn't push as far and fast as they could have. The Thais had problems with the Burmese, and were also distracted. Otherwise they would have probably finished off the Khmers. The Thais were much more aggressive to begin with, moved much faster, and came earlier. The Vietnamese were caught up for a long time, blocked by the Chams. Geography was also against them. They were on the other side of the mountains, while the Thais simply came straight down the river.

If you look at the Mekong River today ... north of the Cambodian border, you have the Laotians. Now Laotians and Thais are the same people. They had come right down and were on the verge of moving in. They were all over the Khmers already. That's why they are still arguing about the Preah Vihear Temple on the border. That was a Khmer building that the Thais took over. In fact, many Thai temples were originally Mon-Khmer temples.

OKB: So the temple issue was frozen by French colonialism.

WGW: Yes, that's right. The French drew the present border between Laos and Thailand. There were no borders before that. The people there were all related Thai tribes, with different little chieftains and so on. But the French wanted to control the Mekong in order to have another route into China. There was already one by land from Vietnam, and having one up the Mekong would have been an added advantage for them. In the course of doing that, the French wanted to draw a boundary. They thrashed it out with the Thais for a long time, and the boundary is now on the Mekong itself. But the fascinating thing to me — something that didn't click in my head before — is that the majority of the so-called Laotian people are actually in Thailand. They are on the western side of the Mekong. But because the French, against Thai protests, drew the border at the Mekong, they left the majority of the Lao people in Thailand.

OKB: The country of Laos is actually at the fringe of the Laotian nation then?

WGW: And Laos, east of the river, is actually thinly populated. Between the Thais and the Vietnamese is this range of hills, occupied by different small tribes. They live on the top, separating Vietnamese space from Thai/Lao space, as it were. And to the east of the Khmers were the Chams. The Chams are a fascinating people, a coastal Austronesian people. They could have been a naval power — they actually had a bit of naval power, like the Malays. But they didn't have powerful states, so they didn't develop great navies. But as seamen, they were naturals. So when you look at the fragmentation of Southeast Asia, the northern part was being absorbed into the overland continental system, which left the archipelagic side even more peripheral.

So there was never a single region here. Right down the middle in the north, there was a historical if not a geographical cut. We've been spending the last decades trying to give Southeast Asia a sense of region because it wasn't there in the tradition. They never thought of themselves that way. And therefore the Malay world was a very fortunate world — they were left alone. The continental part didn't bother them because they were oceanic! The Mon-Khmers and the Chams were less fortunate.

The first continental power to stretch deep into Southeast Asia was the Thais! When they began moving down the peninsula, they did have a navy. There is no doubt that it was their naval power that Javanese naval power confronted. Srivijaya Majapahit did in fact run into Thai naval power.

After reaching the Menam Valley, the Thais absorbed some Mon-Khmer technologies. The Mon-Khmers presumably had some ships, and the Thais built on this. When moving down the Malay Peninsula, they found that they needed naval transportation, or at least, trans-shipment. So they built ships that became powerful enough to do that, because the state was now more powerful. It had the resources and the political, administrative and organizational structure needed to build a navy; something the Mon-Khmer didn't seem terribly interested in.

So the Thais pushed down to the point of being a threat to Malacca. The Malays then turned to the Chinese; and to that extent, Admiral *Zheng He* contributed to the rise of Malacca. It helped that *Zheng He* himself was a Muslim, and was sympathetic to the new polity. There were already Muslims throughout the region — Arabs, Persians, Indian Muslims, Javanese Muslims, and

Chinese Muslims going to Java to trade. The treasure ships that have recently been discovered show that the Arabs were very active, but mainly as merchants, and so were peripheral to the politics of the region.

From what we can see, *Zheng He* supported the independence of Malacca from the Thais so that he could use it as a base for voyages to the Indian Ocean, just like Singapore and Penang also serve that purpose today for travellers going west. In his case, he used Malacca in the middle of the strait instead of the two ends, which gave that city a fantastic chance to develop. So when you look at it that way, *Zheng He*'s voyages were again just projections of continental power. That also helps to explain why it was so temporary.

In the end though, the continental pull was too great, and the *Ming* did not push out further. The same went for the Thais, who did not thrust down too persistently. They did take Pattani, Kelantan and Trengganu, no doubt, and these were obliged to pay tribute to Thailand, mainly because the Thais had some naval power.

The Burmese, on the other hand, never developed naval power, as far as I can tell. We don't have any record of Burmese naval power. On land, they were definitely powerful. They certainly defeated the Thais and took all the Mon areas. This was all the extension of the continental system rolling down into the Malay Peninsula ...

OKB: ... until they hit water, and had to stop.

WGW: Yes, like the Chinese, who hit water and didn't want to go beyond that. So the Malay world was very fortunate. They were left alone and they went their own way and therefore didn't develop a great urban civilization, except for Java under Indian influence, where you have Borobudur and other kingdoms.

OKB: Even there, some influence would have come from continental Indian culture.

WGW: A bit of it. The Indians also stopped. They weren't that interested in the sea either. You see, only the Cholas, the Tamil group, did that. They had a naval empire for a while, but then in the end they found that their real enemy was on land. At sea they had no enemies. They showed the same thinking as the Chinese — they sent out ships but found no enemies, and so decided to withdraw.

The Chola Empire (300s–1279) had navies. They probably defeated the Srivijayans, and reached Kedah and the Straits of Malacca.[7] They probably controlled parts of the Bengal coast as well, but after a while they saw that there was nothing much to worry about; there was no need for big naval systems. The Malays were as always willing to trade with everybody, and so the nature of the relationship essentially became mercantile and peaceful. There was no need for warfare.

For the Cholas, and later on the Vijayanagar Empire (1336–1646), their major enemies all came by land. The Moghuls from the north were a continental power, no question about that. They almost reached Tamil Nadu, after taking most of India, and having moved into Bengal.

The Moghuls were quite content with what they had achieved and never thought of going to sea. They built the beautiful Taj Mahal and all the great cities in India, collaborated with the Hindus and became quite integrated in a way, and had a working relationship with the Hindus, who paid tribute and acknowledged the Moghul Empire (1526–1857). So the Moghul Empire didn't actually run what was called the Moghul Empire. They sort of decentralized it, and these Hindu rulers became their agents.

The Maharajas no doubt fought many times among themselves, but in the end none of the battles were transformative. They basically held the line between what the Moghuls actually controlled and what the Hindu rulers actually controlled, and then peace was settled by one paying tribute to the other. But it was still about continental power. In that context, the coming of the Europeans was what had a major transformative effect. People do say that the Europeans didn't actually impose their system until the late eighteenth century. There is truth in that. Basically the Portuguese, the Spanish and the Dutch were on the whole just accepting of the locals, and were just trying to fit in. Nevertheless, their impact was gradually to bring a different world view to the region — a world view that included naval power, and where trade was not just trade. Trade was armed trade. We now had guns; guns on ships!

As far as I know, the practice of having guns on the Portuguese men-of-war and the Spanish galleons was not known in this part of the world. There were sailors bearing arms, but not guns fixed on ships ... cannons screwed to the deck. This was a decisive innovation. It defeated the Arabs and the Persians in the Persian Gulf and in the Indian Ocean. It wiped out everybody in the way. The Chinese had no navy to speak of, and the continental powers of Southeast Asia didn't have any either. So the Europeans were just dealing with the Malays, who couldn't match them. As we know, the Portuguese took Malacca easily. Malacca had cannons, no doubt, but not on ships.

The skills of the Portuguese engineers quickly came to be widely recognized. All the rulers realized the need to employ them to build cannons. Portuguese cannons were superior, and they could be used safely on a ship. Even the Chinese employed them during the late *Ming*. So the Portuguese actually made themselves very useful as professional gunmakers. They may have come out on Portuguese ships, but they actually left their service to work for Burmese kings, Thai kings, the Vietnamese, the Chinese ...

OKB: But they were not backed, like the English later, by the power of their state ...

WGW: No. This was private enterprise. The Portuguese state didn't exercise strict control. The King of Portugal and notable merchants in Portugal would merely fund a ship, and recruited anybody who would go. Who would have wanted to go? This was a very dangerous journey, and once you went, you were not back for three years or more. Those who went were adventurous types, and they were not all Portuguese. There were Frenchmen, Italians, a lot of Dutchmen, and Englishmen. People who knew how to sail and were not afraid of the sea went to Lisbon to enlist and to come out. You see that in the early records.

But that was how the Dutch and the English knew so much even before the formation of their East India companies. These companies could be formed partly because there were these people who already had been with the Portuguese, who came back to tell their countrymen what it was all about. So they said, why should we leave it all to the Portuguese to make the profit? We will go in ourselves. That was really the turning point.

After all, who was Christopher Columbus? He was Italian! The idea of nation states didn't exist. They were not nations. They were just a bunch of people who shared the same religion — they were all Catholics. Linguistically they used a kind of Spanish-Portuguese lingua franca, which was not so different from Italian. Even the Dutchmen could understand it, and the British could learn it. They were, after all, the Holy Roman Empire under a Holy Roman Emperor, who happened to be Spanish at one time and then French at another and German at yet another.

OKB: Recently I read a book on white slavery, on how the northern African states captured thousands of Europeans as slaves, to build their palaces.[8]

WGW: Yes, that is why Gibraltar was so important. The British got there quite early, with the help of the Portuguese. But that's a very big story again, you see! That was how the Mediterranean became so crucial to modern history. The Arab world conquered the southern coasts, and the Christian world hung on to the north. The line remains more or less the same today. Now, that in itself is really remarkable.

You can see how significant it was when the Arabs took over the southern Mediterranean. It changed the whole pattern, because up to that point the Roman Empire controlled both sides, or at least tried to control both sides. But when the Arabs gained control over the whole southern stretch and moved into the Iberian Peninsula, they forced the Christians to come together on the northern side. In the end, the Spanish and Portuguese succeeded in pushing back, but the whole process took hundreds of years — from the eighth to the fifteenth century. During that period, the line hardened. It is now an absolute line.

The crusades were a very good example of the Christians trying to push back, but failing. And failing not because of the Arabs, who were really not that strong. It was the Turks they had to face, coming out from the deepest parts of the continent. Here again, we see the coming together of land and sea power in a balance. One land power supported the southern Mediterranean, and others — the Germanic, Slav, the French, the Latin lands, the Iberian, the Anglo-Saxons — all supported the other side. And that line became harder and harder with every crusade. The push went forwards and backwards, forwards and backwards — and the line grew firm.

This process stretched into the nineteenth century — with Greece gaining independence from the Ottoman Empire — and into our time. The Ottoman Empire itself stretched into the northern Mediterranean from the east, into the Adriatic, and what would become Yugoslavia.

OKB: So allowing Turkey to join the European Union today, seen in the context of this centuries-old conflict, would be quite a leap in the imagination for many.

WGW: It would be quite traumatic. I was very struck the first time I went to places like Munich and Vienna by how they still proclaim this business about the Gates of Vienna, etc., being where first the Mongols and then the Turks were held back.

OKB: I have Yugoslavian and Hungarian friends who proudly claim their ancestors as the gatekeepers of Europe.

WGW: ... and of the Catholic world, too. The Orthodox world lost out, and it was the Catholic world that defended Christianity. Greece fell, Yugoslavia fell. Much of today's Russia came under the Tartars and the Mongols and then the Ottoman Empire. So in the end, it was the Romans who stood their ground. That is where Western Europe came into existence. The whole concept came after the fall of Constantinople in 1453. After that, you had the Renaissance, followed by the Reformation (1517–1648).

Now, what was all that about? *Well, it was the Western world redefining itself!* For the Western world, the eastern border was Central Europe, not Central Asia. On one side was the Europe that was lost, and on the other was the Europe that was protected and saved for Catholicism. The latter combined continental and maritime powers — and here you see how decisive the absolute division of the Mediterranean was. The Ottomans took the other side of the Mediterranean, and isolated Europe from Asia altogether. The Mongols had started doing that, but it was the Turkish Empire that sealed it, and that cut Europe off totally.

The Venetians tried their best to break this blockade, but all they could do was trade, make peace, be very nice and diplomatic and so on, and do business with the Muslim world. And that's why the Europeans have been suspicious of the Venetians because they were not one hundred per cent pro-Europe. They were on the borders, on the frontiers. But in the end, the fact was the wealth was in Asia. They knew that. The wealth of the Arab world was obvious; there was the spice trade that was so important to Europe, and there was trade with India — the textiles and the gold and what not. The Europeans were being deprived.

So, what do you do? You go to sea! You see, the Portuguese then explored the African coast, which had been completely neglected until then. Sub-Saharan Africa had been completely neglected, and was considered a hopeless place — barbaric, tropical, and disease-ridden, and barred off by the Sahara. Even the Arab world couldn't get there properly by land. The Christian world had to go by sea, and the only people who could go by sea were the Portuguese. They were living right at the southwestern edge of the continent, so it was they who succeeded in breaking this encirclement.

OKB: In this wide sweep, today's state of Israel would quite naturally be seen as an outpost inserted into the Muslim world, would it not?

WGW: All sorts of people occupied Palestine — the Romans had it, the Hellenistic world had it, the Arabs came and took it all, and then the Turks had it. And the European crusaders had it now and then. Everybody claimed it.

What you call an outpost, seen in the wide sweep of ancient history, was actually a corridor. It was a corridor between the continental powers in Asia and Egypt in northern Africa. Egypt after all always commanded great attention, being a great civilization and so on. So Palestine was the eastern Mediterranean corridor that linked up the continental powers. Spain in the western Mediterranean was already clearly dominated by the Moors, but to the east, things were much more miscellaneous and complicated. Palestine was always strategically important. Today, you have the oil element thrown in as well.

CONQUERING THE OCEANS

OKB: The picture I am getting is that the focus of a lot of global economic activity and connectivity through the ages would be on the southern belly of the Europe-Asia landmass.

WGW: ... on the Indian Ocean. There was Roman interest in the Indian Ocean, because the Hellenistic Empire actually touched the Arabian Gulf and went beyond the Suez — the connection went down the Red Sea. You see all that already mentioned in the Bible. Ethiopia was already known, the southern part of Arabia was known. The Persian Gulf and the Indian Ocean were already in the consciousness of the Western empires.

So from that point of view, the Indian Ocean was now blocked off by forces hostile to the European powers. Arab and Persian merchants were the ones who were sailing at that point, and came to be classed together through Islam. Before that, the references were to Persian traders. We know there was very intensive coastal trade between the Arab world, the Persian world and the west coast of India. That's ancient. There are not a great deal of records, but we do know a little where matters of shipping is concerned. The most effective shipping was Arab-Persian shipping. They were the nomads of the sea, as it were. The ship replaced the camel for their trading purposes, and they developed it. But it was not linked to any major political power.

Although the Persian Empire was very powerful, we don't see the Persian kings being involved very much in naval matters. Their interests were always in Central Asia and Europe. In other words, they were a continental power and remained so throughout, as far as I can tell. The sea was more for private enterprise, carried out by lightly armed merchants. There were no powerful state-sponsored war machines, so that's where the Portuguese had their advantage. They were bringing something new to the area — state-backed private enterprise, with a flotilla of ships that could be sustained.

State backing was needed for sustainability. One tended to lose a lot of ships, and that was hard for private enterprise to absorb. A state on the other hand can sustain large numbers of ships, and provide capital and support. The Dutch and the English learned from that, and each of them formed their own East India Company — the English started theirs in 1600 and the Dutch founded the Vereenigde Oost-Indische Compagnie two years later.

Long-distance ocean trade was a totally new innovation. It was a revolution in fact, and the revolution in technology that followed from that was what determined the modern world. It completely changed the nature of power and altered wealth distribution throughout the world. Once you had crossed over to America, you created a completely new set of conditions. Naval power became everything, and for a long time. The Spanish in particular were ahead of everybody else, and maintained the world's strongest navy. The fear that Francis Drake and the English had for the Spanish Armada was well founded. The Spanish Armada was indeed the most powerful fleet up to the end of the sixteenth and into the seventeenth century.

The question as to why the Spanish did not build on that has been argued for a long time. I'm not sure if there is any real conclusion about it, but the major trend is to say that the Spanish failed because they did not develop a middle class — a business class, in other words. The Spanish remained very feudal in their attitudes, and their power base remained a church-based landowning aristocracy that never allowed a middle class to develop its own autonomy and rights.

Now, the Dutch did just the opposite. They hardly had any aristocrats. When the Dutch nation was created, when they got their independence (de facto in 1581; de jure in 1648), it was all thanks to merchants. It was the middle class that created the Dutch nation.

Across the English Channel, it was also the middle class in London that eventually overthrew Charles I (1600–1649) and destroyed the old monarchy to create the new kind of Englishmen. These were based in London, and their *wealth* was based in London. Even earlier, the money was always from London, and it was the London merchants who always had some say! No doubt the aristocrats had the army, so the merchants kept their heads down and negotiated with the help of their money. But by the time of Elizabeth I (1533–1603), there was a new life in the guilds of London; among the merchant classes.

In Spain the enterprises were royal ones from beginning to end, including the sending of Columbus across the Atlantic. The Spanish aristocrats, who would make use of the lower classes sometimes, never gave the latter any say. One of the theories I find attractive — but I am not sure if it is conclusive or not — is that the failure to broaden the interests of the Spanish nation in the naval and imperial enterprises meant that they didn't have a solid base at home. This meant that once the aristocrats got caught up in either bankruptcies or extravagance — once they lost control over their wealth and power — they lost out. On the other hand, the mercantile types in the East India Companies founded by the English and the Dutch were solidly based and cash rich, and were capable of maintaining long-distance trade by being united as traders. They did not compete amongst themselves. They competed with the outside world.

OKB: Keeping to the paradigm of our discussion, the Spanish went over the Atlantic and took over a lot of land, and remained continental even on the other side of the Atlantic. In time, other European powers also settled in America, but the English did not become continental. Instead, they remained sea-bound in their exercise of power on the global stage. Would the case of the Philippines on the other side of the world illustrate your point here?

WGW: That was a really interesting accident of history. It was the Treaty of Tordesillas[9] that divided the world between the Spanish and the Portuguese. The Pope just wanted to make sure the Spanish and the Portuguese wouldn't fight with each other. When Magellan and his crowd arrived at the Philippines from the east, they saw the Portuguese were already in the Spice Islands, south of the Philippines. They came to an understanding, and it was in Mindanao and somewhat south of that island that the Spanish stopped, leaving the Portuguese to have rights over the rest. So the Philippines came into being by accident. The Spanish would not have claimed it — I think, not necessarily — if not for the fact that they had the practice of dividing the world up with the Portuguese. It was linked very much with the Latin America project, the Columbus project, which leads to your point about the interest in landownership in South America. To the Church, landownership was the key to wealth.

OKB: The need to work land also encouraged peasant slavery. I imagine the conquered peoples could have been used as sailors and not peasants if the thinking on power and economics had been different. What about the case in North America? Why did that turn out so differently?

WGW: It looks to me, that for a long time, the English did not get very far. They had thirteen colonies, but their settlements remained coastal. For two hundred years they didn't cross the Alleghenies, partly thanks to the natives! Their enemies were the French, the Spanish and the Dutch, and the fighting was in the Caribbean.

In fact, the Caribbean is very interesting, too, if you compare it to Southeast Asia. The only other part of the world that resembles Southeast Asia is the Caribbean — archipelagic and without its own civilization or political system. The fact that its peoples were wiped out makes the Southeast Asian story very interesting in that the Malay world had enough political structure to resist the West to an extent. They had a mixture of Hindu-Buddhist plus Muslim ideas of kingship, administration, governance, strategic thinking for rulers, and linking rulers to Allah or other divinities for legitimacy.

The Caribbean peoples had nothing like that, so the West simply took over — the Spanish took some bits, the French others, the Dutch theirs, and the British as well. So it could never develop a sense of region.

But in Southeast Asia, there were states. You see that in the end, the colonial powers had to leave; they couldn't colonize it properly. There were peoples there with cultures, with their own ability to resist the European powers. Also, the region was too far away from Europe — there were never enough Europeans here. The Caribbean peoples, on the other hand, were just too vulnerable, and were also wiped out by disease. In Cuba, Dominica, Haiti, Jamaica, and so on — the natives were completely wiped out. So that story ended there.

Southeast Asia was fortunate in that it was both left alone and yet had enough input from outside to give it capacity to defend itself against latecomers. So everything that was adopted afterwards was essentially done voluntarily. They took in Hinduism and Buddhism voluntarily; they took in Islam voluntarily. There were no religious wars, nothing like that at all. All was voluntarily done. The only thing that was not was Western modernization. *That* was imposed on them.

Even Catholicism in the Philippines was voluntary for most people. The Muslims in the south resisted, but that battle is an old one brought there from the other side of the world. It was not local. The locals didn't fight for any other reason than that the churches resisted the Muslims and the Muslims resisted the churches. That was the only case. All other religious and cultural influences were voluntary.

It's extraordinary when you think about it. There was no religious war whatsoever here. The fighting was usually over trading rights, and so on. With that tradition, religion played very little role during the coming of the West. What the Malay world was basically interested in was trade. The continental part of Southeast Asia may have been less so, having a different kind of defence system and political set-up. The maritime world, on the other hand, was entirely a trading world, and the West took advantage of that. What they brought in — the new factor they brought in — was military power; naval power that had staying power and that built bases, be they in Penang, Batavia, Singapore, or even Macau.

Malacca under the Portuguese was the beginning. They inherited the Malay city and turned it into an armed fortress for trading expansion. This was not what the Malaccan empire was about entirely. Old Malacca was a bit of everything. It was a Malay world kind of enterprise. The new Malacca was instead a Portuguese enterprise being carried out thousands of miles from home. They needed armed bases and basically acquired three — Malacca, the little foothold of Macau, and Ambon in the Spice Islands. Further west they already had Goa, and that was all they needed.

OKB: In Asia, the Portuguese were not drawn into controlling huge landmasses the way the British did later.

WGW: If you look at the whole of British history, you see that every time they got drawn into continental control, they lost out. It was never in their interest, but that was what they tended to lose sight of.

OKB: Like in America.

WGW: Even further back. From the Normans right down to Henry V and so on, they were fighting in France all the time. And every time, they lost. Finally, the only thing they could do was to go back to their island and say, "Continent cut off". Their only defence was the Channel.

They always had trouble with continental power, because they are a small country. They had a limited population, and the thirteen colonies in America in a way was an exceptional thing! Canada was part of the same thing. Elsewhere, they inhabited islands. They loved islands. Even Australia is an island! Hong Kong is a very good example, like Singapore. That was where they felt safe, because their own power was naval. With naval power you can defend any island.

They should not have gotten caught up in the continent. So, why did they make that mistake in India? I suppose imperial expansion becomes inevitable if your base is on the edge of a continent, and not on an island. You are not safe if you don't push forward. The "forward defence" idea is understandable. I think the thing that attracted them was to get into Delhi. That was one bridge too far though, but they didn't see that. They then went even further — into the Punjab and into Afghanistan. You see, they were really sucked in! They got carried away by hubris and by the imperial history of Alexander and the Roman Empire.

OKB: A sense of destiny crept in.

WGW: Yes. But of course they did very well, when you think of it. It's amazing that they held on for a hundred years to so much territory with maybe, as most people calculate, a hundred thousand British.

OKB: ... Not to mention the deep cultural penetration they achieved.

WGW: Oh fantastic, fantastic! Had they concentrated on cultural penetration, they probably would have done even better. As it was, it cost them a lot. In the end they didn't make much money out of it. Essentially it was a big cost to them also to run the place. The private merchants made their profits, but for the state, it was a big burden in many ways.

The weakening of British ties to Europe as a consequence of large numbers of talented British spending and losing their lives in India was considerable. In a way, once they got caught in that particular trap, they became irrelevant to European history. They were too committed elsewhere. So you can see that British interest in Europe over time became peripheral. And in a way, this fate is repeated in the case of Japan's relationship to Asia.

They got caught in the same sort of historical trap. The fear of the continent — and the conceptual separation from it — became very much a part of the psyche of the people.

The idea of a continental holiday as being simply going to a holiday resort is as quintessentially English as you can get. You have busloads or shiploads of English people going over to Belgium, all to a single street or a quarter where there are English pubs, and everything is made for these tourists to feel at home. They spend all their time there and then go back home. That's the idea of a continental holiday.

In the early days, the upper classes would make a grand tour of Europe. It was no doubt regarded as a great thing even then. To this day, the common Englander thinks it very foreign to cross to the continent. You can see why the British position on the EU has always been so difficult.

OKB: I remember being surprised when English friends, when they mentioned "the continent", actually meant France.

WGW: That was the enemy, for hundreds of years, a thousand years maybe.

OKB: Speaking of historical hang-ups, in Ireland, the focus on the Vikings remains strong, even today. I suppose the Scandinavians left a traumatic mark there.

WGW: Yes, the Irish are very interesting, because they were on the borders for the English. And this is where the British, I think, are very interesting in themselves. They are torn in that they are a mixture of Celts and Anglo-Saxons. They are Germanic and Celtic, and the Germanic side identifies to some extent with the continent. Their roots are there, their language is Germanic, and so many of their people are Germanic in origin. But then the Celtic side is definitely anti-continental. They do have a special relationship with Europe to help them deal with the Germanic peoples though; the Scots and the Irish turned to France, and the Irish turned to Rome, to defend themselves against the Anglo-Saxons. So did the Scots. Scottish Catholics were quite powerful.

But the essential thing is that continental powers in Europe remained very strong, down to Napoleon and to Hitler. The British were always peripheral, always marginal. In the end, in World War II, the British needed the Americans in order to survive. They really could not identify with the Europeans. Someone like Winston Churchill is a heroic figure because he stood for that sort of separation from the continent. But then, he had an American mother. I think we are talking about a deep emotional and historical thing here, which is very difficult to shake off.

OKB: The North Atlantic is now their pond.

WGW: It's the northern Mediterranean in our context. The North Atlantic is a Mediterranean tying together the Americans and the Canadians on one side, and the UK on the other.

OKB: So in this view of global history, where is Africa?

WGW: Africa is very interesting in many ways. It was taken over to a great extent by the Anglo-French powers, so there is an Anglo-French continuum in Africa. Africans in the south were Christianized, and there's an attachment to the Anglo-French. The French have military units to this day in central Africa; in Chad, Niger, and the Central African Republic. These are completely dependent on France.[10]

There is a conflict there between the Christian world and the Muslim world. Both sides have been proselytizing at fantastic speed. Most of the conversions of the twentieth century of Christians and Muslims were in Africa. So right now, the borders are being drawn. Nigeria is a very good example, with the majority being Muslims and the minority Christians.

OKB: I suppose there is resentment against the Chinese suddenly turning up.

WGW: The Chinese are there for very different reasons, looking for resources and trade. A bit of the base was laid during the Cold War. That was done together with the Russians, in support of anti-colonial Africans against Anglo-French power. The divide was very clear. The Anglo-French were on the American side, while the African nationalists were more likely to look for an alternative. They were not communists necessarily, and were just looking for some defence against Anglo-French dominance. So the Chinese state under Mao Zedong and Zhou Enlai got involved. We see some remnant of that. The Chinese sent a lot of workers to build railways, in places like Tanzania for example. It was a question of whether or not a regime in Africa wanted to show that they were not too dependent on Britain or France. Also, the Chinese did everything they could to befriend the Africans who had helped them get into the United Nations.

OKB: So, modern global conflicts and international relations then, stemmed largely from the European need to get round the effective blockade of Europe. Going south, the Portuguese passed Africa and got round the Cape of Good Hope into the Indian Ocean. Going west, the Europeans found America.

WGW: Nobody knew about the Americas. Columbus was heading for India. But once the Europeans found it, they got distracted. If there had been nothing there, they would have come straight through! No doubt Columbus would have taken a longer time crossing the Pacific, which would have been the same ocean as the Atlantic. But one could sail round the landmass, nevertheless, and it did not take them long to find that out. Magellan did it only twenty-eight years after Columbus reached San Salvador, by going south. You can imagine the excitement when all those reports got back to Europe.

One could have tried the northwest, which they also did! The English were exploring Canadian rivers and coasts to see whether they could get to China that way. They were blocked in the south by the Spanish, you see. They thought they could go the other way.

There is a wonderful book by a former colleague of mine, Oskar Spate, called *The Spanish Lake*, which is a history of the Pacific in the early days.[11] The ocean was Spanish controlled then and was indeed a Spanish lake. The Manila galleon trade — plying between China and Mexico via the Philippines — was the biggest thing in those days.

And that is where the Chinese came into the picture. That story is a very interesting one in itself. The wealth of Mexico — the gold and the silver — was a very important contribution to East Asia's economy. The Hokkiens were already in Manila before the arrival of the Spanish, but they came together and that city became the centre of that trade. Now these Chinese were getting too numerous, making the Spanish, who were far from home, rather nervous. This led to a massacre of the Chinese — twice.[12] The Chinese had small mercantile, lightly armed ships, and could not really fight the Spanish armed fleet. While the Spanish had the fortress of Fort Santiago in Manila, the Chinese, despite their numbers, merely had the Chinese quarter.

But trade was rich. Without that, the Philippines could not have survived. They had no resources to speak of — the silver came from Mexico, and the textiles from China. The teas and other things were paid for with Mexican silver. That's why the Mexican dollar became the basic currency of Southeast Asia for hundreds of years, down to the twentieth century.

Southeast Asia never became a Mediterranean, though. I argue that it's only a semi-Mediterranean, because the Mediterranean as a power system, as a basis for civilization, required power to be exerted on at least two sides, counteracting each other. That's how a kind of status quo, a strange stability comes into being, with each side remaining united in peace and war, remaining integrated.

But not in Southeast Asia — the Chinese up north looked away and the others just lived their own lives. So the two were separate, although the conditions for a Mediterranean arrangement could be said to have been there. It didn't interest the Chinese world enough. If the Javanese at that point had been powerful enough to represent a counterpoise to the Chinese, maybe the Chinese would have taken more notice. But the Chinese found Champa too small to bother with; Vietnam was under them for a while and was no threat to them; and beyond that, there was politically nothing much for them in the Malay Peninsula. Indians came, some Persians and Arabs came, some Malays came, but that was it. So they just turned away and paid no more attention.

You need a different world view and different structure to take advantage of that geographical given. The Portuguese didn't quite get there, and the Spanish were not really interested. The Dutch were, but didn't have the power. They actually went very far though. They were in South Africa, Ceylon, India, Malacca, Batavia, all the way up to Taiwan and Japan.

So that chain was there long before the British. The Dutch, being on the continent, unlike Britain, were not safe. They had continually to watch out for the French and the Germans, not forgetting the Spanish, who were still in Belgium. It was still the Spanish Netherlands after all. They were originally fighting the British in faraway lands, but realized in the end that they could not afford to do that. They made their peace after several Anglo-Dutch naval wars. As a continental state, they were vulnerable in a way that the British were not. It was only a matter of time before the British would replace the Dutch as the major sea power. By the eighteeenth century, the Dutch had indeed given in.

SMALL ISLANDS, BIG EMPIRE

OKB: How important was it to the imagination of the maritime British that they managed to defeat Napoleon, the great European power at the turn of the nineteenth century?

WGW: The naval battle was the important thing. Once they controlled the sea, they were able to muster continental support from Spain and the Germans against Napoleon. So it was by sea and by diplomatic means that somebody like the Duke of Wellington could actually defeat Napoleon at Waterloo. By themselves, the British could not have defeated the French on land. On land, they were actually always under tremendous pressure.[13] It was really the allies, led by Wellington, no doubt, who were solid and reliable, and that was because of British control of the seas. In the end it was still naval power that made the difference. The fact that the British could defeat Napoleon in the Mediterranean was very important. They had Gibraltar, they had Cadiz in Spain, and they had the Portuguese. Anglo-Portuguese ties had been very good from the beginning because the Portuguese always needed help against Spain. Basically they stopped Napoleon in the south, and the Germans, realizing that disunity made them vulnerable, got their act together with the Austrian-Hungarian Empire. In the end, everybody was France's enemy — first you contain the French, then you fight them in a land battle. But the crucial thing, I think, was still the naval battle.

The French had virtually no power in the Indian Ocean when the Napoleonic Wars started. They had no navy to speak of, and the defeat in the Mediterranean ended the French Navy for a long time. The fact that the Napoleonic Wars allowed the British, on behalf of the Dutch, to run Java, made it more natural that they would later pick the Riau-Lingga archipelagic area for their base. Stamford Raffles realized that if you didn't control the southern end of the Straits of Malacca, you were never really in charge.

Small islands were really important to the British, irresistible to them. The secret of British naval power — and imperial power — was the use of small islands. And it's quite remarkable. The perfect example I can think of is Guadalcanal in the Solomon Islands in the Pacific. In this group of islands, there is one big island and a number of smaller ones. But where did the British choose to put their base? They picked the tiniest little island off the main island, Tulagi. In other words, the main island was too big. So, even islands could be too big for their strategic purposes. So here, they took the smallest one for defensibility.

OKB: That reminds me of the founding of the colony of Hong Kong. Captain Charles Elliot, who negotiated for the cession of Hong Kong to the British in 1841, was apparently given a scolding by his superiors in London for choosing such a small island for a base.

WGW: It's a rock.

OKB: It's a rock, yes. But given the mentality of those who were actually building the empire, a small island was just right, wasn't it?

WGW: Yes, yes. And Tulagi is much, much smaller than Hong Kong! I have actually been to the Solomon Islands. I went there when I was based in Australia and I saw it. It's very defensible. They built a fort there, some government buildings, and the jetty. All you need do is place one well-armed ship there, and nobody would be able to cross.

You also have the case of *Xiamen*. There, the British built all their offices on *Gulangyu*, a small island off *Xiamen*. *Xiamen* itself is an island, but it was too big for them!

OKB: Taiwan would not have been interesting to them.

WGW: Too big! The Dutch failed to control it. In the end, they had to let go. The island was too big for these maritime powers. Their imperial principle was to maintain small islands that they could defend, given the lack of manpower. If you look at the many studies about how the Dutch lost to *Zheng Chenggong*, the *Ming* loyalist fleeing the mainland in the face of the Manchu invasion, you will see that the Dutch actually had stronger military power.[14] They had a good fortress, and they had well-armed ships that were actually more powerful than *Zheng Chenggong*'s. Theoretically, they could have defended it. But they failed, and in the end they blamed it on the governor for making a number of blunders and mistakes and for surrendering. But the point is that it was not for lack of capacity. Simply put, the Dutch could only control the fringes of this big island.

So the whole nature of the modern world is based on this idea of controlling small islands off the mainland. That is why Singapore is still relevant today — it is just that, you see. When the Malayan Union idea was to be implemented in 1946, the British thought they should hang on to Singapore, not because the Malay leaders didn't want the island because there were too many Chinese, but I think it was also because the British felt they had a chance there. They couldn't retain both Penang and Singapore. All they needed was one island as their base in Southeast Asia.

As it turned out, they had to give up Singapore as well, but of course they didn't expect it to become as successful as it has become. They couldn't have achieved that themselves anyway, because they didn't have the legitimacy. But in any case, an island was something that they understood, and they hung on to Hong Kong for as long as they could.

So you can see why Southeast Asia is so interesting today, and why it was neglected for centuries. It took the Europeans hundreds of years to realize that the whole of Southeast Asia could be something significant for dealing with India and China, the two big powers in the region. It was only on the eve of their departure that they understood this. When the Japanese took control of Southeast Asia, the Europeans realized that the whole of Southeast Asia could be one entity in between China and India. So with the setting up of the South East Asia Command under Mountbatten in Colombo,[15] Southeast Asia began to be seen as a region. That was also when the first books on Southeast Asia were conceived, with E.G.H. Dobby and the geographers, and D.G.E. Hall and Brian Harrison, all writing about a place called "South-east Asia".[16]

Significantly, when D.G.E. Hall did that, he left out the Philippines. He was in the South East Asia Command, which didn't include the Philippines. The Philippines was under the Americans then! But later on of course he made up for it. They had come to understand that it should all be seen as one.

And this is strategically very important. Once the world is globalized, you have one enormous country on one side — China — and you have an India created by the British and now left to the Indians on the other, and you begin to have this image of a Balkanization of the region. It was during this time that there was talk of, and a fear of, a Balkanized Southeast Asia. In trying to avoid Southeast Asia developing into the Balkans of Asia, the idea of making all the countries work together developed — from its humble military origins, as it were.

OKB: I see. So, in time, ASEAN grew out of that.

WGW: Before ASEAN, we had the Southeast Asia Treaty Organization, SEATO. The Cold War was raging, and the Western powers were all contemplating a divided Southeast Asia. Their concern was to contain communism. Already, Vietnam and Myanmar were outside Western control, while Cambodia and Laos didn't really count. In order to protect the colonial territories, Thailand was the key; it had to be protected. So the first thing they did was to bring Thailand into SEATO.

Now, the American idea of Southeast Asia is not the same as the British idea. The Anglo-French idea was what ASEAN is today. The American one was not — it was either East Asia, or a Southeast Asia that stretched all the way across the Indian Ocean to Iran. That was why SEATO included Pakistan. It was because the Americans simply wanted to contain Russia and China. So they formed a long arc. With SEATO, they tried experimenting with different solutions. ASEAN came at the end, after Sukarno fell and was succeeded by Soeharto.

Sukarno was the one they were frightened of. He was too pro-communist, and the communist party was too strong in Indonesia. I remember in 1965, talking to people, how very alarmed they were that Indonesia was going to go communist. Before the actual coup, the Indonesian communist party, the PKI, looked very powerful. This alarmed a lot of people. *Liu Shaoqi*, the vice-president of China, was being entertained by Sukarno in Jakarta, the PKI and the Chinese CCP were in cahoots, and Sukarno had at the same time a lot of left-wingers in his government.

I was in Australia then. Alarm bells were ringing everywhere. The communists were on the borders of Australia! So they talked a lot about "forward defence" and about sending troops to Indonesia. That was the language of the time, you know! I remember there was one infamous remark made by an admiral in New Zealand, which is part of the ANZUS pact.[17] He stated that their frontier was the Mekong, and someone had to point out to him that the Mekong begins in Tibet, in China! But that was the mentality at the time — "forward defence" — and this was all because of the fear that Indonesia could become communist.

Modern strategic thinking is for the really big powers to fight through their proxies. The Cold War was certainly like that. Since World War II, everybody had learnt that when big powers fight, the damage is too great. This was even more impossible once the Russians got nuclear weapons. Once we were there, strategic thinking had to be about balance. And conflicts were fought out peripherally. The periphery became important.

On the global scene, maritime power is crucial, and is now as important as land power. So the maritime periphery became the proxies. It's still true today, even though the Soviet Union is gone. With China having arisen, we still have two major powers. These cannot fight, so they will always talk, talk, talk, and once in a while say rude things to each other, but basically they both avoid fighting, and instead let proxies fight it out.

Today it is the United States that controls the maritime regions, and they know that's where their advantage lies. The Chinese are trying to get their foot in, but every time they do that, they get scolded. The West has had this historic advantage ever since *Zheng He* pulled back five hundred years ago.

How are the Chinese to remedy that? It's an almost impossible task for them ... very tough, very tough.

Notes

1. "A Two-Ocean Mediterranean", in *Anthony Reid and the Study of the Southeast Asian Past*, edited by Geoff Wade and Li Tana (Singapore: Institute of Southeast Asian Studies, 2011), pp. 69–84.
2. The Battle of Salamis took place in September 480 BC in the cramped waters between Piraeus and Salamis Island, near Athens. The Greek allied navy under the Athenian Themistocles managed against the odds to triumph quite thoroughly over the Persian navy under Xerxes. This turning of the tide soon led to Persia's demise.
3. Lars Brownworth, *Lost to the West: The Forgotten Byzantine Empire that Rescued Western Civilization* (New York: Three Rivers, 2009).
4. The Greek city states were defeated by Alexander's father, Philip II of Macedonia (359–336 BC) at the Battle of Chaeronea in 338 BC.
5. The so-called Mauritius Campaign of 1809–11 saw the British defeating Napoleon's navy in the Indian Ocean, gaining complete control of the Indian Ocean and securing the sea trade routes to India and beyond.
6. The Khmer Empire lasted from 802 to 1431.
7. Attacks on Srivijayan cities came during the reign of the Chola king, Rajendra Chola I (1012–14). See Herman Kulke, K. Kesavapany, and Vijay Sakhuja, eds., *Nagapattinam to Suvarnadwipa: Reflections on the Chola Naval Expeditions to Southeast Asia* (Singapore: Institute of Southeast Asian Studies, 2009).
8. Giles Milton, *White Gold: The Extraordinary Story of Thomas Pellow and North Africa's One Million European Slaves* (London: Hodder & Stoughton, 2004).
9. Signed on 7 June 1494.

10. See Thomas Pakenham, *The Scramble for Africa* (London: Abacus, 1991).
11. Oskar Spate, *The Spanish Lake* (Canberra: ANU E Press, 2010).
12. According to George H. Weightman, there were systematic government-sponsored massacres in 1603, 1639, 1662, 1686 and 1762. See his article, "The Philippine Chinese: From Aliens to Cultural Minority. In *Journal of Comparative Family Studies* 16, no. 2 (1985): 131–79. The two major ones were the Sangley Rebellion that took place in Manila in October 1603 and another in 1639–40. In both cases, over 20,000 Chinese were killed.
13. For a good understanding of the financial and political exhaustion the British faced under French pressure, and how close they were to final defeat, see Roger Knight, *Britain against Napoleon: The Organization of Victory, 1793–1815* (London: Allen Lane, 2013).
14. *Zheng Chenggong* (1624–62), also known as Koxinga, was the loyal commander of *Ming* troops on the maritime front, who spent the last sixteen years of his life resisting the Manchu invasion of China. He expelled the Dutch from Taiwan in his last campaign in 1661–62.
15. South East Asia Command, 1943–46.
16. See E.G.H. Dobby, *South-east Asia* (London: University of London Press, 1950); D.G.E. Hall, *A History of South-east Asia* (London: Macmillan, 1955); and Brian Harrison, *South-east Asia: A Short History* (London: Macmillan, 1950).
17. The Australia, New Zealand, United States Security Treaty (ANZUS) came into force in 1952, binding the three countries to cooperate on military matters in the Pacific Ocean.

Chapter 3

SOUTHEAST ASIA AND FOREIGN EMPIRES

EAST AND SOUTHEAST ASIA IN MODERN TIMES

OKB: May I suggest that we continue discussing Southeast Asia as a concept?

WGW: As I mentioned earlier, the term really came out of World War II, from the Mountbatten Command in Colombo, which was called the South East Asia Command. The term stuck, and it did so because of the advent of decolonization. The British and the Americans found it useful, and I think the French and Dutch followed thereafter. Decolonization made them think of the region's future, which they feared would be similar to what had become of the Balkans — fragmented, and in effect a power vacuum. European experiences were transposed on to the region, and the notion was that, where there is fragmentation, big powers would intervene. So a quick look around showed an independent but fragile India on one side, and on the other, Communist China, one of the five powers in the United Nations Security Council.

The strategic planners saw a potential political vacuum, and to get down to work they needed a coordinated bigger picture. Identifying Southeast Asia as one region helped them visualize the future. This didn't happen immediately, by the way. The Americans took some time to accept it because they thought in terms of East Asia, or the Western Pacific. They never looked at South Asia much, the way the British and the French did. On their side, Europeans saw India and they saw China; and they saw the region in between as a residue. So the French used the term "Indochine", which is very interesting because it showed that the French had understood the area to be a bit of China and a bit of India. For Western powers that had been moving eastwards, this area would have indeed been orientated through references to India and China.

OKB: In the early days, the British were denoting the region as "Farther India".

WGW: Farther India, yes. They were thinking in terms of the projection of British power out of India, an extension into the Malay Peninsula and into Burma. Burma was actually managed as a province of India, a tail end of India; something the Burmese have never forgiven them for. So their view was always India-centred. The Americans however were concerned with the Philippines and Japan, and tended strategically to be China-centred.

It is significant that "Southeast Asia" is really a British conception. The Americans eventually saw that it could be useful, but even then, this was more among the academics. The strategic thinkers still largely thought in terms of East Asia. Even the universities subsumed Southeast Asia under East Asia; only a few took up the idea of Southeast Asia studies, such as Cornell, and then eventually Michigan and Berkeley. But many other universities didn't! The British were very early on that front. Take London University's School of Oriental and African Studies (SOAS) for example, which immediately had a Southeast Asia division, alongside South Asia, and East Asia. I think London University already had that clear idea about this, while Oxbridge took a little while longer, because they were not that interested, and they were looking at the classical era. So I would say it's a post-war British conception, which was eventually accepted by everybody, and by strategic thinkers.

OKB: Did the old Chinese term *Nanyang* have any strategic sense to it?

WGW: Not really. You see, *Nanyang* is actually a very modern term for China. I used the word *Nanhai* for my *Nanhai Trade*, and people have even argued whether or not the Chinese actually meant South China Sea.[1] It's one of the problems we have today. In the past, there were no exact definitions for anything. No specific maps, no borders, certainly not in the sea. Borders on land could be discerned to an extent; but borders in the sea? Those were quite impossible to ascertain. So, all these modern quarrels over borders are very new problems.

Essentially, the terms were very broad. For example, the term *Nanhai* did exist, but it was not accurate. I had actually given it a new focus by calling it and equating it with the South China Sea. But they had many other terms. Up till the seventeenth century, the Chinese term was *Dong Xi Yang* — the Eastern and Western Oceans. The Eastern Ocean meant Japan, Korea, the Philippines and Sulu. The Western Ocean, in other words, meant the South China Sea, the Java Sea and the Indian Ocean. So the line was actually drawn, roughly looking down from *Fujian* Province, from places like *Quanzhou*.

So *Dongyang* is very much geared towards Japan, and areas to the east. And then on the other side, you have the Malay Peninsula, the South China Sea, the Java Sea and the Indian Ocean. So even as late as the seventeenth and eighteenth centuries, references to *Dong Xi Yang* were still used. When Admiral *Zheng He* went on his trips, it was to *"xia Xiyang"* — going down the Western Ocean. That was already a common term by the fifteenth century, though it was not defined. But the *Dong Xi Yang Kao* (Treatise on the Eastern and Western Oceans), a book from the early seventeenth century, does draw a line.

So *Nanyang* — Southern Ocean — was a recognition of something in the south. I think it came from the nineteenth century, when the Chinese began to develop a navy. They had had no navy to speak of; they had only coastal fleets. After the defeat by the British in the Opium War (1839–42), they realized that they had to do something about it. So people like *Zeng Guofan*, *Li Hongzhang* and *Zuo Zongtang* set up a naval dockyard. They tried to get help from the British, who refused. Then they got the French to train them. They decided to have two fleets — *Beiyang* and *Nanyang*. The *Beiyang* fleet operated out of *Tianjin*, which was controlled by Beijing, while the *Nanyang* fleet was based south of Shanghai, more or less, and the headquarters either in *Fuzhou* or looking south from Shanghai. At least three ports had been opened up by the West in the region — Shanghai, *Ningbo* and *Fuzhou*. Only after that do you find the term *Nanyang*, often used in describing all those people who departed from *Xiamen* and Hong Kong as *"xia Nanyang"* — leaving for the Southern Ocean. There were no boundaries suggested. You could probably include the South Pacific as well; you could be going to Fiji or to Papua New Guinea, and maybe even Australia.

It denoted trips in that general southerly direction. So it is not exactly Southeast Asia either. In fact, the Japanese used it the same way — Nanyo (*Nanyang*) definitely included the South Pacific. Their idea was "south" — all the way south to Australia, crossing Southeast Asia and the South Pacific.

So *Nanyang* did not have any political, security, military, naval connotations as such. It had a naval link in the sense of two Chinese fleets facing different directions. For the Japanese, almost all their naval activity was in the *Nanyang* anyway, in the south. So they were basically active only in the Nanyo.

OKB: Did the catastrophic naval war against the Japanese in 1895 involve only the *Beiyang* fleet?

WGW: No, the whole navy was wiped out. Even the *Nanyang* fleet was sent up north. The Japanese navy actually completely destroyed them, all in a matter of a few days, a few weeks at most if you include the trip up. It was pathetic really. It woke the Chinese up, but it was too late to do much anyway, and the *Qing* Dynasty soon fell. The newly founded republic was in a terrible state, with no central government to speak of, and with factions fighting each other. Where was there time to speak about navies or to build up a national defence? They tried, but it was mainly talk or at best small weak efforts done without enough funding and without enough training and facilities. All this occurred utterly at the mercy of the Anglo-Japanese alliance.

Then came the Washington Naval Treaty of 1921–22, signed by Britain, America, Japan, France and Italy, to curb a potential naval arms race. They came to an agreement as to the proportion of tonnage of ships allowed in Asia. The Japanese were very aggrieved at this, and felt that the Anglo-Americans were limiting them. But nevertheless, they accepted the conditions because they were in no position to argue against those two great naval powers. At that time, Britain was still the number one naval power, with America close behind. So Japan was sort of quartered, and signed unhappily.

But where was the Chinese navy? All this was being done at the expense of the China coast. So this registered in the mind of the Chinese, and one day they were going to do something about it. In the meantime, they were fighting a civil war — all on land. The thing was, the Kuomintang at least tried to build a small navy. But when did the CCP have any kind of navy? The People's Liberation Army, the PLA, was entirely a continental army. Right up to the moment, of their victory in 1949, they didn't have a navy.

OKB: When the Kuomintang expounded the eleven-dotted line in 1948, there was a power vacuum in the South China Sea, wasn't there?[2]

WGW: There were no claimants at that time. The French had a vague jurisdictional line off the coast of Indo-China. Sabah and Sarawak were in the middle of changing hands. They were not even controlled by the British government before the war — Sabah having been managed by the North Borneo Company and Sarawak by the Brooke family. So basically, the Anglo-Dutch Treaty[3] was all they had at hand, which divided the Straits of Malacca down the middle. The Americans never bothered to claim anything. Down to this day, the Taiwanese can't find any maps.

This is why I think it is very significant that the only time the South China Sea had ever been under one jurisdiction was under the Japanese. By early 1942, they actually controlled the whole coastline of the South China Sea: Indonesia and Malaysia, of course; Thailand was basically their puppet; French Indo-China was under their control; the Philippines had been conquered; and *Fujian* and *Guangdong* in South China were under the Japanese command. Hong Kong had been taken, and Taiwan had been theirs since 1895. So for the first time, you can conceive of the South China Sea as a unit, and as being under one power. So I've been asking Taiwanese and Chinese friends to see if they can find any documents in their archives about this, but the Taiwan scholars haven't found anything in the Kuomintang archives, or they don't want to talk about it.

My own speculation about why they do not wish to talk about it is that they were influenced by what I have just described. When they took over the Japanese territories, the Japanese records in Taiwan referred to this "Nanyo" that was under their control. The Governor-General of Taiwan was essentially the power behind the whole war in Southeast Asia. They were operating out of Taiwan while the other command was dealing with the Pacific, and I think it is this perspective that the Kuomintang just accepted when they in turn drew their map. There was a Japanese map, a very clear one, in which you can see that the South China Sea was a Japanese lake! So I think it was this process that influenced the immediate post-war situation, not any basis in any international law or any larger conception.[4]

OKB: What you say sounds very probable.

WGW: That was how they would have perceived it. But they never explained it that way, at least not to my knowledge. And when the communists took over, they simply took over the same map. They didn't think further about it either. They simply said that that was Chinese territory — the estate they inherited from the Kuomintang. So now they are insisting that that's the basis on which their own nation was based. The map of the Kuomintang, the map of China, was what they inherited. The only bit which was left somewhat controversial, but to which the Communist

Party agreed and to which the Kuomintang was forced to agree because of the Sino-Soviet agreement that the Kuomintang signed with Stalin, was the acknowledgement of the state of Mongolia. Except for that, the China that the communists inherited was the *Qing* map plus the Japanese maritime map of the South China Sea.

OKB: The tradition in Chinese history had been for succeeding dynasties to inherit the conception of China handed down by their predecessors.

WGW: Yes, each dynasty inherited the empire from the previous one. It did not matter if the predecessor was a conquering power. You see, this is where Chinese historiography is interesting. Chinese historiography is not a national history. It is a *Tianxia* historiography; and *Tianxia* is the reach of the emperor, who is *Tian Zi*, the Son of Heaven, in so far as the Confucians acknowledge him as such. According to the orthodox interpretation, the Son of Heaven had command over the territories under Heaven — theoretically everybody, but they were concerned in practice only with those people who belonged to the family of the Chinese peoples. But this was all very vague and there were no clear-cut borders. Essentially the borders were fluid, so they were always fighting to define the borders between the Steppes of the nomadic confederations and the territory where the Chinese agrarian armies could hold their positions — on this side, civilization; on that side, not. The whole of Chinese historiography is based on that.

The question of national borders never came into it. So when you introduce a new element like the nation state and nationalism after 1912, the problem becomes very difficult. And then the Chinese Communist Party aggravated the problem by accepting

Stalin's definition of nation and nationality. Because the Russians recognized numerous nationalities, Mao Zedong and the Chinese communists, in order to be seen to be progressive internationalists and accepting of the Comintern, took Stalin's categorizations generally, and in 1952 asked a group of anthropologists and ethnologists — *Fei Xiaotong* (1910–2005) and all the others — to work out how many nationalities there were in China.[5] But the assumption was that China's borders were set. So it was a question about the number of nationalities inside China, and they were all Chinese by definition — thus the phrase *zhonghua minzu*. It meant territorial Chinese and not national Chinese, and measured the extent of the Chinese borders.

But this term has never been understood outside of China. Outside of China, *zhonghua minzu* simply means Chinese, and Chinese means *Han* Chinese. And the Chinese don't know how to get over that problem. How do you translate *zhonghua minzu* except as "Chinese". And how do you get out of "Chinese" being equated with *Han* Chinese, which is how outsiders would define the term, including even the Chinese definition outside of China. When you talk about Chinese you mean the *Han* Chinese. You still don't see the Tibetans or the Uighur or the Dai as Chinese. You don't. So this is the basis for a lot of difficulties for the Chinese. And even today, the literature in China is still thrashing it out — what are we to make of this *"minzu"*?

But in truth, the *minzu zhengce* — the nationalities policy — really came out of Stalinist practices. They invited applications over two or three years from different peoples claiming they were Chinese or something else. In the end, they had over 200 categories, which *Fei Xiaotong* finally simplified to 55, alongside the *Han* Chinese. They've never changed the categories. They had a broad category for all the indigenous people of Taiwan, no doubt, but that was not under their control.

So who are not *Han*? According to Stalin's concept, each nationality was given certain rights. Once you were identified as a nationality, you were given certain rights, including some autonomy. You would have your own chieftain, which is again traditional. Traditionally, at Chinese borders, there were chieftains carrying certain titles and exercising some self-governance over their own areas. So the communists combined the Chinese tradition of autonomous areas with the Stalin nationalities project, and created a new idea of territorial nationality. Territorial is the key word, because once a certain area was allocated to you, you produced your own chieftains, and you were allowed certain subsidies from the central government along with certain exemptions and certain privileges about schooling and health care. So a lot of groups wanted to be recognized, because once you were recognized you had followers, and you had demarcated areas that were self-governing. You have *Guangxi*, which is a *Zhuang* autonomous province, and you have Tibet, *Xinjiang* and *Ningxia*, the latter having that status for the *Hui* people for a while. Further down, there are a lot of *zizhizhou, zizhixian, zizhiqu* — self-governing areas at various levels. So those rights were much appreciated, and that was why the ethnologists and anthropologists had a difficult time trying to limit the number. There was a lot of dissatisfaction, and even till this day, I know of groups that still protest against being wrongly placed under some other group.

Some cases get very tricky. The most interesting one is the Manchu. You see, the Manchu have been so Sinicized that there were hardly any Manchus left who spoke Manchu amongst themselves or who were clearly identifiable as Manchu. Through looks you simply couldn't tell; and even their names would have been Sinicized to a great extent, following their aristocrats, who at the fall of the *Qing* all adopted Chinese names. So how do you go about classifying them? To start with, relatively few registered themselves as Manchu. But once it was clear that the advantages were great, people started turning up saying, "My grandfather is Manchu." Soon, these linked up, and the number of Manchus shot up.

So you can see it was an administrative bureaucratic issue, rather than a genuine ethnic one in most cases; with the exception of the big populations such as the Mongols, Tibetans, Uighurs, and a few other very strong ones like the *Zhuang*. But even the *Zhuang* — the largest minority group — has been Sinicized to a great extent now. Of course, they keep some customs and they still speak the *Zhuang* language. For most Chinese, that *Zhuang* language is not very different from, say, Cantonese. Speakers of Cantonese and Mandarin can't always understand each other anyway. But they are sufficiently different, and have maintained their own ways.

OKB: The *Hui* must have been a problem as well.

WGW: Yes. Basically, they are *Han*, but they have religion as their main difference. And I think the Chinese made that an exception because right at the beginning when the *Qing* Dynasty recognized five major races, the *Hui* was one of them. The *Hui* at that time meant all the Muslims, including the *Xinjiang* Uighurs. But later on, the *Hui* became identified as just the "Hanized", ones — the *Han Hui*, the *Han* Muslims who are quite distinct from the Uighurs and other minorities like Kazakhs and Kyrgyz along the *Xinjiang* border. They were not the same, and so wanted their own identity, and the Chinese gave it to them. So the *Hui* are now the only ones who are *Han* in every respect except religion. They are very few now, compared to the early days of the *Qing*, when the Manchus recognized the five races of *Man*, *Han*, *Meng*, *Hui* and *Zang*.

OKB: While China was trying to shift from imperial conceptions to nation-state conceptions, similar processes were also happening here in Southeast Asia.

WGW: Here, of course, it was done under Western tutelage. The territories were actually run by the Dutch and the British, and the categories were determined by them. I think you've seen some of the writings about how the British counted people on the Malay Peninsula.[6] To start with they were counted as Bugis, as Minangkabau, as Javanese — each one separate from the other. Melayu was one specific group among many. Even Kelantan Melayu was different from Johor Bugis. And for the Chinese, there were Hokkiens, Cantonese, and so on.

Then at one point, this changed. We began having large groupings under the headings Malays, Chinese, Indians, and others. Now, where the term "Indians" is concerned ... if you are looking for a group word that will cause you trouble, that would be one.

After that, these groups became politically significant. Exactly why the British adopted those changes, I have never been able to make out. It was partly for simplicity, I think. You had all these Bugis, Minangkabaus, Bataks, Achehnese coming over from Sumatra, and you had the Javanese as well, causing a lot of difficulties because they intermarried. In the end, how do you count them? You lump them together as Malays for administrative convenience. Although, if you look at the actual records, they were quite clear about who the real Malays were — who had reservation rights and who did not. The others were migrants, and so had no such rights. These rights protected agricultural land. So if you look at the land regulations in the various Federated Malay States, you find the mention of Malay reservations. Not even Europeans could touch those purely meant for agrarian use. Those were meant for Malays.

But then, of course, some of the Malays had foreign origins, and they also intermarried. The lines became increasingly hard to discern. So in the end, the British called them all Malays. I think what it boils down to is that the distinctions were not significant; these were all people of the Malay Archipelago — the Indonesian Archipelago, as they call it now.

THE RISE OF THE NATION STATE

OKB: This brings us again to a discussion of the nation state.

WGW: The word "nation" is a very tricky one. In the European context, it is very blood-based. It is not just race; it is narrower than race. It is genealogy-based; it is about bloodlines. You are descended from the same people, to start with. That's a kind of biological fact. Then you share one language, which is one of the key defining factors. Then you have the same religion. And finally, you have shared occupation of the same territory over a long period of time; it's your history. So "one language, one religion, one history" clinches your nationality. That was eventually the definition on which the first nation states were built up.

The Dutch in a way captured that very well when they fought against the Spanish Netherlands Empire. You had one language — Dutch. And you had one religion — meaning the Catholics were not counted; these ended up in Belgium, or the Spanish Netherlands. So you had "one language, one religion, and one territory". The territory was of course what they fought for. They battled for nearly a hundred years to mark out that territory, and also to show that they were not Germans either. Having lived there long enough, they had history as well. So you have your nation. In that sense the Dutch on the one side and the Portuguese on the other were the beginnings of it all.

The Portuguese case was not as clear-cut, because their language is close to Spanish and their religion is the same as Spain's, and furthermore they had shared one king for a while. So that made things a bit vague. In the end the Portuguese were actually dependent on the English, who supported them against the Spanish. So Portugal is a political creation with some legal and jurisdictional history behind it.

The Dutch case was really a war of independence. So the first anti-colonial, anti-imperial war of independence prior to America's thirteen colonies was fought by the Dutch. And what a battle that was. It took a very long time to determine. It was at the end of the Thirty Years' War, with the signing of the Treaty of Westphalia in 1648, that they started to define this idea. Thereafter it became more and more widely used.

But it was still not accepted, as seen in how the Germans continued to have numerous states. Where was the German nation? Things couldn't quite click for them after the Reformation. Martin Luther started something, but they continued being under different kings. And there was no unity in religion, only unity of language. Where history was concerned, they were definitely separate territories.

I would say that the Dutch may have started the nation state, and the Portuguese may have had something similar; but the most important event was the French Revolution (1789–99). The French Revolution essentially saw a major power determining itself as a nation state. And not only that, it cleared one thing out of the way — religion. The new France was secular. Its people were basically Catholic, of course. Napoleon's France was still about ninety-five per cent Catholic, but they had basically moved away from the religious definition. It was now about language, territory, and *the state*! So the link-up between the nation and the state — if you want to find a date for it — was absolutely achieved by the French Revolution. You see, that was what inspired the Germans in the end to create the German nation. It was a response to Napoleon, who had bashed them to such an extent that they were nearly all destroyed.

The Prussians began to move towards creating a German nation state, in contest with the Austrians. The Austrians were hampered by inefficiency, corruption, and just general confusion because they were mixed up with the Hungarians and the Slavs, and so on. While the Austrians had an imperial system, the Prussians were almost a hundred per cent German. So it was the Prussians whom I think essentially cleared another barrier; namely, you didn't have to have one religion, as long as your diverse religions were Christian. So, the Catholics and the Lutherans were brought together under the German state. Now, this is Napoleonic, this is French — religion had indeed become less important.

Because of the secularization of power after the French Revolution, the German product was able to de-emphasize religion. And so the Germans could be united, and the Bavarians could be brought in. How else could one bring in the Bavarians? They were Catholics. But the Protestant majority accepted that and so the Prussians attained the German nation state. In the end, Bismarck clinched it. The goal of defeating the French was what clinched it for him.

OKB: We started by talking about the difficulties China faced in the twentieth century in trying to move from dynastic empire to republic. Republicanism was just as radical a process in Europe in the late eighteenth century. It was a vehicle for a proper break with the past, and hard to accept for many.

WGW: "Republic" was an even more profound definition than "nation state", because it went one further step beyond the idea of a nation. It sought to bring together citizens loyal to one state. So the "state" was emphasized. The "nation" part was about the bloodline, but the "state" part was the structure of government. The French state was a unitary one, under one central bureaucracy with its capital in Paris. All this followed from the absolute monarchy, and it became the main model, with a participating citizenry and a definition of every person's rights. That was French, and that was new. At that point, the Germans didn't have it; nor did the British.

But I would again say that the Dutch started it. They already had the republican ideal. During the sixty, seventy or eighty years of fighting against the Spanish, they developed the idea of a dedicated national citizenry. So there was not only a nation, there were also citizens who had rights because they had participated in a war together.

The American Revolution (1775–83) derived from all these ideas. Everybody was a citizen, and the rebellion was a citizens' rebellion. It was not kings and churches and states fighting. It was citizens revolting against the structure. The French Revolution, of course, went so far as to cut off the king's head. The British had actually started that — they had cut off their king's head first. But then they managed to balance things and recover to some extent. And so, their revolution was not quite as revolutionary as the French one. In France, no doubt Napoleon restored the monarchy, but after several decades they finally got the church and the monarchists out of the way to create a true republic.

In that sense, the idea did not triumph properly until 1848, the year Karl Marx's *Communist Manifesto* came out. It was only in 1848 that you see the beginnings of a truly secular citizen-state. And finally, with the Franco-Prussian War (1870–71) as the climax, there was no question of France being a monarchy ever again.

OKB: And the Italians followed the Germans in constructing a nation state.

WGW: Italy and all the others were inspired by France. To that extent I would say that the classic model of a nation state was France. The British never quite had it, you know. Till this day, they still have their monarchy, and the citizenry of Scotland, England, Wales and Northern Ireland are still uneasy about each other.

The idea of Britain, of the United Kingdom, took a long time to develop. In fact it was the empire project that encouraged it. The British Empire gave them a purpose to act together as British, and the fighting against the French united some of them. But even then, the Scots and the Irish were never totally behind the English rivalry with France. So the British were in a way the classic example of people who knew how to compromise and to work towards a balanced solution. In that way, their political culture is the opposite of the French one. The French like clarity, consistency, and clear definitions. The British think it better to compromise and come out with a mixture of things that everybody is more or less comfortable with, or more or less uncomfortable with.

As a result, British nationality is not as solid a thing as French nationality is. The idea of a nation state is still a bit vague. You have the English, the Scots — among whom secession is still a possibility — and the Irish, who never accepted the English.

The British treated the Irish probably worse than they treated any other colonial subjects. That is why Irish resentment of the English was probably stronger than in many other places. Think of the centuries of mistreatment! Think of Oliver Cromwell and Elizabeth I, who really hammered the Irish — conquered them and treated them as inferior people; made fun of them and looked down on them. There was religion behind it as well, because the

Anglican Church broke away with the Catholic Church. But they actually just drove the Irish to become even more Catholic.

OKB: When we now talk about the English-Dutch relationship, I remember that New York was originally called New Amsterdam. What was the significance of that name change?

WGW: The Dutch were not there for very long. The story went like this. The British in the seventeenth century were fighting the Dutch in Southeast Asia — in the Moluccas, in the Spice Islands. The British back then controlled one of the Spice Islands, while the Dutch controlled the rest. Now, the Dutch were very unhappy that they didn't have total monopoly of the spice trade, and that the British were getting their goods separately. So they fought on many occasions. There was even a massacre in Ambon (1623). Well, the British called it a massacre, while the Dutch refused to admit that.

Eventually what happened was, at the end of one particular war, they came to an agreement. They would do a swap. The British would give up their spice island in exchange for New Amsterdam. And the Dutch took it; they accepted that deal! So that was how the Dutch gained total monopoly over the Spice Islands, and were very happy about it. Rather shortsighted of them, but that was where the money was — in spices.[7] The British, on gaining New Amsterdam, changed the name in 1626 to New York.

OKB: So the Dutch and the British swapping Malacca for Bencoolen in 1824 had a precedent.

WGW: Yes. The Anglo-Dutch relationship was a very old and bitter tale of rivalry, until they became allies against the French. At the beginning of the seventeenth century, they were fighting for naval power. The Dutch navy, through the Dutch East India Company, was stronger than the British at that point. But they would weaken.

Basically, they were too small, and their resources were torn between sea and land. They still had to watch out for the Germans and the Belgians, and for the Spanish who still begrudged them their independence. While the British, safe on their island, could build up their naval power. They did not have to bother with the continent. That was their great advantage, one that they had enjoyed for a long time, even till this day. They have never been happy or felt secure about being part of the continent.

OKB: That insecurity must have fueled their anger with the Irish for not giving in to them.

WGW: And the Irish going to Europe, turning to France, to their Catholic brethren, upset the British greatly. The Irish were creating a threat to them by bringing in foreign allies to their side, while the British would have liked to see all the British Isles come under one administration. They even had the King of Scotland become the King of England, the King of the United Kingdom, which helped the Scots accept the union of course. After Elizabeth I (1533–1603), the Stuarts who took over were Scots, and that brought about the union of Scotland and England. So there was never a nation state, there was only a marriage of two nations, under one state. To this day, there are Scots who still feel that to be the case. If you insist on one nation, then they will get very uncomfortable.

Never call a Scot English. That will upset him greatly. He accepts being British, but never English. As you know, in the World Cup in football, there are four separate teams from the

British Isles — which never win, no doubt. Well, only once, when England won back in 1966.

OKB: Is the French Republic more a state nation than a nation state then, in essence?

WGW: It is not as clearly cut as all that. The former colonies in Southeast Asia are more like state nations because here we had the state first and no nation. So the state then became the instrument, the vehicle through which a nation is built. That's why we talk about nation building. For the European states, the phrase didn't really come in. It didn't have to, because by definition either you were or you were not. Through the Treaty of Westphalia and thereafter, the nations determined the state. We, being elsewhere and wanting to copy that, had to reverse things. So we had the state, and then we try to create a nation.

All those gaining independence faced the same problems. You just had the territory passed down from the Dutch, the French and the English, and you tried to make a nation. This was the case even for India, which had a system somewhat like the Chinese *Tianxia*. The Moghuls ruled an empire populated by autonomous Hindu rulers who had to deal with the imperial system. Multi-ethnicity in an empire is really not a problem; you just have to be loyal to the emperor. Now, the British inherited that system after the Indian Mutiny, and they took over the role of the Moghul emperor.

In the meantime, anti-colonialists perceived the nation state to be the model to adopt and develop: "Why should we not have a nation state like you Europeans? The nation state is a powerful mechanism, proven by the fact that you dominate the world — you French, British, Dutch and Germans".

It is true that when the nations became nation states, they did become stronger. That was what inspired the Germans to become a nation state. They were tired of being pushed around by the powerful French state. The Italians did the same thing. They were otherwise grouped in many city states and regions, like Piedmont, Venice, and Milan. Again they were responding to the show of strength by the French. In that sense, the France of Napoleon was a fantastic creative and destructive force. It destroyed the feudal systems and created nation states that soon proved to be mighty weapons for achieving unity of purpose and cohesion, and for the drive towards wealth, prosperity and power.

OKB: That involved an excluding mechanism that the old systems did not have.

WGW: Yes, of course. Citizenship participation is the thing. Deciding who a Frenchman was, was probably the first attempt that really clicked. The French had to define themselves away from the Spaniards, the Germans, the Italians, the British and the Dutch. It was a very successful process despite the fact that they are still fighting over who is or is not a Frenchman today. But they were the ones who made that process so important, and the rest of the world has all been influenced by it. So when we in Asia were being anti-colonial, what could we replace the colonies with if not with nation states?

In fact, what we were doing was to accept the colonial state and use it to create a new nation. That is the struggle we are still caught in.

OKB: Yes. I find your article on party types in the region very interesting.[8]

WGW: We are struggling to do it in different ways, and using the party as one of the necessary instruments within the nation-state framework. I am not criticizing this in any way; just saying that that's the origin of it. It all comes very unnaturally to us; we are after all trying to do something with institutions that are imported, and we are not fully aware of how best to use them. For the people, there is no strong sense of belonging, or ownership. And so you can change party quite easily. You take your coat and put on another one and move over to the other side. But this was not the norm for the party state. The norm was the opposite, in fact.

OKB: Were parties not guild-based at first?

WGW: Yes, but it was also about extraordinary loyalties. In the beginning, of course, there was a class base. But then families became loyal to the party, be it the Labour Party or the Conservative Party. Belonging to a party was an act of loyalty in itself. For Asians, loyalty was completely unchangeable to start with, such as Japanese loyalty to their emperor. They were prepared to die for the emperor. The idea is that a country is indivisible; so how can you have parts within it? A party is a part; and one part would contest against another part.

In the West, the party was a device perfected in the process of developing British democracy. The device posits that the best way for citizen participation to have real consequences is to share; and the best way to share is to work out through debate and argument what the best solution is. Open debate eventually developed the idea that whoever wins the debate should be given a chance to implement his ideas. If he fails, he is chucked out, and others will have their chance. But the loser still survives, and no one is killed. This left behind the tradition of the murderous Wars of the Roses.[9]

And that was really a good idea. After the Tudors,[10] the English tried to centralize, and have a democratic system. They had their civil war (1642–51) no doubt, but they were always looking for ways to prevent military collapse, looking for a civilian solution. And so constitutional compromises became a brilliant solution to their problem. I have been very impressed by British scholarship aimed at showing that the development of the legal profession and the idea of the law was what led to the idea of the constitution and then to the political thoughts of John Locke (1632–1704), and so on. They all link up — the lawyers and the constitution. Of course, one could go back to the Magna Carta, which limited the power of the king, but that was a feudal product. The new way was through citizen participation governed by the law and constitutional rules. It was brilliant.

Constitutionalism was basically a British invention, perfected into an instrument of the state to ensure social cohesion and prevent bitter division and war. Everybody had to agree to the constitution. When there were disagreements, then you took one part and I another, and we thrashed it out. In the course of this thrashing out, these parties — the Whigs and the Tories — emerged. Eventually they solidified and became identified with class, gradually with regions, and eventually you had the Labour Party and the Conservatives. All this evolved over hundreds of years.

The British don't have a written constitution, but they piled up all previous answers and gradually built up a sense of right and wrong. A sense of justice grows because you were testing all the time, you debated in the court of law, you never resorted to arms, and you sought a peaceful solution to every issue. It is all a very civilized way of fostering a participatory people whose divided opinions can be worked out together. And whoever wins the argument has the chance to actually implement his ideas. If he fails then others take over to show that they instead are right. Because the process was so gradual, the base is very solid. Underlying it all is a long period of continual debate and agreement on rules and passing of judgments. What emerges is a shared political culture where everybody can disagree on policy and yet maintain the same values about the institutions. They may disagree on a specific debate, but they move together to thrash it out each step of the way. The mechanism is really quite a sophisticated and elaborate one, but it is not easy to reproduce.

So, real democracy came from centuries of fierce debate. Parties are the clarification of diverse groupings of people who have represented different causes over time. But they are united in their political culture and agree on how solutions are found. This is a very different tradition from the one with a unitary structure with a single ruler, where the winner takes all. The victor ensures that the defeated never has another chance. That was how the Chinese system was. There was no "The King is Dead, Long Live the King", where everything continued with little change. Instead, whoever won destroyed the defeated completely.

There have been many varieties of monarchy, but none of the others developed political parties. In Southeast Asia, the shared political culture is very vague, and most systems shared some kind of Indian political culture. They inherited it from the Hindu-Buddhist tradition, no doubt, but the way they implemented it was not Indian. They may have a recognizably Southeast Asian way of doing things, but that varied a lot nevertheless. For example, there was a great difference between the Javanese style and the Malay style. The Malays were coastal, agile and mobile, and had no real centre, while the Javanese — and the Khmers for that matter — were agrarian based. So, geography and the ensuing economic system played an important part.

The parts of the Hindu-Buddhist tradition that were emphasized produced different shapes and forms. The Chams were very Hindu, the Khmers were more Buddhist, and the Javanese became very Hindu — the Buddhist element didn't last very long there. You see remnants of that in Bali. The Malay area didn't have agrarian states. They were totally dependent on mobility, on maritime activities like fishing and trading. They founded ports and never bothered to go far into the interior, because that was the way they maintained great flexibility and mobility. They could take off when trouble came and move to another place. If Malacca falls, they go to Johor. In Srivijaya, when the Javanese attacked, they moved somewhere else. So that gave them a very distinct political culture, very distinct from the Southeast Asian mainland.

The mainland culture — and I think recent studies support this — was ultimately influenced not only by the Indians but also by the Chinese. Vietnam was definitely strongly influenced by the Chinese, but even the Thais and Burmese came from areas where they were dealing with the Mongols and the Chinese. They were nomadic, but over time they inherited a kind of continental power system and brought it down south, where they destroyed the Khmers and the Mons, and entered the Menam and Irrawaddy valleys. They brought with them a system that was different, and although they had Buddhist ideas, these were incorporated into their Eurasian power structure, which was naturally very different from the ones found in maritime societies.

Tibetan, Mongol and Turkic influences coming down the rivers from *Sichuan* were very different from those of the *Yue* moving through *Guangdong* and *Guangxi* into Vietnam. But all of these were nevertheless continental and Eurasian. The Thais learned some maritime manners after getting to Bangkok and coming down the peninsula, and the Vietnamese did the same on their side. In the end though, neither really developed much of a maritime mentality. The Burmese never had it either. They had barely reached the coast when the British arrived.

THE MALAYS AND MARITIME CULTURE

OKB: Maritime political culture in the region was therefore unique to the Malays.

WGW: Yes. The Indians didn't have it, being influenced basically by the Eurasian continental model with its very powerful idea of the king, a son of heaven surrounded by nobles and wielding imperial power instruments. So for them to build an empire in Southeast Asia was not a straightforward matter. The Mandala Theory from Oliver Wolters was an attempt to show the derivation of ideas in Southeast Asia from the Hindu-Buddhist tradition.[11] But I wonder whether it was native — and inherent in the fact that the people here were seafarers. The whole Austronesian migration down to these islands had built a framework into which political ideas came and went, but inside it was the fact that they never converted to agrarian power, apart from the Javanese. The Javanese are very interesting in that sense, and sometimes it is very hard to quite fit them in. They seemed to have taken an aspect from the Hindu-Buddhist tradition and magnified that into a state system based on agriculture. The Acehnese in northern Sumatra didn't, and the Minangkabaus down in southern Sumatra didn't either. They could have, but whatever the reason, they decided to remain coastal and maritime. So what made it happen in Java, we don't really know. They did create a different kind of state, and the Javanese remain a very distinctive group among Indonesians, and they are the most powerful.

Quite frankly, if you don't have the nation state today, you can't survive. World War II extended the whole system globally, and solidified it through the United Nations. The earlier League of Nations didn't mean much, being a grouping of colonial powers. Now, to be a member of the United Nations, you have to be a nation state. So, to qualify, you have to somehow make yourself look like a nation state.

For example, when Singapore was kicked out of Malaysia, the first thing it had to do was try to get itself recognized in the United Nations. Only then was its legitimacy as a state assured.

OKB: Yes, nation states are equal today except for those in the Security Council.

WGW: That was a victor's formula, of course. The great powers could not agree to be treated the same as, say, Luxembourg. That's why Germany and Japan were left out. They were and are powerful states, but they were defeated. China was simply lucky because the Americans insisted that it be made a member of the Security Council in the face of British and French opposition. Today, they would probably have insisted on Japan being made a member. In those days, Chiang Kai-shek was a loyal ally, so China got in as a matter of strategy. It was not really a major force in the victory except for its size and vastness tying the Japanese army down. The French got in because the British insisted on it, and the Americans wanted it too. Otherwise, what qualifications did they have? Charles De Gaulle was sitting in London during the war.

So this was really a reflection of the Anglo-French division of the world in the nineteenth and the first half of the twentieth century.

OKB: The next step in the evolution of the United Nations would have to involve the Security Council.

WGW: There are books galore about global governance today, and more and more are coming. I have just been reading the latest one, which is by our friend Kishore Mahbubani.[12] He was in the United Nations at a time when Singapore was in the Security Council, and so he really has a first-hand understanding of the actual practice of the council — what it means and what the sense of injustice felt by others is like. He is not alone though. People have been talking about it for a long time. Other big countries have been wanting to join the council — India, Japan, Brazil and South Africa. But once you bring so many in, then the thing may become meaningless. What if the powers in there can never agree?

OKB: For geographical reasons, Southeast Asia was left alone, as you said. But now the Big Powers are getting interested, and this puts the region in a challenging situation.

WGW: Well, we were left alone because we were not part of the Eurasian continent. World history is really derived from the Eurasian continent, including the Mediterranean and North Africa. That is where all the history was made. The rest of the world was left alone to a greater or lesser extent. It was only from the fifteenth and sixteenth centuries that it began to cover the whole globe. Even then, things did not settle down until the nineteenth and twentieth centuries. The global history of nation states is indeed very new.

FROM NATION STATES TO NATIONAL EMPIRES ... AND BACK

OKB: Now when I think over what you said about the Dutch, the nation state developed in that fantastic way as a defensive mechanism. To what extent can one look at history over the last five hundred years as a struggle between the imperial element and the nation state element?

WGW: A nation state works both ways. It is a defensive and also an offensive thing. With the backing of a nation state, you can create an empire. You see, the empires all became national empires. I have written about this.[13]

There are traditional feudal empires; the Roman Empire is a good example of this. There have been many variations, but the essential feudal one is based on the monarchy and all the sacrosanct institutions that go with it. In different places, they evolve somewhat differently, but the essential idea is that you have one ruler.

Then you have the modern thing — the commercial empire like that created by the East India Company. You can even start with the Portuguese and the Spanish, but I think theirs was ambivalent and was actually royal intervention in commerce. But the East India Company was outside of the state. It was commercial and it had no intention of building an empire. But out of their successes and desire for commercial monopolies, similar to what the Dutch and Portuguese had, they created an imperial system that was commercial. Now, based on that, many of the early scholars of empire said that we moved from the feudal empire to one that is essentially capitalist-industrialist. So you have Lenin's idea of imperialism as an extension of capitalism, and it was capitalism that turned the feudal empires into capitalist empires, based on the economic power unleashed by the industrial revolution.[14]

This is true. I don't deny that was a major factor. John A. Hobson was the first to explain it and Lenin took it up and developed it.[15]

I would add a modification that, in the course of that, these empires also became national empires, because after the Treaty of Westphalia was signed in 1648 and the nation states became what they were, each of the empires took on the characteristics of the nation state that ran it. And again, the best example was France, followed by Britain. Especially after the thirteen colonies broke away, the British Empire became more and more based on British people — it was led by Brits. Whether it was deliberate or not, the people who ran the empire had to be British. The same with France, although the French tried to blur that a bit by saying that one could *become* French. The British didn't even do that. It was very difficult for anyone else to get in. Only an odd few Indians may have done it in the twentieth century.

So it was not simply an evolution fueled by capitalism and the industrial revolution. The empires became national empires, which explains why the colonies sought to become nation states in our day. The reaction against the national empire was to create your own nation state to distinguish yourself from the British and the French, and to use that as affirmation of your own independence and autonomy. In order to be your equal, we reproduce ourselves as a nation state.

If we don't include that modification, it will be harder to explain why all the colonial regions became nation states. They were reacting to national empires, not feudal empires. Those were no more.

The Irish response to the British Empire was what inspired the Indians and others. You see, the Irish were an early case of a national response to a national empire. The national empire didn't include them, so they had to have their own nation state. And so, anti-colonialism and anti-imperialism became identified with nationalist movements. And that can only be explained if the fight was against a national empire. That's why I say that Lenin and Hobson did not emphasize the concept of national empires sufficiently. I would say that to be correct, to understand better the post–World War II situation, you have to recognize that the fight was against national empires. And it was national empires that determined the way we have become nation-building states. In fact, the whole phenomenon of the United Nations is an expression of all that. Before that we had the League of Nations, which was determined by the national empires. Nations, they say; but in fact they were national empires.

OKB: It would have been more correct to call it the League of National Empires then.

WGW: Today we have a global system of nations, of new nations. You cannot explain how that came into being just through reference to capitalism and industrial revolution. That can only be explained by recognizing that the empires that were created and the wars that were fought down to the time of the League of Nations, and to global decolonization and nation building, stemmed from the fact that the early nation states had become empires. And that's what we are up against. We want to create a world where nation states do not become empires. So that's why we have the United Nations. Each nation has its own sovereignty and that sovereignty is sacred, and that should make sure that there will be no more future empires. But then things begin taking another form. We don't call them empires anymore, but the fact remains that some are bigger than others, and the big boys and the small boys behave differently towards one another.

OKB: So American presence in the Pacific is all right, but not Chinese presence.

WGW: It's arguable. Some would argue that China is still an empire. It is not a nation state, while America is, as are Britain and France. Now, the British Empire has ended, and the British have pulled back into their nation state. The French have also gone back into their nation state. Only the Chinese haven't gone back to anything; they are still an empire.

This is how the argument runs. The Chinese inherited the *Qing* Empire and they are continuing as if the *Qing* Empire is their nation state. The *Qing* Empire is still the basis, and they are not allowing the natural decolonization and anti-imperialism to take place within their territories, unlike what had happened in other empires.

Now, the Chinese counterargument is this: No, we were actually conquered by the Manchus and we inherited the empire the way Indonesia inherited the Dutch empire and India inherited the British Raj. We are no different. We are nation building based on post-imperial conditions.

So you see, the argument can work both ways, and the Chinese stand is actually quite reasonable. So it depends on what you want to emphasize; it depends on what you want to depict. If you depict pre-republican China as a Chinese empire, then present-day China has to be reduced to a number of nation states. That's one argument. The other side claims they are nation building under post-imperial conditions, just like India and Indonesia. And in the Asian context, that also makes sense.

I think this is the basic debate going on now about China. The idea for Tibetan independence comes from one argument, while the Chinese are arguing that they inherited these borders, and their task, their sacred task, is to protect the sovereignty of what they inherited, and to make a nation out of all the peoples who are inside that area, just like in Indonesia and India. So what is the difference? It's hard to reconcile the two.

OKB: Are there not additional elements introduced into how we define new nation states today? I'm thinking of democracy as a component that helps define a real nation state, for without democracy, you tend to have suppression of minorities.

WGW: That is an argument used. Well, the nation-building argument is that they will eventually arrive at that position, but it will take time. This is an argument that applies to Malaysia, Indonesia, China and India. It will take time, and meanwhile you will have lots of pain, lots of disturbances, and a lot of people will feel disenfranchised, and so on. The defensive argument is that you've got to give us time to sort it out, and we've got to sort it out in our own way. The more you interfere from outside using external criteria, the more you make it harder for us to arrive at a peaceful solution now.

Those who argue the opposite way say that you've got it all wrong to begin with. You've got to have different nations.

But then there is a break in the argument. If you say that all states are states first of all, which are trying to nation-build, then why are you not allowing the Chinese to do that? You are allowing others to. For example, the Bengalis and the Tamils don't feel the same way as the Hindus of Uttar Pradesh. The Indians implement tremendous decentralization, which the Chinese also do. Both are not federal systems. The central power is there, with reserve power. In China the centre may look much more powerful, but what it has is also reserve power because all these party secretaries who are provincial heads actually have tremendous autonomy. Their autonomy is not that much different from the autonomy of Tamil Nadu or Kerala. It's just that they are not elected.

So your democracy point comes in, which is on the legitimacy of the provincial leader. But he is still appointed from the centre, and he can be removed. Actually, India can intervene as well if something goes wrong, and replace a chief minister. That's constitutionally possible, so the difference is probably a matter of degree.

OKB: The argument of being given sufficient time is quite strong given that many young democracies actually don't function very well as an economy, like the Philippines perhaps.

WGW: Yes, that's another complicated argument, because the idea that democracy actually helps economic development is proven wrong in Asia. In Asia, it seems to be the reverse that works. The Japanese developed under the Meiji, not under a democracy. The fact that they succeeded so well after the war was because they already had the base. And Korea and Taiwan were all under a dictatorship of one kind or another. China as well, of course. But those that are very democratic, like the Philippines, have tremendous difficulties. They are getting there slowly, but it is a tremendously expensive and painful manner of economic development. Their democracy in the end allows for too many private interests to intervene in the development process. Especially now when transnational religions are coming in. If the state is not strong enough to resist them, then the economy will continually be fragmented by forces that are against nation building.

So what is your priority? Is it to build a nation that is at the same time economically developing, to develop economically and forget about the nation, or to build a nation at the expense of economic development? All these are choices that have to be made.

The nation state is not only a defence against the imperial. States are now defending themselves against each other. The imperial is gone now, with the exception of America still with the capacity to intervene.

And, therefore, the claim to absolute national sovereignty is a way of making sure at least of being left alone to develop my nation. There is the tough job ahead of building this nation, and interference simply makes things more difficult. However, globalization is taking place at the same time, and international pressures on each nation are very strong now, unlike the way it was when nations were built up in Europe in the seventeenth and eighteenth centuries, where each one had the capacity to do it, and over time. Here, there is a shortage of time, because while you are working at it, your economy has to function globally. You have to endure external pressure on ideals of freedom, democracy, human rights, minority rights, justice, and so on. So you've got to do the nation building within that framework. Some countries can, but others find it very difficult and feel that these ideals would actually lead to disunity rather than aid national development.

These tensions are very, very strong right now. Every country faces them, except for those who are already strongly united, like the Japanese and the Koreans, who have been pretty much mono-ethnic right from the start. Their basis for building a nation is much stronger.

OKB: They fit the ideal much better.

WGW: They are a more natural fit. Japan is an island, so you can understand that.

OKB: Well, China is not too far from it.

WGW: If you stay with the original eighteen provinces, then you would have it. But inheriting the *Qing* borders doubled the country's size. The new areas were not the same as the eighteen provinces. To the northeast, in the extension that is Manchuria, the *Han* Chinese are there; in Mongolia, they are now the majority; and *Gansu* and *Qinghai* already have a *Han* majority. So only Tibet and *Xinjiang* are left. Everywhere else has a *Han* majority. Even *Guangxi* has a *Han* majority, as does *Yunnan*, even with the twenty-five nationalities found there lumped together.

So they are doing it in a different way. But it takes time. Of course the world outside feels that something wrong is being done to the Tibetans and the Uighurs. I think that is understandable. They have great sympathy for Tibet, particularly because the Dalai Lama is such a highly respected figure. So the Chinese will have to handle that part with some delicate moves. But they don't know how to do it yet.

COMPARING INDIA AND CHINA

OKB: Some analysts, in comparing the amazing economic growth rates in India and in China, have argued that China paid the price of modernization by struggling through the communist era where a lot of old habits that might have stopped modernization were eradicated and altered — the role of women, for example. India, on the other hand, never went through such a revolution. Would that in the near future act as a brake on how India can develop as a modern nation state?

WGW: The revolution argument has been made. Yes, I think there is an element of truth in it, but I don't know whether that is the whole picture, because underlying it all, perhaps just as importantly or even more importantly, is the fact that the Chinese were more or less unitary all the time. Essentially, although they had conquerors and they had different ethnic groups, it had always been a unitary system that grew and grew and grew. The Indian system has politically been just the opposite; it had always been fragmented in different groups with a foreign conqueror on the surface, but not making that much difference to the social economic structure. Underlying it all was a very strong religious culture, which persisted through everything, and which was very meaningful to Indian peoples in a way religion was not to the Chinese. China's growth is dependent on and identified with the state.

The Indian case never depended much on the central state. All those who were inclined to trade formed a caste. They were the ones who continued to trade no matter who the Kshatriyas or the Brahmins at the top were. They were nationwide and didn't depend on the state being unified or not, as long as it left them alone. Basically they had light government, and I think that remains the case. In fact it couldn't be anything else even if it tried. The central government can only do certain things, and doesn't have the tradition of intervening below a certain level. The structure of autonomous trading groups and castes operating successfully throughout the subcontinent remains to this day. These groups are the ones who continue to develop the economy, in a way. Despite the state and despite a religion that doesn't emphasize trade but worries instead about the next world, they operate according to their own commercial culture.

Chinese economic growth has always depended on the central government, and when the central government did not emphasize trade and treated traders badly instead, the economy became agrarian and stagnant. Resources were not properly utilized. The state didn't allow the merchants to be too powerful, because when they were rich and powerful they could intrude upon the Mandarinate. Those reservations and limitations actually hampered economic development. That very narrow framework was blasted open by Western penetration and by revolution, leading to the complete collapse of that particular kind of agrarian economy and to the coming of thorough industrialization under the communists. Mao Zedong started it, using the Soviet Model, and Deng Xiaoping inherited it. After all, the economy of the Soviet Union grew tremendously in the 1920s and 1930s. That was why so many Western Europeans became communists. They admired the Soviet model greatly until 1945. That sympathy began failing only in the 1950s and 1960s, when the Soviets started to compete with the United States.

OKB: They were the first to put a man into space.

WGW: Yes, they were fantastic. So Mao Zedong had grounds for using the Soviet model of industrialization. Eventually he found that it didn't quite work for China because the peasants couldn't adapt to it. The Great Leap Forward was a way of trying to speed up the whole thing. Mao got very impatient, and got the whole party galvanized to push harder. Of course, it created havoc instead and was totally counterproductive. Tens of millions died unnecessarily, but he still persisted. With the Cultural Revolution, he took another approach, and again he essentially wanted to make sure that the party would be dynamic in pushing for economic development. But he took very extreme measures. Throughout, the revolution was led from the top, and central power was decisive in economic development.

This was opposed to the Indian case. Even the British never tried to control the local economy in India. They inherited the Moghul system, and essentially left things alone. They just had a few British around using the local people to run things in the different states. Only in Calcutta, Madras and Bombay did they try to do things themselves. Outside these, things were run by the Gujaratis, the Tamils, the Bengalis, and so on. The British had companies located here and there, but the number of Brits was small. In Delhi, members of the Indian Civil Service were mainly Indians. Even the garrisons were full of Indian soldiers — Muslims, Hindus, Sikhs and Gurkhas. Outside, the basic cultural mix remained solid, and economic development followed traditional lines.

Would revolution have made a difference? How could they have run a revolution, I ask you? They had communist parties in all corners of the continent, but that got them nowhere.

OKB: It remains the Argumentative Continent.[16]

WGW: Yes, the whole cultural heritage is not susceptible to revolutionary change. Revolution was successful in China only because it was centrally based, as was the case in Russia. I remember being very struck by the fact that when Lenin came to power after 1917, one of the sections of the tsarist system which he did not change was the secret police. He kept that because he realized how necessary that was to his ability to control the country. So, while he got rid of all kinds of bureaucrats, the secret police was left more or less intact. He did put in some of his own men, but he kept the machinery of surveillance and control, and so on. This was not accidental. China in many ways did the same thing, because when the communists took over they retained a lot of the Kuomintang officials, while getting rid of those who were obviously hostile or unwilling to join them. They kept the system and gradually modified it. However, Mao Zedong was dissatisfied with that way of doing things because it couldn't help to take them to the next stage of revolution. That's why there was the Great Leap Forward. In other words, the earlier revolution was not revolutionary enough. The old system had to be broken up and replaced. And so he did that from the top, using state power.

Nothing in the whole of Indian history allows for that kind of top-down revolutionary change. Different parts of India operate almost independent of each other, and a tremendous amount of freedom and initiative is possible among the people there because of this loose structure. In that way, we see why Oliver Wolters tried to apply the Mandala image in Southeast Asia, an area without central power. In India, the Mandala system was already clear. There was never a central power there either.

The Chinese were always the opposite of that. So in that way, when we go back to our original discussion about the Eurasian continent, there were all sorts of varieties of political structure. The Western European case had the Greek city-state idea that the Roman Empire did not totally destroy. After the Roman Empire fell, city states as a political structure remained until the creation of the nation state. The nation state was something in between the city state and the empire. It was a compromise that soon produced the national empire. And even today, cities have tremendous rights.

OKB: A city state expanding into its rural surroundings is the beginning of a nation state, in that sense.

WGW: Yes, you are right. But on the Asian side, nobody created a nation state. There was always an empire with the agrarian masses as subjects. In between, in the space where what we might call civil society today would be found, there was nothing much. In the Indian case the caste and religious systems decided a variety of roles between top and bottom. The central space in the Chinese case was filled by the family, which is not part of the civil society concept. The family is about genealogy; it is a bloodline concept. Similarly, the caste system is a bloodline system. It is very strict and rigid, as is the family system. You do not belong to my family unless you marry into it. Otherwise, it is always my clan against yours.

OKB: Can one describe Southeast Asia historically through Silk Road, or trade routes, politics? The ports were not sufficient in themselves. Instead, they were quite peripheral in the larger context, and survived because they were part of the trading activities going on between the empires.

WGW: That's a very interesting way of describing it. It is apparent where the continental side is concerned. Where the maritime side is concerned, we are dealing with a very new perspective, with the Silk Road image being transposed on to the sea. The Silk Road in the north was still basically a Eurasian power system, with areas in between and with powerful states at both ends. So it was always the part in between that expressed the relationship between different ends.

I won't say the maritime system in Southeast Asia was like the Silk Road. We think of the Silk Road as having the Roman Empire and the *Han* Empire at the far ends, and in between there were the Iranian Empire, the Arabs and even the Moghul Empire. The routes in between all these were in areas nobody took the trouble to control, since they were based in oases surrounded by desert. And they were not agrarian like these powers were. There are similarities enough for us to apply this pattern to the maritime region in Southeast Asia. But the one was the Eurasian centre, while the other was on the edges and was not regarded as significant. In terms of political power and even wealth generation, Southeast Asia was not that important. The essential economic power came from agrarian surplus supporting the political system, the army, the garrisons, and so on.

OKB: Today, ASEAN groups together a number of states, all of which know how vulnerable they are individually. For them to stay united and enhance their credibility, they have to be each other's peers and to always make decisions unanimously.

WGW: This is a by-product of being between India and China. From day one, decolonization took place under the shadow of the great powers and was affected by how these were planning their own futures. Even though unspoken, the underlying thought which the British had already come up with — and in that way we are still a product of that imagination — was that sooner or later the region as a whole will be clamped between India and China. So what do you do? If you are Balkanized, you will always be subject to one or the other. They sold the idea that they could help us, which they are still doing. The Americans joined in, and so Britain and America basically offered a guarantee that if we welcomed them, they would help us against the two powers. The Cold War, of course, increased the sense of urgency throughout the region. One side had become communist, and the other side was capitalist.

So decolonization taking place during the Cold War was the full context. The underlying idea was that these places between India and China offered a strategic opportunity for the West. And now we have President Obama's pivot to the region. India is no threat today, so they focus on China. You have a counterbalancing act going on, and this is where Australia comes in. Whether they like it or not, Australia represents the West. They are here in the neighbourhood! So if Australia participates, then the West is in the region.

OKB: They are more than just deputy sheriff to the Americans then?

WGW: They are actually integral to the whole set-up. Having U.S. marines in Darwin doing elaborate surveillance from the south is not accidental. It is an extension of the whole process, and the justification for that is that Southeast Asia needs protection. At the same time, the Southeast Asians who worry about India and China feel that the only chance they have is to let the West in. If you look at the economics alone, the whole of Southeast Asia is not as strong as China or Japan, or even Korea. India still has some problems in South Asia, and Bangladesh and Sri Lanka create some awkwardness for the Indians, but basically the gap is still frighteningly big, and so the Southeast Asians feel justified in allowing the West a role. It makes them sleep better at night.

That is why we have the business of ASEAN being in the driver's seat. The language is very interesting, because putting it that way justifies the third leg — not only India and China, but also the West. This centrality of Southeast Asia is based on an assumption that this will *forever* be the only way that Southeast Asians can feel secure, locked as they are between those two. This proceeds from the post-1945 process of decolonization. There is an extraordinary and interesting continuity here, and I would say it is the brainchild of the British — British idea, American capacity and Australia as the instrument of their partnership; altogether guaranteeing security and stability for the Southeast Asians.

OKB: They handled their retreat very well, didn't they, the British?

WGW: Beautifully! Look at the British Commonwealth. It was a brilliant invention. Most people now dismiss it, but I would advise against that. The idea is extremely powerful. It doesn't depend on power; it depends on diplomacy and negotiated agreements and a sharing of insights about what the future should look like strategically. And if you look at it that way, then the Commonwealth has a different, though seemingly minor, function. It is there to provide a backdrop upon which a lot of other things can take place. A sense of sharing of political culture can continue via the Commonwealth. It doesn't offer any clear alternative, but it is an alternative, to either India or China. That's all you need, actually.

The Commonwealth remains peripheral though, because in the end you do need a solid territorial base; and that is why ASEAN — the Southeast Asian Ten — was an extraordinary step forward. It has not been very long since the last member joined. Cambodia came in 1999, only fifteen years ago. So it's too early to say whether it will succeed or fail. It's just beginning, just growing into a three-sided reality, with Southeast Asia in the centre. It's brilliant. The ASEAN peoples all know this. So do the other players.

OKB: The common tendency to study ASEAN by comparing it to the EU misses the point entirely then.

WGW: The EU is different. I think the EU is only important to us in the sense that we look at how far one can go without getting into big trouble. We watch what they do and learn from their mistakes, and if there are ideas there which will help us, then we can take them. But it cannot be a model; it's a totally different story. ASEAN is entirely strategic. The EU had strategic origins as well, what with NATO and the Cold War; but that is all over, so it is a different story now. The dynamics are different.

I use the Mediterranean concept because I think what will make the Anglo-Americans and the Indians even happier is if they can complete this arc from Japan all the way down to India, and so contain China. They would then feel safe. You would then see the South China Sea as a real Mediterranean. Keeping the Chinese out of the Indian Ocean and the western Pacific is part of this policy of containment. So the South China Sea remains the final region needed to complete this picture. Should they succeed, then you will have a Mediterranean setting stretching from Japan and Korea down to Java and the Malay Peninsula, dividing two sides completely, just as the Muslim and Christian worlds are separated by the Mediterranean. The West knows that they cannot incorporate China into their story. China is too big, too powerful and too rich, and it has too much of its own history. This is the reality that they have to accept.

Now, on the Chinese side, many of their leaders accept the reality that they are not able to challenge the United States. What they want is to be sure that they are safe from external attack and intervention. That's all they want. To do that, they must have a very special relationship with the United States.

In between, however, there are many proxies, so who knows what will happen there. That's a situation that has to be managed. It is in a way the expression of a long stand-off between those two sides. How big or small the arc will be, and who will be included or excluded is for the future to decide.

OKB: Going back to what you said about how the political-economic structure of China differs so fundamentally from India's, the fact that China's growth is based on a strong state means the chances of a huge crash in China is much greater than in the case of India, where the political and economic structures are so diverse. Would you agree?

WGW: Yes. That's true. India may have more limitations to its growth than China, but China can crash. As Roderick MacFarquhar and many others such as Susan Shirk have said, there is a kind of fragility in the Chinese system.[17] One may choose to exploit it or one may not, but there is a fragility there that makes it difficult for the Chinese to develop their country into something totally stable in the long run.

Notes

1. Wang Gungwu, "The Nanhai Trade: A Study of the Early History of Chinese Trade in the South China Sea", *Journal of the Malayan Branch of the Royal Asiatic Society* 31, pt. 2 (1958): 3–135.
2. This was drawn as a nine-dotted line after the communists took over.
3. Treaty of London, 1824.
4. See Wang Gungwu, "China and the Map of Nine Dotted Lines", *Straits Times*, 11 July 2012.
5. See Fei Xiaotong, *From the Soil: The Foundations of Chinese Society, A translation of Fei Xiaotong's Xiangtu Zhongguo*. University of California Press, 1992.
6. See, for example, Charles Hirschman, "The Meaning and Measurement of Ethnicity in Malaysia: An Analysis of Census Classifications", *Journal of Asian Studies* 46, no. 3 (1987): 555–82.
7. See Japp Jacobs, *The Colony of New Netherland: A Dutch Settlement in Seventeenth-Century America*. Cornell University, 2009.
8. Wang Gungwu, "Party and Nation in Southeast Asia", *Millennial Asia: An International Journal of Asian Studies* 1, no. 1 (2010): 41–57.
9. This was a series of English dynastic wars fought in 1455–87 between two rival groups — Lancaster and York — within the ruling House of Plantagenets.
10. The Tudors were of Welsh origins, and ruled from 1485 to 1603.
11. O.W. Wolters, *History, Culture, and Region in Southeast Asian Perspectives*. Studies in Southeast Asia No. 26. Cornell SEAP Publications, and ISEAS, 1999.

12. See Kishore Mahbubani, *The Great Convergence: Asia, the West, and the Logic of One World*. Perseus, 2013.
13. Wang Gungwu, "Keynote Address: Southeast Asia: Imperial Themes", *New Zealand Journal of Asian Studies* 11, no. 1 (2009): 36–48.
14. See Vladimir Lenin, *Imperialism, the Highest Stage of Capitalism*. Zhizn'i znanie, 1917.
15. John A. Hobson, *Imperialism: A Study*. Cosimo, 1902.
16. See Amartya Sen, *The Argumentative Indian: Writings on History, Culture and Identity*. Picador, 2006.
17. For Roderick MacFarquhar's views on this subject, see, for example, Verna Yu, "Reform Unlikely, says China Expert Roderick MacFarquhar", *South China Morning Post*, 31 October 2012. See also Susan L. Shirk, *China: Fragile Superpower*. Oxford University Press, 2008.

Chapter 4

CHINA'S STRUGGLE WITH THE WESTERN EDGE

ADAPTING TO THE WORLD ORDER

OKB: We are now in a situation where the eastern edge of the Europe-Asia landmass meets the western edge. It would be interesting at this point to discuss China again. Perhaps we can start with an article you wrote a while ago on China trying hard to adjust to a world order it had no part in creating.[1]

That is in fact the process that China has been going through for a long time, starting with the Opium War, followed by the fall of the imperial system, then the rise of the Kuomintang, and then the triumph of *Mao*. It was Deng Xiaoping's reforms after 1978 that finally brought remarkable economic growth to the country. All this took a hundred and seventy years. But now, in its new position of power and influence, functioning well at the global level in all areas becomes extremely important for China. There is also a fall in confidence in the West, which in a way opens up space for the Chinese to actually *tweak* the world order wherever they can. This begs the question: to what extent is Confucianism — or Confucian thinking — still at play here? After all, in the bigger scheme of things, communism will probably just be seen as an anomaly.

You told me the other day that you see yourself as a Confucian, and that you were raised that way. I'm one of those who believe that the contribution that Confucian thinking can bring to modern life is actually quite enormous. But because of colonialism and the rise of Western science and technology, whatever knowledge that was not Western was pushed aside as being essentially misguided. I am hoping to hear your views on that.

Also, China is now ranked the second-largest economy, and aiming to be first. But we know for a fact that the American system is much more stable, and even if it should someday rank only second in terms of certain statistical figures, it's got strong institutions and it's got impressive unity in ideology. On the Chinese side, things are rather chaotic and fragile. So the figures don't tell the whole story, and I would venture that they are in some ways being used to incite fear of China.

WGW: That's quite right. I think a lot of the debate that argues from the figures can be very misleading. I think the thrust of the Chinese experience is that their underlying world view is being restored, and that world view does stem from their Confucian heritage. But there's a lot of misunderstanding about the Confucian heritage. Most Chinese in my generation and the generation immediately before me were very sceptical about Confucianism because we were identifying Confucianism with the Chinese imperial state. Making that connection was certainly correct because the Confucian philosophers and scholars accepted the imperial state as the norm and in fact did their utmost to preserve it and to work for it loyally. In fact it was their loyalty that ensured its survival for so long. All those centuries, were it not for the Confucians, the imperial state could not have managed as well as it did.

So their contribution was that they laid down the foundations for a particular kind of state — which they didn't invent. It was invented by others: by warriors, kings, the legalists and others. But they didn't challenge it. In the *Han* dynasty, they built on it. They felt it was the given condition. It was potentially strong and effective, so the Confucians who emerged then thought that they could actually improve on it, and enable it to function as a moral and righteous state. So all their aspirations about their responsibility to help to govern, to help make society better, to enable people to have a fairer life and better chance of a good life, continued. It was just that the structure of the state was now different from what they originally imagined, but they accepted it. As a result though, they were complicit in building that imperial state into the kind of power that it became. And again and again, they were forced to make concessions about what the nature of the state was and what the role of the emperor was; and each step of the way, those concessions actually consolidated into a very rigid bureaucratic system that was highly elitist and that benefited the Confucian literati. But they of course paid a price for it. They served the emperor loyally in order to preserve their elitist and privileged position, a position that they thought was deservedly theirs because they served the state well.

Now many of us in the twentieth century rejected *that* Confucianism, which may be called "State Confucianism", and which had become the orthodoxy of the imperial state. That set of ideas, most Chinese thinkers of the time rejected as being totally out of date or totally dysfunctional and no longer needed by the Chinese. So they turned away, looking for other things.

In looking for other things, they experimented with many ideas, none of which really worked in China. They experimented with the Kuomintang structure which drew on the West. In fact, both the Communist Party and the Kuomintang drew almost entirely from the West; it didn't matter that people said that Chiang Kai-shek was a Confucianist trying to go back to the past. In fact he was drawing on the Japanese modelling of the West. He had studied in Japan, and behind a lot of his rhetoric was a structure of centralized power, which the Japanese had perfected. There was no democracy in Japan either. Also, the militarism which he had through his military training also led him to admire the Germans, too. So the nationalism-militarism part of the Japanese model, which many Chinese saw as the secret of Japanese success, was commonly adopted. If Japan could be successful in that way, perhaps the Chinese could follow suit. The Japanese way of absorbing certain Western ideas — particularly technology and military skills — and the Meiji's imperialistic view about the importance of wealth and power was proving successful. "Wealth and Power" was a Chinese idea, but the Japanese developed it to a high point. The first generation of Chinese nationalists actually accepted the logic of that success. Of course, so did the communists.

The communists actually were not communist in the sense that Marx had had in mind. Nor were they communist in the Lenin mould. They were in fact more communist in the Stalinist mould. Lenin, to an extent, built the communist state on the tsarist structure, and basically departed from what Marx had in mind. Marx was very much a Western European intellectual trying hard to predict the future of Europe after decades of capitalism, and all the terrible things that *naked* capitalism could do to society. He was quite right in describing what the consequences of untrammelled capitalism were. He did see the alienation that was occurring around him, so he predicted a kind of workers' revolt against capitalism, which would eventually lead to ideal communism. But as we all know, it didn't happen like that. The West found solutions; they found ways to get out of the bind. Capitalism adjusted and, through socialism, actually compromised in many ways. In fact those measures prevented revolutions from happening.

Revolutions could only occur, and did occur, in countries that did not have much capitalism. That's a fact. Revolutionary movements were successful where there was no real capitalist proletariat to provide an alternate structure. So they had to build it on the *collapse* of an agrarian structure, and upon that collapse, they could impose something new. I think that model finally attracted the Chinese, and not because of its communism. Some Chinese communist intellectuals did talk a lot about it. Some of them of course learned it from living in Stalinist Russia. Mao Zedong himself read a lot of Stalin's writings. But I think in the end, someone like Mao understood that success in China would depend on taking advantage of the Chinese agrarian system and relying on the tradition of peasant rebellion. They did not identify the weakness and failure of the Kuomintang to be its nationalism. The nationalism was all right. What was wrong was that the Kuomintang was trying too hard to be partly Japanese and partly Western European. Sun Yat-sen had introduced China to all kinds of miscellaneous ideas that Chiang Kai-shek restructured to support his party. The militarism, for example, became much stronger than Sun Yat-sen had envisaged. Sun had been converted to a degree of militarism in the revolutionary army, but never fully. On the other hand, Chiang Kai-shek, being military trained, felt that there was no alternative but to use military power to consolidate political power.

So neither of them were really successful in adapting what they understood from the West. They got it all by accepting a little bit here and a little bit there; like the militarism Chiang

Kai-shek learned from Japan and Germany. As for liberalism, they were very hesitant. On the surface they had many other things that were Western. They had a lot of capitalism, but they also adapted it to become nationalistic capitalism. They were very much against foreign capitalism, but they accepted capitalism! They were using capitalist methods, inviting a lot of foreign firms in but at the same time controlling them and trying to minimize their power on Chinese soil. They were committed to building up *Chinese* capitalism to take over from Western capitalism. They had a kind of relationship between state and capitalism, which in the end failed for all sorts of very complicated reasons. But most of all, looking back at it, one can see that what the nationalists put together might not have failed; it might have had a chance had it not been for the Japanese war.

So it is true to say that the Japanese war with China played a big role in the ultimate destruction of Chiang Kai-shek's nationalist government, and helped the communists greatly. Of course one could also say it was the failure on the part of the nationalists — they were not ready to fight the war.

There's no question that the Japanese were much more powerful than the Chinese, and if you read Chiang Kai-shek's diaries and writings, you will see that his thinking was actually very traditional: "Don't fight if you cannot win." This is very much *Sun Zi* talking. Chiang Kai-shek kept on saying he didn't want to fight the Japanese, because he knew he would lose. He wanted to be ready first, and one of the reasons he thought he would lose was because he thought he would have to fight the communist party at the same time. His undoing was that this stance then made him look like he would rather fight the communist Chinese than the Japanese. So the communists took advantage of that and in their propaganda used that very skilfully against the nationalists: "You would rather kill Chinese than Japanese?" He had no answer to that because, in his private moments, he knew that he couldn't fight the Japanese and win. But he would have a chance if he could destroy the communists first and unite the Chinese under him. That was his logic. But the communists managed to turn that around against him. And so you had the *Xi'an* Incident (in December 1936), when he was kidnapped and forced to admit that fighting the Japanese was a matter of national interest and should be the first priority.

He now had no choice but to fight the Japanese, whose argument was also interesting. They said, "We didn't start the war. We kept on telling the Kuomintang that we wanted to combine with them to help destroy the communists. We're on the same side. The enemy is the Soviet Union, and the Communist Party of China is being directed by the Comintern, by Stalin." Incidentally, *Wang Jingwei* — Chiang Kai-shek's opponent within the Kuomintang — did accept that argument and did work with the Japanese. But Chiang Kai-shek was caught in an impossible position. In the eyes of the Chinese, the Japanese were invaders on Chinese soil, just like the Manchurians had been. How could these people be regarded as allies now? So in a way, geopolitically, it was a no-win situation.

After the *Xi'an* Incident the Japanese knew that it was now the communists and the Kuomintang *together* who would fight them. It was a question of whether they would be thrown out of whatever they held in northwestern China and in *Shandong* Province. Just north of the Great Wall, in *Hebei* Province, the people were already restless and worried about further Japanese incursions. The conditions for war were there. The Japanese argument — which the Chinese didn't accept of course — was that they never actually declared war on China. Fighting did start in the *Luguoqiao* Incident — the Marco Polo Bridge Incident — on 7 July 1937, but no, there was no declaration of war.

Put in perspective, the failure of the Western model in China was not just because it was Western but because it was associated with Japan as well. Japan represented the West. There was never any real rejection of the West among the Chinese. Despite all the reasons they had for doing so, the Chinese never really hated the British or French. And they never hated the Americans either! The Americans were actually very much on their side, although there were disagreements about various things. But the Chinese were never against "The West" as such. What they rejected were the Japanese. In that war, the confusion was that the Japanese-West and the American-West constituted two choices of the West. But they were both "The West".

On the other side were the Russians. I don't think most Chinese ever understood why they should be allied to the Soviet Union, no matter what Mao Zedong said. He tried his utmost to convince the Chinese that the Russians were their greatest friends. I think that to this day it's not how the Chinese are inclined.

But that the West should be associated with Japan, and that Germany was also the West, really confused the Chinese people. It really made the question "What is the West?" a profound issue. You see, today we try to simplify it so that the United States represents the West; and all the great inventions, new ideas, liberal freedom and so on get associated with that country. Today we've isolated certain things to represent the West. But that was not how the West was seen in the 1920s and 30s. It was associated with gunboat diplomacy then; it was associated with power; and it was associated with militarism. The West denies that bit about themselves now, but fascism was part of the West, as was communism.

OKB: There were many Wests.

WGW: Yes. There were many Wests. Sometimes we forget that the Chinese did not reject the West. They were choosing from the West. One side of the West now rejects its other side and argues that the Chinese don't understand the West, and that what they chose was not the real West. But I don't think that's a legitimate argument. They're all the West. As far as the Chinese were concerned, they were just choices. Even in the West they were making choices. Look at how the intelligentsia and the intellectuals in the West were also debating whether or not to be sympathetic to Nazism and Fascism. Today we take it for granted that these were all "baddies", but that's because we're not in the 1920s and 1930s now. There were lots of British intellectuals who were quite sympathetic to Germany and Nazism, and they were *very* disgruntled with what was happening to liberal democratic systems. Many found Soviet Communism appealing. If you read the literature of that time, and study the people who fought in the Spanish Civil War, you can see how utterly confusing it all was.

So it was never about East versus West. It was about how Asia — China in particular — chose from among alternatives provided by the West. In that sense the rejection of its own past by the West was pretty thorough. The Cold War was a perfect example of it. The Cold War put *two Wests* in stark contrast to each other. This or that. There was nothing else; the West in its entirety was dominant. The choices were between Team A and Team B. That was the case until the 1990s, so we're talking about something very recent!

And the Chinese were in exactly that position. They've rejected one West now — West B, meaning the Soviet Russian Communist model, which turned into such a tragic thing for the people. They're not so sure of the other West, West A, especially when they are now being attacked by that West, and being regarded as suspect in its eyes. Most Chinese people are perfectly happy in the West. If you put them in Western countries, they would be delighted — if they were only treated equally. What they are unwilling to accept is to be treated as second class. What has kept them from totally accepting the West is that the West looks down on them. The pride of the Chinese people cannot accept that. If they are treated as equals, they have absolutely no hesitation about accepting the West. Always, at the back of it all, is a glass-ceiling problem; the basic feeling that Western people are patronizing. That is something that they cannot accept; that is the hesitation. But in the meantime China is doing well without exactly following the West, and instead taking only selectively from this West whilst retaining something from the other West. And they're finding that this mixture is working. But while it is working, they also feel that something is missing. They are basically taking the methodologies and technologies of West A and West B, but their heart and soul are not in it. The sense of belonging, the sense of being fully part of it, is missing... because it isn't Chinese. They know that it is not. So the West A–West B mixture, even if it works, is still lacking something.

OKB: That's where Confucius becomes relevant again, I suppose.

WGW: This is where the Chinese turn back to their own past. After a hundred years they're now coming round to not rejecting Confucianism anymore. They tried so hard to reject it, but it keeps coming back. The reason why it doesn't go away, as many people will say, is that there is a lot of basic truth in it. There's nothing fundamentally wrong with the ideas of Confucius.

The moment you separate Confucius and his fundamental ideas from Confucianism as a state orthodoxy, then you see it with different eyes. And that's the interesting thing about it; that always, through those long two-thousand-odd years, even when the Confucians were making all sorts of compromises to support the imperial state, individual Confucians always looked to Confucius, and privately knew that there was a *real* Confucius to which they were attached. But in real life, they had to adjust and adapt to the Confucian ideology that the state supported. So they were torn between being good Confucians and being only that part of a good Confucian which is to serve the emperor and the state, and be useful to society by becoming part of the system.

So there was a private Confucian and a public Confucian. And you can see this in the way Neo-Confucian philosophy developed. The philosophy in itself went in one direction, but the reality was that individual Confucians had to make choices. They could concentrate on being filial to Confucian principles or choose a public career to serve the state and be a good Confucian in the eyes of the state. These were the *"Ru"* (Confucian gentleman) in distinction from the *"Guan"* (Mandarin). And you find both kinds of Confucians throughout Chinese history. There were those who never served the state, who spent their lives teaching and serving their own local communities, and who feared that they would have to make too many compromises and become so corrupted by political demands that it would make a mockery of their own ideals. So the difference was always very clear to most Confucians. But it was a Hobson's choice if they wanted to serve. To serve is after all also part of the Confucian ethos.

You see the same sort of thing emerging again today. They're done with Confucianism, while "Socialism with Chinese Characteristics" is coined to give some legitimacy to the Chinese Communist Party. They cannot throw that out, or else they have nothing at all. But what is the substance? They have acquired now the methodologies of the West. Whether it is West B or

West A, they've mastered it; they've understood it now. But now what they want to recover is some Chinese core. What should be revived, and what deserves to be kept?

Now that they have the methodologies to maintain a strong state and a healthy economy — assuming the economy will stay healthy — they need more. They are human beings. It's not enough to have a strong state and a good economy. The challenge is that the West not only brought methodologies and technologies, it also brought a set of ideals, much of which came from Christianity, from West A. The Chinese Muslims remain Muslims, not growing very fast in number as far as I know. The Chinese Buddhists are turning to Buddhism. Other Chinese, who don't have anything else clear in their minds, are turning to Christianity. So if the Chinese system fails to make Confucianism relevant again, people will go back to one of these religions, and the two major ones will be Buddhism and Christianity. Christianity has been making a lot of headway today because there is a spiritual hunger somewhere. That's quite clear. The intellectuals today are working very hard to restate Confucian ideals in terms attractive to the young, but they're not succeeding.

But then there's the other part — the serving part — which serves a socialism with Chinese characteristics. That system is not Confucian at all, but because serving society and the state is part of Confucianism, they make their compromises.

What's fascinating to ask now is how much of the private Confucianism is still relevant, or viable? And in what ways can the public service part be the basis for the evolution of a Confucian Socialism, or whatever can be a better name for it — a Socialism with Confucian Characteristics — which will make it possible for them to be both Confucians and socialists? Can they make the socialist state Chinese by adopting some Confucian ideas? What *Hu Jintao* tried to represent with his notion of *Hexie* (Socialist Harmonious Society) was a move in that direction, but that's using socialism with Chinese characteristics — imbibing and accepting something to make things more indigenous, recognizable, and comfortable for the Chinese people.

And this is the real test. It is an internal problem for them. As for dealing with the outside world, the technologies of the modern world are mechanical in many ways. You learn them and you apply them where appropriate. Chinese understanding of the rules of geopolitics and their expertise in international relations are pretty good. They sent some of their top brains to study all this. They know what it's all about and they know that it does not entirely satisfy China's needs, but they can live with it. Over the last thirty years there have been many examples of how the Chinese have actually accepted the rules and tried to make the rules serve their interests. That's well known, and some people even argue that they're actually following the rules of the United Nations better than the United States sometimes. The United States doesn't always bother.

The Chinese are not too unhappy with the rules, because these are techniques only. So what is important are not the rules themselves. Fighting hard to change the rules is not worth the trouble. Interpreting them, or hiding behind them, using them in flexible ways to fit different situations is to be preferred. And this is in a way like everything else — manufacturing or marketing, and so on. You don't try to change the rules. You master them and you pick the bits that help you most and you manoeuvre within them. So I don't think that they're too unhappy about the rules. If others wish to change the rules, then they're willing to change if necessary. But they don't want to take the initiative, because they don't want to be seen to be challenging the rules or even questioning them.

This is where it comes back to an interesting difference in attitudes towards the law. The West probably has a much more pious attitude towards the law. I call it piety because it also involves a lot of hypocrisy; piety in the sense that you pay tremendous reverence to something and you treat it as sacred. The Chinese don't have that kind of piety. They don't treat the law as sacred. Law is just one of the instruments of the state, of society, of any group of people where you need rules. Law is an extension of rules. It's a higher order of rule-making perhaps, but it's no more than a set of rules.

PRAGMATIC VERSUS PIOUS LAWS

OKB: There's no concept of Natural Law, like in the Germanic world.

WGW: I don't think they believe in something like Universal Law or Natural Law in the absolute sense. Law is just a set of rules that are necessary for certain purposes, and they can be changed. But this is true of law in the West, too! In reality the West is very realistic about the law. They don't say rules are absolute; their rules do change accordingly. So if you both understand that, if both take that as a basis, then it is a question of degree which rules you want changed at what time, and that is often guided by one's interest.

The difference is very interesting: the Chinese do not have this idea that law is sacred at all, to them it is just an instrument. The other side makes the rule of law an absolute thing, but in practice also recognizes that it has to be flexible. You get different camps in the sense that one is a bit more cavalier about the law while the other makes a lot of fuss about its sacred qualities. But when it comes to facing reality, I believe that most human beings — whether Chinese or Westerners — are quite open to changing the rules, if necessary. Look at how many new rules we have had since the United Nations was established. International law has been evolving all the time. So the Chinese are ready to look at new rules.

OKB: Global trade mechanisms have been changing, certainly.

WGW: And continually, obviously trying to improve. That means if it doesn't work, you improve it. So they find it very strange when people come to them with a scolding, "This is the rule, you're not observing it." It doesn't make a great deal of sense to them. But of course it creates a lot of misunderstanding. We have here two very different starting points. One is that once you have an agreement, it is forever. But that idea has never been part of Chinese culture.

OKB: What you say about the pious attitude on the side of the West and the more pragmatic approach on the Chinese side reminds me of Confucianism again, and the centrality of the concept of "*Li*", of rituals. In an important sense, laws (*Fa*) are a form of rituals. International laws are more clearly so, and are newly initiated rituals where there is agreement to do certain things in a certain way. *Li* comes before *Fa*.

WGW: I think that describes the Chinese attitude very well. Law is a kind of agreed upon, accepted ritual, and the Chinese put the emphasis on the ritual side, instead of the absolute side of law.

OKB: So there's no place for conceit. A tentative attitude is required since we are dealing with an agreement on ritual. A more pious attitude to law attempts to assume authority from beyond the agreement itself, or postulates that there is really no mutual agreement, just an inspired discovery of that law on somebody's part.

WGW: The Chinese don't have that transcendence. You see, it's not part of their tradition to say that there's something over and above that determines a universal or natural law, and from which you cannot deviate. And then, of course, when the Chinese find that the protagonists also change the law when it suits them, despite their pious attitude, then they will say, "There you are, our approach is more justified!" The Chinese have experienced enough of that in the last two hundred years, and are now saying, "Your idea of the law is also not that different from ours; we have a different attitude towards them but the actual reality is not that different. We start by assuming it; you start by asserting it. But in the end, we're all practical and pragmatic, and we're prepared to look at it and make adjustments. From there, we can converge."

The Chinese position is more realistic, although the Western position has its justifications. You *need* some certainty from which there's some measure of how far you can deviate. The Chinese approach is very flexible; it's all a matter of negotiation and arbitration, and working out how two sides can agree. For the Chinese, there are no fundamentals, while the West argues as if there are such things.

I think this difference towards the notion of law is the source of a lot of misunderstanding. The Chinese state, the Chinese Communist Party in actual fact, has been *extremely* pragmatic. There's nothing dogmatic about the CCP, not since Deng Xiaoping came back anyway. And Mao Zedong was not actually dogmatic either. He was just egocentric and idiosyncratic. If you look at the history of the Chinese Communist Party since its founding in 1921, the dogmas actually came from the West, from Lenin and Stalin. In China, *Chen Duxiu, Qu Qiubai*, down to Mao Zedong and Zhou Enlai were just negotiating among themselves, and when they finally found that Mao had everything so well knitted up, they couldn't challenge him and decided to accept him as a kind of emperor. But that was because he was politically so very skilful. He manipulated everybody to the position where "if you don't accept what I say, off with your head" — which is the imperial position.

OKB: It was more that, than any understanding of Marxism then.

WGW: It had nothing to do with Marxism. So in that sense, the Chinese Communist Party has never been dogmatic. It's not correct to say Deng Xiaoping made it more pragmatic. It had always been pragmatic, susceptible to the peculiarities of the top man.

OKB: I am fascinated by the CCP's decision in recent times to limit their presidency and prime ministership to two terms. That is quite impressive a change.

WGW: Technical again, it's all a device. There is no principle behind it. It's a device for modern governance. And they decided that, first of all, you want to prevent any one person from becoming all-powerful again, so you need a kind of collective leadership. Secondly, how do you ensure that this kind of collective leadership knows when to leave? The best way is to disallow any one person from staying in power too long.

Again, mechanisms, devices, technologies, methodologies — and these are all taken from the West. The British Parliament uses five-year terms, the Americans use four years, the Australians three. So they basically took the British practice. From the Americans, they adopted the limit of two terms. The only thing they've added, which is not found in the West, is the upper age limit. That is new, and was introduced by Deng Xiaoping.

Nobody should continue beyond seventy. That was laid out and implemented by Jiang Zemin. He was past seventy, so he had to step down. So now all the personal career calculations orbit around the question: "At what age can I become president?", or whatever position one is aiming for.

OKB: So by sixty one should have become president.

WGW: Yes. If you're not president by sixty, you've missed out. You can see these are techniques. It's got no principle behind it. Everybody can do sums: "So okay, these two are below sixty, they get ten years. We put in five others who are above that, so they can only last five years." Now, in the Standing Committee of the Political Bureau, we know well beforehand that two of them will last ten years, that the other five have to go after one term, and that there are five new guys waiting out there to replace them.

In many ways things have become more predictable. The mechanism is a much more predictable one than any election in the West. In America you have serious uncertainties about who's going to be the next Republican leader, for example, and who are going to stand for elections. And there is no need for huge amounts of money to be spent, as is the case in America. The present Chinese system sidesteps this. Right now we have Xi Jinping as president and Li Keqiang as prime minister for two terms, and we know the other five are going to step down. Once you have decided on the rules that will work, you work within that set of rules.

Modernity, the Chinese seem to realize, is a set of technologies deriving from science and technologies in the West, which Westerners have completely accepted as the norm. And that's now part of Chinese life too, and it is working. Again, what is lacking now is the soul — the feelings, the humanistic side.

THE GLOBAL IS MARITIME

OKB: You're talking about the dialectics over the last two hundred years between the Cultural Essence (*Ti*) and the Practical Means (*Yong*), are you not? In the process of mastering the *Yong*, the *Ti* seems to have been lost, or is not apparent anywhere.

WGW: This is because they took so long to work out where the *Ti* was. They chucked out the original *Ti*, tried to find a new one, and failed! But the *Yong*, they have mastered. So now they have got to find the *Ti*. Interestingly, what they said in the beginning when confronted with Western power and when trying to reform the dynastic system — and they went about it with the greatest of conviction — was, *Ti* comes first. We retain the *Ti* while we master the *Yong*. But the *Ti* was actually abandoned, and they tried to find a replacement. If you put it in mechanical terms, they tried to replace the heart. It didn't work! So now they are trying to repair it. They are finding out that it can't be replaced.

You cannot avoid adopting those technologies and methodologies — you cannot survive otherwise. Both society and state cannot survive without the *Yong* that comes from the West. So, in that sense, the Great Convergence, to use Kishore Mahbubani's term, is a convergence of all these methodologies. But, underneath it all, each civilization and culture wants to keep something of its beating heart. It doesn't matter if it is Islam or Buddhism — they all want to keep something of their own because it is what gives things meaning.

So the challenge is, how can we have all these methodologies and technologies and yet keep our original heart? And if we can't, how can we find some new ways of meshing or merging the two, having the two to coexist? One can go so far as to integrate the two. The West in a way is the result of an integration. The West does not articulate any conflict between their *Ti* and the *Yong* the way others do. The conflict is apparent everywhere else.

So when you talk about the West versus the Rest, my understanding would be that the biggest difference is this: the West is integrated, everybody else is not. Everybody else is struggling to match the methodologies, and yet not wanting the soul of the West. At least, they are not comfortable with it, and they want to retain their own. The West, in the meantime, is trying to sell the whole package, but the others are buying only the methodologies.

That tension will remain for Asia, for East Asia, for our part of the world. For me, the example of Japan is of great interest. Japan has been ahead of the rest of us. The Chinese may say all sorts of negative things about the Japanese, but actually they know that the Japanese are leading the way for East Asian cultures. There, a mixture of Confucian and Buddhist ideals exists alongside a total acceptance of Western technologies. They're still keeping the Japanese way of thinking — which may or may not survive, which may or may not work in the long run — but they're doing their best and they've succeeded up to a point. There's nothing un-Japanese about the Japanese people, but their mastery of Western technology is complete. Nobody else in Asia knows the West as well as the Japanese do, and yet, when you meet a Japanese person, you do understand that he is definitely Japanese.

So the Chinese say, "Why can't we be like that?" And the thing is, right now, I think, the very smart ones in China are saying, "Yes, we can still be like them, and adopt a few more technologies and methodologies like democracy and human rights without changing our souls." The West will say, "You can't! If you take our human rights idea, you must take the integrated thing", to which the Chinese reply, "Okay, maybe, maybe not, but let us see what can be done."

Democracy, they can definitely take as a technology. The Japanese have taken it, and it hasn't changed the way they relate to one another. Maybe the spirit of democracy there is different, but their technology is absolute. They are performing. Singapore is another good example — we have taken the technologies, and the country works like a British Parliamentary system. All the rules are exactly right.

So the Chinese are also interested in that: "If you can do that, we can do that. What the Japanese can do, we can do." Now, how to do it in China? The population is huge in China, and their inequality is not just inequality of income; it is also inequality of technologies between those who are so very advanced in the high-tech areas, and those who are still agrarian. So you can't just talk about inequality of incomes. That's only, again, one of the technologies. The inequality in the understanding of modernity — that gap — is very big in China. This is not true of Singapore, and certainly not true in Japan. When there's no such gap, then you have everything you need to move ahead.

The spiritual side is a different matter. Japan is a much better example for the Chinese. Singapore is not because it is a multicultural, multilingual, pluralistic society. There's no one soul; there are many little competing ones who are not very comfortable with each other, but who put aside their differences to concentrate on the mechanisms. In Japan, however, there is integration of modern technologies with Japanese ways of thinking — and I believe the Chinese would like to achieve that. That is the real challenge, the real test.

Now, if we move back to our original discussion. The balance between the continental and the maritime is just another way of looking at things. The Chinese have to adapt to the fact that the global is maritime. Eurasia today is not global; it's continental. And for thousands of years, China had been continental, brushing aside maritime concerns as being secondary. Now they have to face the reality that modern globality is a maritime phenomenon. So the technologies they adopt carry with them a new perspective, which is global in the sense mentioned. This is a totally new experience for the Chinese. In the past they were made painfully aware of Eurasian globality, if I may use that word here, of which they were an outlier. They were on the fringe of this continental expansiveness, at the peak of which was the Mongol Empire.

No doubt the West was an outlier as well in the face of Eurasian clout, but thanks to its maritime power, it created its own globality. They could not have become a global power were it not for the sea. Mastery of the sea and ruling the waves is the secret of becoming a global power. Now, the Chinese don't know how to do that. They are beginning to learn, but only beginning. And the moment they began paying attention to it, everybody began jumping on them.

OKB: Yes, they get accused of becoming imperialistic.

WGW: It has nothing to do with it! I understand enough to see that this has nothing to do with being imperialist. It's just that they're beginning to realize they cannot afford not to do it. Just to be a modern state in a globalized world — to be global — you have to pay attention to the maritime, otherwise you have failed. People look at the Chinese Navy now and note that it is quite insignificant. But don't forget, the Chinese have the largest merchant marine in the world. Why? Because they need it — for trade, marketing their goods, bringing back resources. They can't develop otherwise. The whole economic development formula has led them to understand that the sea is the secret to a global economy — not the air, not land. Of course they are building railways internally, but that doesn't link them to the global world. They can never be international on land alone.

OKB: So Africa comes into the picture here.

WGW: And Latin America; even Europe and America. Their merchant marine is important. They cannot depend on other people's merchant marines. I was quite fascinated to discover that the Chinese merchant fleet is the biggest in the world.[2] They have been quietly building it, because they need it.

And the Chinese are very good at it. The shippers in Hong Kong are from Shanghai. It was the Shanghai people who went into shipping a long time ago. The merchants, whether from *Fujian, Zhejiang, Zhoushan* or *Ningbo*, were in it. But the centre reined that in. The *Zheng He* expeditions were a good example of this. The capacity was there, but the central world view was against its use. The centre wanted to build a Great Wall up north instead.

Now, when Xi Jinping, as the new President of China, goes to Russia, what does it signify? I think it's a kind of balance. Jiang Zemin had gone to America in his time. The fact is that they're reminding their own people that the continental still exists, and that their continental concerns are real.

You see here the fantastic advantage that America has. They are a continental power with no enemies, and they are a maritime power that dominates two oceans, even three oceans. The Chinese are a continental power, but with *lots* of enemies — continental enemies, thousand-year-old enemies. They are always vulnerable. And now when they want to be part of the global economy, how do they defend their huge maritime interests? They have to have a navy. The merchant marine is not enough. In fact, because they only had a merchant marine and no naval potential, people say they are free-riders. This is true, I suppose; they are effectively freeloaders. So the Americans have been complaining. But then, to participate in sea security, they need a real navy. But the Americans don't want that either — it's a threat to them. So it all becomes contradictory. The Chinese say it's hypocritical.

From the beginning, since the Opium War, maritime encirclement had been the strategy against China. The British did that. After all, the nature of global power is maritime. But how should the Chinese respond to it? In the early days they locked their doors, but then saw them blown up. So that was not the way out for them. The solution was to participate in the global process and the global economy. But if you have no navy, you have no bargaining chips. You're just at the mercy of people with navies.

As we know, China was at the mercy of the British navy and the French navy for about fifty years. And, at the end of the nineteenth century, they were at the mercy of the Japanese Navy. Those three navies destroyed China. The sea was totally in the hands of others. And the Chinese couldn't recover. If you look at the whole period from 1895 — when the newly built navy was destroyed — until 1949, the Republic of China, the warlords, the Kuomintang, were all quite helpless without a navy. All that time, China was *utterly* helpless.

And as I pointed out on different occasions, the People's Liberation Army (PLA) was a continental force. They didn't have a single ship. They won entirely on battlegrounds on land. This was the traditional Chinese way, not different from the *Qing* Dynasty or the *Ming* Dynasty. It all happened on land, without a single ship being involved.

OKB: The PLA had no air force either, which could have attacked enemy ships.

WGW: Nothing, no air force either. They took a few from the Russians in Manchuria, but that was very late in the day. And the first ship they actually had was a surrendered ship from the Kuomintang. In any case, Kuomintang ships were second-hand ones passed to them by the Americans.

And how were they to train a navy? From 1949, when the communists came in, entirely by land, I must add, and over the next thirty years from the Mao regime to Deng Xiaoping's time, all the naval powers of the world were allied against the Soviet Union. In the Cold War, the Soviet Union was the Eurasian power and America and the rest were the maritime power. And who won? Russia couldn't break out of the maritime blockade. They had Vladivostok, but that was too far up north. On the other side of the world they were locked in by the Baltic, the Black Sea, the Mediterranean and the Arctic. So, it remained a purely Eurasian power.

Now China can be caught in the same position. But China has a warm water coast, unlike Russia. China is the only country in the world — and this is something the Americans are very clear about — that is both continental and maritime, apart from the United States. The only power! India, yes, but India is not a continental power. India has always been peripheral, because of the Himalayas. And they'd always lost out on the northwest frontier, where invaders would pour in.

But China is different. They have access to continental power, although they have always treated that as a threat in the past. They instead built the Great Wall to protect themselves. The thing is, they have been vulnerable in a way that India is not. The Indians are vulnerable only through a narrow path on the Afghanistan-Pakistan route, not elsewhere. But China has always been wide open.

China *has* to be a continental power. The Indians don't really have to. That's why they call India a subcontinent; there's some reason for that. China on the other hand is continental. But it now wants to be more balanced. That is why the United States is very concerned about the Chinese getting maritime power.

But the untouchable advantage that the Americans have is that they are completely free to concentrate entirely on maritime power. So when President Barack Obama says, "pivot" to Asia, he means just naval power. Its "forward defence" with naval power is quite unmatched, and the Chinese have no way to counter that. All they can do is to make sure that in their coastal area and in the seas between Japan and Southeast Asia, they have some say. And for that, they are going to pay a price. Everyone's going to join in a chorus to say that it must not be allowed. So they're caught in a terrible position.

When Xi Jinping goes to Russia, it's in a way symbolic. But what he also does is to go to Africa. Why? That is a reminder of the fact that the merchant marine and the maritime link are actually vital. Going to Russia is a reminder of the continental routes of Chinese history, and going to three countries in Africa is to say, "We're also global and we want to be part of the global economy."

That trip is a balance. I'm trying to understand what it means. Symbolically it is the growing Chinese awareness that lack of credibility at sea of any kind is a handicap they cannot afford if they want to be a global player. And also, they cannot perform their global role if the Americans ask them to do so, if they have nothing at sea. So the Americans are also caught in that one. When they ask the Chinese to participate more, they are telling the Chinese to do certain things, but at the same time they don't want the Chinese to do certain other things in doing those things. But the Chinese will say, "You want to be G2 partners and so on, so we must be able to do the things that you do." But the Americans say, "No, no, we didn't mean that." They want the

Chinese to help them in Iran and in North Korea, but to be hands off about the rest. The Chinese say, "That's not a partnership." That's why the Chinese turned down the G2 idea — not because they're hostile to Americans, but because it's not meaningful. The Americans really mean, "We work together so that when we tell you to do things for us, you will do it." Of course if they ask the Americans to do something for them, then the Americans will probably say: "Ah, but that's not in our interest."

OKB: The Americans want another Britain.

WGW: In a way, yes. The Chinese know the G2 is not for real. It's a G–one and a half.

CHINA'S CONTINENTAL FRONT

OKB: At this point can we take a look at China's land borders today and perhaps discuss the significance of the Chinese being so touchy about Tibet and *Xinjiang*?

WGW: Their inland frontiers are very vulnerable. The *Xinjiang* people are related to the Turks in Kazakhstan and other states there, while Tibet is an issue with India. There are over 100,000 Tibetans in India who claim that their home is in Tibet. The Indian government does not give them citizenship, and they are in their second and third generation now. They're educated as Indians in Indian schools, and they have the outlook of Indians. So how can the Chinese ignore that? The Indians know this too, and it has been a source of tension for a long, long time.

There is no easy solution to it. The Chinese put a lot of troops in Tibet and the Indians have troops at the borders. That's a reality. I don't think they'll ever fight, because it's ridiculous to fight up there. There's no point, but at least it helps keep the status quo. And that's all the Chinese want — the status quo at their frontiers. It's a very expensive status quo though. Fortunately, the Mongolian one is not a serious problem, and I don't think the Russians at this point wish to change the situation in any way. The two don't trust each other, but it's relatively easy for them to be cordial to each other. Neither side will gain from creating any trouble. The instability lies with the Turkic side, the Muslim side.

OKB: What about Myanmar and its surprising reforms? Are the Chinese worried?

WGW: The status quo there is changing, certainly. They have had a good relationship with Myanmar, but they were always aware that Myanmar was playing them against the Indians. That was always very clear.

I think the picture of Myanmar being bullied by the Chinese is overstated. The Burmese are very skilled in playing one side against another. In a way this is like the North Koreans, who are a very clever, very independent people. And the Burmese are certainly that as well — a very independent people. They have been observing their own interests since the West placed sanctions against them. So they turned to China. They turned to India, too, and the Indians were very quick to respond, so relations with them are very good as well. Now, what Myanmar has succeeded in doing is to bring in the West as well. This has improved Myanmar's bargaining position all round. Of course, it's also made it more complicated for its leaders. Aung San Suu Kyi, if she becomes president, is going to have a difficult time running the country.

The Chinese were always aware that the Indians were very active in Myanmar, and they knew that it was a matter of time before they had to adjust. They may not be comfortable and may be very unhappy — some of their projects there are left hanging — but they will adjust very quickly. It's again about being practical. They helped the Burmese build a port, but what they're really interested in is not so much the port itself, but the pipeline to *Yunnan* for oil coming from the Middle East. The Chinese are concerned with where the pipeline goes and about its security. Now that, I think, is of genuine interest, but that has nothing to do with geopolitics. If Myanmar's government is stable, then everything is all right. What the Chinese are afraid of is instability in the government. Should the military reject Aung San Suu Kyi and change its mind about Thein Sein's rapprochement with the West, and civil war or fighting breaks out and all the different ethnic groups start to take advantage, then that would certainly worry China. In a way it's like Singapore preferring Suharto as ruler of Indonesia. For thirty years you knew who was in control, and so you could do business. After Suharto, things became much more complicated.

In Myanmar the Chinese got used to this bunch of military people and just learned to do business with them. One side knew who the other side was, and so both could plan. But once things are opened up, they become much more uncertain. This is what I think the Chinese worry about: "Who will protect the pipeline, and how can we be sure?" If it's Aung San Suu Kyi, can she really control the country? I don't think they're against Aung San Suu Kyi; they just have doubts about her ability to run the government. Will the military allow her, really, to have power? How much power will they yield to her when the dice are thrown? It is still uncertain. The Western approach opens up a lot of possibilities, but it opens up a lot of uncertainty as well. Even the West is uncertain. People are pouring in, trying to shore up different democratic forces inside Myanmar, but who knows how the country will actually function.

OKB: The Japanese and Koreans are very active in Myanmar as well.

WGW: Oh yes, sure. But that, I think, doesn't worry the Chinese, because if the economy really picks up, it's also good for the Chinese. They will buy Chinese things too. *Yunnan*, after all, is next door. India will benefit, everybody will benefit, if Myanmar really works. What the Chinese are worried about is that things may get uncomfortable again. What if the military starts acting up? They haven't gone away; they may just have had a change of tactics.

Also, the Indian Ocean is a strategically important place. Penang, for example, at the top end of the Malacca Strait has suddenly become geopolitically more significant. Francis Light didn't get it wrong; he picked a good spot for a port. Looking across the ocean from the other side, Penang was ideal. Seen from the South China Sea, Singapore had the advantage. But the fact is the Chinese don't just depend on Singapore anymore, and they want to have some say in the Bay of Bengal as well. Then again, the Chinese interest in ports is because of the merchant marine, not the navy.

Everybody seems to be watching the navy. That's wrong. It's the merchant marine and its energy that is interesting. They're building ports in Sri Lanka, Bangladesh, and Myanmar; and they are all linked together.

OKB: The British Oriental Pearl of Islands is facing the other way now?

WGW: Except that it's not a string of pearls anymore, because each of these are owned by different countries. They're not owned by the Chinese; the Chinese just have access, be this in Myanmar,

Bangladesh or Sri Lanka. They would like to have it in India too, but the Indians have disallowed it. In fact, the irony of it all is that Sri Lanka first invited the Indians to develop the port for them. The Indians turned it down, because it's near Jaffna, and this was in the middle of the Sri Lankan civil war. The Indians were very sensitive about the fact that a lot of Tamils were being killed. So when the Sri Lankan government offered the port project to the Indians, a kind of geopolitical move on their part, the Indians turned it down. So the Sri Lankans asked the Chinese, who agreed. This upset the Indians, of course.

Chittagong is another case. That's the part of Bangladesh that is as far away from India as you can come. Chittagong is near Myanmar's border, near Arakan, a politically very sensitive area. The Chinese have a port there. Again, they're interested in the future, and they're also very careful. They don't want to be completely dependent on one country. The more pipelines they have, the better. Why be dependent on one source? On the other side of India there is the port of Gwadar in Pakistan, being managed by the Chinese, and from which there will be links into *Xinjiang*. That has upset the Indians also. The Port of Singapore Authority (PSA) was managing it for three years, until 2013. It was a money-losing venture, being very exposed to Baluchistan, where there is hostility towards foreign interests. The PSA gave up on it and the Pakistanis offered it to the Chinese, who agreed to run it.

Are we seeing a string of pearls? You can say that, but it isn't real in that it's just business, and it has nothing to do with military strategy.

OKB: If we now turn to China's maritime situation in East Asia, it is indeed significant that the first Sino-Japanese military conflict in 1894–95 was a naval one.

WGW: Japan is a country of islands, like Britain. There was no way for it to become a continental power, and it was never part of the Eurasian story. It was a *real* outlier.

The Japanese had of course known of the British victory over the Chinese in the First Opium War of 1839–42, and that it was achieved with advanced warships. However, the black ships that arrived in the Bay of Edo were Americans. Unable to get into China, they went to Japan instead, and forced the Japanese to open up to them. This was in 1853. The British — and the French — were never interested in Japan. In the Second Opium War in China, which soon followed, the British and the French again subdued Beijing. Seeing all this, the Japanese realized that a new world was dawning, and it was a world that fought from the seas. Being an island people, they recognized the significance of that shift. The Chinese didn't.

In the years leading up to the Sino-Japanese War in 1894, the Chinese response to the sea was still lukewarm. They were totally confident about their control over the empire. For example, they spent almost all that time confronting the *Taiping* rebels, clobbering the *Nian* insurgents, suppressing the Muslims in Yunnan, and fighting a major Muslim war in *Xinjiang*. These took ten to twenty years and cost millions of lives. All that time, they fought on land. The war against the *Taiping* armies was a close shave, but Beijing won every one of those wars.[3]

They lost the ones at sea though, and these were against foreigners. Yet they thought nothing of it: "Well, we didn't have a navy. Anyway, the foreigners wouldn't have really dared to come in." Of course, this was true! They wouldn't have dared go in. In actual fact the foreigners just wanted the coast. So the Chinese remained completely confident, until they realized that this was more than just a question of a few ships. Once you have the ships, and if you're nearby like the Japanese, you can land troops.

Britain and France were far away; so was America. There was nothing to fear from them. But if the Japanese defeat you at sea, their troops can come straight on to your land. And so Taiwan was lost (in 1895), and control over Korea would soon go as well (in 1910). Only then did the Chinese wake up. But they were already forty years behind the Japanese. From the time the black ships arrived in Japan, the Japanese had planned their naval revolution, sending their best young men to England to study.

CHINA AND SOFT POWER

OKB: May I prompt you to discuss the concept of "soft power" and how it bears on what we are talking about now?

WGW: It's a difficult term. I can't say I fully understand what it should or should not mean. The major different interpretations rest on soft power being different from hard power understood as military power. But I don't think that's what Joseph Nye meant.[4] He recognized that hard power was a much bigger concept than military power. There's political influence and economic power, but soft power was in addition to all that. It is cultural values, ideals, principles, dreams; the humanistic side of things. Even he couldn't draw the line very sharply. But the underlying insight — and this is a major interpretation of Nye's term as I understand it — is that behind soft power, there must be hard power. In other words, you cannot have soft power without hard power. But the other interpretation is that hard power is the bad guy. You isolate hard power — understood as military power — and everything else can be regarded as soft power. This will include, then, economic power. So business becomes part of that. These are two quite distinct interpretations. And people can't agree about this.

My understanding is that at the crux is the question of wealth. If you are a Marxist you would think that economic power is everything. The foundations of power are economic, and sustained military power is entirely based on economic power. You can have a little bit of military power, but it cannot be sustained unless you have economic power.

Now, if economic power is also hard power, then China doesn't have any soft power. But if economic power is part of soft power, then yes, China does have a lot of soft power.

If you look at how the Chinese are using the term, you see that they try to separate it from military power. International relations, strategic studies, military power and defence — all that is hard power. Everything else is soft power. Investments, economic arrangements and trade are all soft power. That is also the only way they can use the term soft power, because if you go beyond that, the Chinese really don't have soft power.

Now, the Japanese and Koreans have some soft power, other than wealth. But behind it, there is always wealth. I think Joseph Nye doesn't pretend otherwise. If you read his work carefully, he really takes for granted that there is wealth and power. Wealth and power are the basis for hard power. What he's saying is that this does not *really* matter in the long run; in the end it's your influence and your soft power that matter — and America has plenty of that. So don't just emphasize America's hard power; a lot of its power is soft power, he says. But he recognizes that this soft power would not have been possible if not for the wealth and the military power. So wealth and military might are probably inseparable. The moment you see wealth as part of power, then the Chinese argument for soft power fails — and, therefore, the Chinese don't want to see it that way.

I have read Chinese writings on soft power closely, and they all talk about business. Business is soft power; it is not hard power:

"We're not using guns; we're not using ships or missiles. Our outreach is 'soft', because it's business." But this is a controversial matter. I'm not dogmatic about it, but the Chinese case rests on defining soft power to include business arrangements, commercial matters and the merchant marine. I'm not quite sure if that's a correct understanding.

OKB: What's their term for it?

WGW: *Ruan shili*. *Ruan* is soft. Easy enough. But then they use *shili*, which means "power", literally meaning "real-strength". So even in Chinese it sounds contradictory. They can't get round it because they didn't invent the concept; they're just translating. How can you avoid using power? Can power really be soft? And if it's soft, can it be power? These are contradictory terms.

Joe Nye is brilliant in putting out that possibility. In a way it's a beautiful reflection of the crux of Western civilization; the missionary part of it. That part has always been seen as the soft side of imperialism. Cultural imperialism has always been separate from imperialism because it's the soft side. But it follows the flag, nevertheless. Without the flag, things would not have been as easy for missionary workers as it was.

Now, real soft power, the highest standard of soft power, is Buddhism. A group of monks arrives in China, from India, from Central Asia, and converts the whole of China, converts the whole of Southeast Asia. There was not one gun in sight; no money either. It is not based on trade either. If anyone wants to define soft power, an undeniable case is the spread of Buddhism.

Christianity had all those guns behind it. Islam was marked by fighting. Joseph Nye is saying that soft power is part of his Christian background: "There was always something there which had nothing really to do with guns and so on." This is also true to some extent. After all, the Catholic Church sent a lot of priests to the Mongol empire, unarmed. They didn't make many converts though; they were not very successful when not backed by wealth and power. When they were successful, you see that there was wealth and power behind them.

Most Chinese whom I knew in the early days converted to Christianity because it was associated with success. The Chinese are very practical people, just like the Europeans. When the Europeans converted, it was usually the kings who converted first to bolster their power; to have the Pope on their side. It gave them an extra dimension for defeating their barbarian neighbours. With the Pope on your side, God was on your side. The spiritual appeal lay in how it could help military power.

Association with real power is probably what Joseph Nye understands; I think he understood that very well — that it doesn't stand on its own, and that it's an extension of higher power. But the Chinese are trying to read it the other way round. And this is why I think it's a difficult one to judge. They have had the experience of Buddhism; they know it is possible to have soft power take over — and Buddhism did take over completely. Wherever it went it was very successful, except in India. In India it was destroyed by the Hindus, and by various other sects. For those who believed in Krishna, or Vishnu or Rama, Buddha was a most dangerous competitor. Buddha was gaining at their expense, so they fought back and destroyed Buddhism — and they were pretty aggressive in doing so.

OKB: It's not so much that it got subsumed back into the Hindu body then?

WGW: It was destroyed; the Buddhist monasteries and so on were all destroyed. In point of fact, the argument that Nalanda was destroyed by the Muslims or by the Hindus is not settled. The Hindus blame it on the Muslims, but we have no record of it. All we know is that the whole thing was wiped out. But by that time it was already clear that there was a bunch of Hindus out to destroy Buddhism. We have a record of the Hindus actually having a campaign on this. Various groups of Hindus ganged up, including the Jains, against the Buddhists. What needs explanation is that all the numerous other sects survived in India, but not Buddhism.

OKB: ... and yet Buddhism has been strong everywhere else.

WGW: In no case was there any military involvement. Today, they can be violent because now they're part of the state, part of wealth and power. But, before that, Buddhism was entirely a message. I don't think anybody can deny that this is soft power.

OKB: But is there not something in most other religions which is beyond wealth and power, and which attracts people at a basic level?

WGW: It's very hard to define. Some cases are very simple. The spread of Islam is associated with the way the Arabs came out of the deserts and conquered everybody. That was the initial push. But if you look at some of the conversions to Islam, very simple means were used. A lot of Malay people were converted through the fact that their rulers were converted. But many of them were never really converted. They didn't really know Islam until recently; with influences coming from the Saudis and the Iranian Revolution.

The Malays were very relaxed about it in the past. Their conversion could be very simple. I came across it when I was in

Sabah a long time ago. I went to a district in Keningau, in interior Sabah. The District Officer, who was a Catholic, took me to visit a kampung and he explained how that one kampung had become Muslim, while all around, the other Sabahans were either Catholic or animists. What happened was, during the war, a Brunei Malay who was running from the Japanese, escaping from something he did wrong in Brunei, came to Keningau and went into hiding in this village. The villagers didn't mind. They watched what he did every day: he prayed, he washed himself, he did very simple things, refused pork, asked for nothing. They got curious and asked, "What do you do? Why do you do all this?" He explained and he talked to them about Allah, Muhammad, and so on, and how he prayed — prayer being a device for linking up with some superior being. And the whole village converted, based on them respecting him and thinking him a saintly man.

OKB: He must have exuded sincerity.

WGW: Absolutely sincere. And the whole village asked him to teach them. They followed him, and as far as they were concerned, they were all Muslims. There was no preacher, no church. This man didn't have a building, he prayed by himself. Eventually they did build a mosque.

And this District Office, who was a Catholic, was quite fascinated, because when the Catholic Church comes along to preach, they demand that you give this up, you give that up, you must study this, these are the things you must memorize, and these are the rituals — all very elaborate stuff to be done before you are allowed to join the Catholic Church. For the other, if you pray five times, wash yourself, say that Allah is your only God and Muhammad is the Prophet and you don't eat pork — you're a Muslim!

OKB: Simple enough.

WGW: And that whole village remained Muslim. So it was not just a question of the ruler alone. There was a simple message of sheer sincerity. Now *that* is an example of soft power.

I think the Christians also had it. But there was a missionary part that Islam didn't have. Muslims weren't particularly involved in missionary work. The Christians were. They set out to convert people through example and so on. It was a mission. In Islam it's not even necessary. I have begun to understand how Islam spread in Africa. It was not done through war. Many were converted in the jungle, particularly West Africa. It was not through military force, not through fighting. Some just converted, and in large numbers.

Soft or hard power moves along a *range*. I think as long as the Chinese believe that commerce and business are not hard power, then they believe that they're doing well in soft power.

Now, another thing that to me is very important is that the Chinese have always been successful in wealth-making. Wealth-making, technical skills and manufacturing were what Chinese civilization was about. It was a wealth-producing culture, which the Confucians managed. Confucians themselves were probably not good at making money, but they integrated a kind of non-money-making side to the money-making side, through serving the political military machine, which was the state.

Ultimately, wealth and power stood side by side. To me, they were and are inseparable. But because the Chinese state was so powerful and controlled private businesses and wished them to serve the state, the commercial people never really had a free hand to develop. They always functioned within limits. And what we're seeing today is still something like that: the state-owned enterprises are really state-protected, and are encouraged, defended, and permitted to be much more adventurous because the game is now global. The state is backing this, so to call that soft power is problematic to my mind. I think the Chinese have to twist the words around to make their point because the state — hard power — is actually behind them. The commercial people in China should understand this, since all through history the state had been either for them or against them. It either gave support or it withdrew support. If it withdrew its support, you were finished. If it gave you support, you advanced. So, commercial people learned to work with the mandarins, very carefully, no doubt. In fact, from the *Song* dynasty onwards, members of the literati replaced the aristocrats who had owned land and who had wielded hereditary power. These literati had come up through learning from business families, and therefore had a much more positive and cooperative relationship with them. As long as you knew your place, as long as you recognized that the scholar (*Shi*) was well above you, and you didn't make any effort to challenge them, as long as you worked this relationship carefully, everybody profited. That was the kind of thing that evolved through the *Song*, the *Ming* and the *Qing*: the relationship between the commercial people (*Shang*) and the scholars (*Shi*) became very intimate.

I think even today, a Chinese entrepreneur, however private he may have started out being, knows that he has to work very closely with the high official (*Guan*). The official in turn knows that the state has to take the initiative to either expand or contract commercial enterprises. These extensions of commercial pursuits and the search for resources or markets and so on, are not entirely free from the state; it is in fact perfectly normal for the state to be involved in that. This upsets fundamentalist capitalists all the more. They say, "No, no, no, you must be all private." But there's no reason why this should be the case. Why must capitalism be private? Capitalism just means a way of using capital efficiently.

OKB: For a small state like Singapore, for example, to take on the MNCs you need state support; otherwise you're finished.

WGW: Otherwise you're finished! You'd have been swallowed up long ago. How can you separate the state from large-scale enterprises? If you want to open a little shop, then it doesn't matter. There, you can talk about being private. But a large corporation that operates beyond its country's borders? These MNCs are bigger than many states. Certainly, if you place them in the list of United Nations members, they'd be up among the top fifty.

So, the biggest Asian banks are all government backed. That's why all the infrastructure done in China is entirely based on state banks providing the loans. We're not talking about a million or two; we're talking about billions of dollars. Each time, several billions of dollars, sometimes hundreds of billions, are involved. Building a railway structure, for example, requires hundreds of billions of dollars. Where is that capital to come from? Only state banks can handle the funding. In that sense it's like Singapore's Government Investment Corporation (GIC). Everything is done on a business basis, but behind it is the state that decides whether to go in or not. In the end it is the state that carries the burden of protecting the capital.

When Joseph Nye talked about soft power, he was speaking in the Western context. He saw it as an area that is beyond the state. In short, hard power has to do with the state; soft power has nothing to do with the state. Now, in the Chinese context, that is almost inconceivable. I hate to always go back to the fundamental differences of world views of where it begins or how it begins, but that is how it is. But where Western thought is concerned, we are dealing with a very analytical approach towards everything, which categorizes everything. Religion, philosophy, what have you; everything is defined and bordered. You're either Christian or you're not.

It's quite different with the Chinese. Are they Confucian or Buddhist? The thing is, they can be a bit of everything — it doesn't matter. Their whole attitude towards all aspects of living is as inclusive as possible. And this is something the West finds puzzling and somewhat sinister. It goes against their understanding of how things should operate.

OKB: The West has an obsession with certainty.

WGW: Yes. You can see it running through everything. You see that Western departments of philosophy never accepted Chinese traditions. There is no Chinese philosophy — there is just Chinese *thought*, and that's not philosophy. Unless you follow Greco-Roman tradition, it's not philosophy. And now, of course, they're beginning to teach a bit of Chinese, but grudgingly. And they are still calling it "thought"; they are still reluctant to call it "philosophy". Singapore institutions do use "philosophy" for Chinese thinking, American ones are beginning to have it, but it took a long, long time to come. There are still philosophy departments in American universities which are entirely limited to the Greco-Roman tradition.

So it is as fundamental as all that. How then can such a fundamental difference be simply ignored or brushed aside? It runs through everything people do. So the nature of government, the nature of Chinese society, the way they respond to the West, the way they are going to shape their modernity, all come out of this inclusive world view, which doesn't draw clear boundaries between this, that or the other.

OKB: ... highly organic in how they see things.

WGW: Yes, that's a nice word for it. Yes, it is organic.

OKB: In talking about these two powers, we cannot get away from actually discussing two world views. Here, you have one that has an inclusive kind of mind, and there is the other that is dualistic. That's going to lead to some misunderstandings.

WGW: It is a genuine problem. That goes even for this continental–maritime dichotomy we were talking about. I'm being very Western in distinguishing between the two, because to the Chinese, it's all one; they also don't quite see the distinction. But I am drawing the attention of my Chinese friends to this because that's how it is seen from outside. If you're not aware of it, you may fail to grasp the significance of what's happening to you.

OKB: I think that a dualism does not necessarily polarize matters. It depends on how you get the two ends to relate. They can have a *Yin-Yang* relationship, for example.

WGW: The whole thing comes together; you must not think of them separately. Now, this is very interesting where Japan is concerned. I don't see it happening elsewhere in the same way. In Britain for example, naval power was all important. But it was never about naval power being superior to army power. It was always balanced. In America, the defence services argue sometimes; they have rivalries, but these are all very minor. But in Japan, they got into a big problem. If you look at Japanese history in the 1920s and 30s, the rivalry between the navy and the army was real. The army went into Korea and Manchuria, and took the lead. The navy, on the other hand, was in Taiwan and further south. They had the same militaristic thinking, no doubt, but the way they saw themselves was different. They competed for resources, and their rivalries were very severe, as were their attitudes towards each other. The thing was, the two couldn't relate.

For one thing, Japan had the Daimyos fighting each other; so in that way, the army had a long history. But there was traditionally no such thing as a Japanese navy. Naval power was new to them, and their new navy had a global view quite unlike that of the military guys. The army was thinking of securing Korea and Manchuria, while the navy was warning them: "Don't stretch too far. The navy can't help you if you do. We can only bring your troops across, but we can't help you beyond that." The naval power had to think in a different way, and the two never quite reconciled.

So right through the war you had two opposing views. Take the attack on Pearl Harbour, for example. That decision was made by the army. General Tojo ordered the attack, while Admiral Yamamoto, who was head of the navy, realized that that would be suicidal, and said so. But then he was ordered to do it, and it would have been cowardice for him to disobey. So he had to go. But we have records to show that he knew it was a disaster. You provoke the Americans, who have a far superior naval power, and sooner or later the Japanese will be finished. But the army didn't understand that because they were thinking of land battles. So, having two different outlooks within one country led to disaster.

OKB: Is that difference in outlook enhanced by the fact that the navy was English-trained while the army was German-trained?

WGW: Yes. And the deeper point about it is that it's the maritime versus the continental. The Germans and the British didn't see eye to eye either, and now the Japanese had that conflict within one country. They actually fought each other — the continental mind against the maritime mind. Having that battle in one country, in one cabinet ... you can imagine the stresses and strains.

I don't know how it will play out in China in the near future, but I think such a conflict is unlikely. The PLA is definitely a continental force, and the maritime perspective will always be subordinate. This leads to the next question: Will that mean that the Chinese navy will always be weak, and therefore will fail to perform their role properly?

The navy will always be a minor force in China, as far as I can see. Can it then ever deal with a major maritime power like the United States, or Japan, or all the others who think in maritime terms? The Chinese will always be at a disadvantage; they will lose every time they deal with maritime matters. Whether it's about Senkaku or the South China Sea, they don't *think* in maritime strategic terms because they're essentially not a maritime force.

These are factors which will eventually influence events even in our neighbourhood. Till this day, for example, the Chinese can't even coordinate what is happening at sea, between their coast guards and their fisheries. This has been pointed out several times. They don't think in maritime terms, you see. This confusion is not possible for a maritime power. Japan would never get into such embarrassing situations — the same goes for Britain or America. Everything about the sea is handled in one particular way, and very systematically — clear divisions, analytical and with a definite chain of command. The Chinese don't have that; but I think they are now finally beginning to realize what's happening.

OKB: This seems to tie in with the Chinese understanding of soft power. Since effective military power in the global context is maritime power, the Chinese cannot possibly even begin to be a challenge to other big powers. But their business side can move much faster, in some cases even faster than Western companies can, thanks to Chinese state support. So that's where the Chinese can be a force to be reckoned with. Soft power, restricted to mean "business", becomes the best card they have to play.

WGW: Their businesses wouldn't survive in Latin America or Africa without the state behind them. This leads me to think of the contrasting case of the Chinese migrants to Southeast Asia in the colonial period. They had no Chinese state behind them. They either adapted or died. So how did the Hokkiens who came to the Philippines, to Java or to the Malay Peninsula survive with nothing behind them? You can't say it was Chinese soft power. It was their individual success under very difficult circumstances.

Think of those who became rich people, living in Java, Singapore, or in Malacca — how did they manage it? Dealing with the Dutch, dealing with the Portuguese, and dealing with the English ... they were simply fantastically pragmatic and tough people. Looking back, we should really admire them. People don't think about it now, but actually they were really amazing people. They went out with no state behind them, and they made a success of themselves. This is where Beijing's present notion of "soft" misses something.

OKB: I think also of how European tourists travel, often thinking that they are travelling alone and being adventurous, when all the time they are protected by their diplomatic corps, by their mass media and so on.

WGW: Oh, absolutely! And by their military... The *awesomeness* of power. Sure!

OKB: So whenever there's a transgression involving a Westerner, it's global news.

WGW: Absolutely. In China in the nineteenth century, when they killed a Westerner, the Chinese government had to pay compensation. And in the case of a Catholic priest, the French sent in the army. That is why I say that the missionary project follows the flag.

OKB: I worry that analysts of international affairs today, even Southeast Asianists, lack your kind of vantage point for studying the region and the world in a grand historical perspective, and in a multidisciplinary manner. What they fall easily into, almost by default, is China bashing.

WGW: It's very common. I have lived with that all my life, whether in Australia or here or in the United States. Very often the whole language of IR, International Relations, strategic studies and what not, comes up automatically. This is especially so if we use English; and the viewpoint is all Anglo-American today. This carries its own rationale. One gets enclosed by it and can't break away from it. Even the Chinese are caught in it. They send their most brilliant people, some of their best students, to study IR, and these come back using those assumptions.

They do realize it now, and they try to learn from it. A good example is *Yan Xuetong*.[5] He was sent out to study at Berkeley, and was excited by all the new things he could learn. He became very good at what he did, and the Americans loved him. When he went home he tried to persuade the Chinese to do what he had learnt from the West. But over the years he came to realize that what he had learnt doesn't match the reality that China faces. The language — it's not just a question of reality — doesn't actually describe the situation, and is actually framed for some other particular power situation. When the Chinese situation doesn't fit the theory, the language somehow puts the Chinese either as the villain, or as the weak, the subordinate or whatever it may be. It comes out wrong — not factual in any case.

And so *Yan* went back to re-reading Chinese history. Today, he is bringing back the language of China's Warring States period. He's trying to marry the two — not very effectively, but he's trying. I give him full marks for trying. He was entirely brought up in Communist China and in the Cold War and had absorbed it all. Now he's going back to his roots and realizing that there's a different way of looking at things. I'm not sure how well he will manage to persuade people, but it is all very interesting.

Both the West and the Chinese government are watching him, and reading him. Whether he will succeed or not, nobody yet knows. But you can see his problem. The whole language of IR is such that anybody in Asia studying IR will attain an Anglo-American world view. There is no way you can get out of it. You try to, and they immediately quote to you all they can draw from Western history to show the logic of their argument. I mean, Western history does support what they say, but it is stretching it a bit to apply it uncritically to Asia.

Yan Xuetong is a very controversial figure, even in China, but he was certainly their top name for interpreting Western IR theory, and politics generally. After he came back from Berkeley, he was made their professor in IR at Tsinghua University. The point is that he himself realized after a while why things didn't fit, and why what he said just didn't match what the Chinese were doing and thinking. He fought for a while to persuade them to understand what he was trying to say, but soon realized that it was not a question of them not understanding him. It was because it didn't fit their understanding of how things were, and because his ideas were based on Western historical experience.

One very striking case of the bias we are talking about now, that I can think of, is when Vice-President Nixon came to Singapore at the beginning of the Vietnam War. This was in 1958, I think; the war was only just beginning and Eisenhower was still president. We met him, and I actually had a chance to ask him questions. And one of the things he said that stuck in my mind was this: "You know, we've had this kind of experience before. We mustn't allow any more 'Munichs'. You've got to stop them early, or later on you'll regret it", and so on and so forth. And he used the example to justify going into Vietnam. In other words, "We have to stop Ho Chi Minh, otherwise he will become a Hitler." He didn't say it quite so, but that was his implication.

It stuck in my mind because, I said, "There is nothing to compare Ho Chi Minh with Hitler. This is not 'Munich'." So why was he using that kind of language? Did he really believe it? And I found that he really believed it. It was his justification for going into Vietnam.

But what my mates and I understood — and we said it then — was that Ho Chi Minh was only fighting for his own country, because he felt betrayed. He was not anti-American. Where America was sympathetic with decolonization, he was pro-American. But when the French were supposed to withdraw, they were asked by the Americans to stay. He was expecting decolonization, but the Americans betrayed him and asked the French to stay, so he had to fight them.

So he fought them and he defeated them at Dien Bien Phu. After Dien Bien Phu, Nixon came out and said: "We can't allow any more of that. This must stop." And so they shored up South Vietnam. What we heard was his justification, which was to me quite absurd. It was the wrong analogy. And that was what he based his thinking on? What happened in the end? The Americans lost that war; a war they shouldn't have fought. It was none of their business; it had nothing to do with them at all!

Today they're using the analogy of Japan and Germany for China. And I've been publicly calling that a highly misleading analogy. They are saying, "If you don't stop them now, they'll be like Germany and Japan; they will become imperialists." That is the language that everybody trained in the West — including most Singaporeans and Southeast Asians — will react to, thinking: "Ah … yes; just like the rise of Germany and the rise of Japan." The universal rule they assert is that a rising power is a danger to the status quo — it must be watched and stopped. Now, once you accept that as a golden rule, then what can the Chinese do? Everything it does will be wrong.

OKB: By definition.

WGW: By definition, wrong. That is how it's happening today. The argument is being used all over. The example is the rise of Japan, or the rise of Germany. And no matter what the Chinese say, they're caught in a general theoretical field which is sacred. The Chinese can't get out of it because they don't have an alternative theoretical field to counteract it. *Yan Xuetong* is trying to find one through the Warring States literature. Good luck to him on that. All that happened two thousand years ago, after all.

OKB: Education at key universities would be the vehicle passing on this IR bias. Is that soft or hard power?

WGW: You see, Joseph Nye doesn't actually include education under soft power. When he talks about soft power, he's talking about films and art …

OKB: Everything outside the state.

WGW: Everything outside the state. Education is not separate; it is very much part of the national outlook, national world view, national mission. Education is a part of it; not all though, because every education system has its own dissidents and its own rebels. But the bulk of what the universities bring out — it doesn't matter if it's Singapore, China or the United States — are inevitably people the country needs. They reflect a particular world view. So that is why the Chinese universities are now turning away from just regurgitating what they've learnt from the West; they're trying to work out their own way of looking at things.

Here, the Japanese are interesting again. They are the most interesting for us because they have been on the frontline longer than anybody else. They have been there since a hundred and fifty years ago, and they have been absorbing and absorbing. And as they did that, they were also digesting and realizing that they didn't quite fit into the scheme of things. But then they went wrong with the war. They were experimenting: militarism, actual democracy, and also turning away from that back to the Japanese way of doing things. Their struggles give me a feeling that it's something that the rest of us cannot avoid. We'll end up differently, but we will have to follow the same path of adjusting to a dominant world view that doesn't fit our interests. We may or may not get out of it, but we'll all try. The Japanese do have something very distinctive. The Koreans are also now beginning to get there, and I think the Chinese are going to watch them with great interest. In fact I think that if Taiwan had more clout they'd do the same.

REMAINING AT HOME OVERSEAS

OKB: Today China is more willing to accept Korean things than Japanese things.

WGW: Yes, but that's political. In a way the Japanese have gone too far being Japanese. They're now *so* different, *so* uniquely Japanese that nobody else can identify clearly with them. They have become just *too* distinct. And yet, as I mentioned earlier on, technically they are as modern as America. Everything the Americans can do, the Japanese can do.

OKB: What I have noticed, if I think of young Japanese and young Swedish students who I know, a natural science mindset is strongly ingrained in them.

WGW: The Chinese are moving in the same direction. Singapore also moves in that direction through science and technology. But while the Japanese have a distinctive "something" which is their own, Singapore doesn't.

OKB: Their aesthetics are clearly very distinct.

WGW: Absolutely. The way they see the world is distinct. Singapore doesn't have that. China has it, but they've mucked around for so long, over a hundred years, that they don't know how to orientate themselves. But it's there, somewhere.

The Japanese never lost it; they never had a revolution; they never rejected the Japanese core. They took from others, and they built further. The core was actually protected, and has never been abandoned. The Chinese gave it up for a hundred years and now find it very difficult to rework it. There's no way you can stop the Chinese now from being as scientific and technological as the Japanese or Americans. Becoming the second economic power is a product of the fact that the Chinese have mastered everything that has made Japan and the United States wealthy and powerful. What's left is the question, where is the heart, where is the soul.

OKB: What do we do with what we have gained?

WGW: What do we do this *for*? What is it *for*? The "for" is to become a modern Chinese, to be modern. The "modern" side is getting clearer, but what "Chinese" stands for is no longer obvious. That's the real dilemma.

OKB: Very interesting. I think Singapore is actually part of that adjustment, although it's a small country.

WGW: Because it's seventy-five per cent Chinese. They are suffering from some of the same agonies as the Chinese, but without the clarity which the Chinese have because theirs is a Chinese state. Singapore is not; it is a pluralistic state that looks Chinese. People expect it to be somewhat more Chinese, but it can't be; the government cannot allow it to be.

Nevertheless, you can go to some parts of Singapore now and see how *very* Chinese Singaporeans are becoming. The old associations are being restored. I read about the Hainanese Association having internal quarrels, while the Teochews have broken up into different factions. All very familiar. And all that they are quarrelling about are very, very Chinese things. That has never been far below the surface. But each one of those people has all the modern skills. They can do anything: they can run an engineering company with no hesitation, do finance, and they can travel around the world.

OKB: They understand the West.

WGW: Absolutely! But when it comes back to fighting on their own turfs, it's about what surname you are, "You're Ooi and I'm Ong." That's not so easy to change. And why should they change? That's what they are, after all: "I've learnt all the *Yong* but I'm not comfortable with my *Ti*. I'm going to keep trying to find my *Ti*, and you can't stop me. Perhaps mastering your *Yong* more and more will help me find my *Ti*. If I'm totally confident with the *Yong*, I'll find my *Ti*." This is the kind of thinking I find in China, at any rate.

OKB: One concept that is popular with some Cultural Studies scholars is the concept of "authenticity". They like to seek "the authentic', which is a reflection, I suppose, of this gap between the *Ti* and the *Yong*.

WGW: One can take Ben Anderson's view that it is all imagined. Authenticity is a man-made thing. *You* determine what is authentic. Each period will have its own sense of what is authentic. There's no essence that is universal. Much of it is socially constructed for the time and place. Chineseness in Singapore is different from Chineseness in Thailand, or in the Philippines. That, I already learned when young, because I saw it all around me.

The Chinese sometimes understand it, sometimes they don't. They say, "If you're a Chinese out there, you must be like us. Why are you not like us?" That's one approach. The other approach is — within China — they understand that a Shanghainese is different from a Sichuanese. They take that as normal. But if you're a Singaporean, some expectation of the universal comes into play — an outside-Chinese must somehow match the standard of a national Chinese, whereas a Sichuanese won't have to. Now, I have told Chinese friends that this is not right. Why do I take what I do as normal and you take it that I have to have a national *norm*, a national average which is an imagined one anyway? You yourself don't know what that means.

But then they say, "You're different. You're not allowed to be different. You're Chinese." So what's expected of an outside-

Chinese is quite different from what's expected of an inside-Chinese. That in itself has its own complexity. When the poor overseas Chinese goes to China, he is made to feel inferior because the Chinese there suddenly hold up some high standard of the norm which he can't match, and no way can he match it. No other Chinese can either. You know what I mean? It's all an imaginary thing. So the poor overseas Chinese are always going to be looked down on.

Right now a much more serious matter of concern is that we have a totally new cycle of overseas Chinese. And how that will bear on the earlier cycles of overseas Chinese is a question which I'm trying to understand. Now, we're not talking about a few dozen, a few score; we're talking about millions. The original base of overseas Chinese may be about thirty million. Now we have probably an additional twenty million totally new ones straight out of China, who are settling! They're making their homes in North America, Australia, Europe, Africa, or Latin America. How the locals, including those of Chinese descent, respond to them is a serious issue.

What happens when all these Chinese get well-off or get richer? And with China being powerful, a kind of blowback of some kind will almost certainly occur here and there. What scale it will take, I don't know. Of course, the "provocateur" element of the West may appear. If the West wants to play that game — not right now; it's not in their interest to play it right now — but if it turns out to be in their interest to play that game, stir up the Africans, or the Americans *against* the Chinese, *"senang saja"* ("that would be all too easy"), as they say in Malay. There can be all kinds of repercussions. I have no idea how it will turn out, but does the Chinese government anticipate that, and does it prepare for it? And how can they prevent it from happening?

I don't know if people have thought it through yet. It's only just emerging, but it could emerge very quickly. The Chinese were doing extremely well in Southeast Asia up until the middle of the nineteenth century; all the Peranakans in Thailand, in the Philippines, in Indonesia, in Vietnam, in Malaya — they were doing fine. But what happened then was the settling of Hong Kong, along with the opening of Shanghai and all the treaty ports. Chinese labour then came in large numbers. You suddenly had a huge jump in the Chinese population overseas, and then the problems began. Fifty years later, the racial problems remain serious.

OKB: The process of integration stopped taking place.

WGW: It couldn't continue. The pace was too fast and the size was too big.

OKB: So you expect racial tensions to increase in the near future?

WGW: How can you avoid it if you're talking of millions? You can't integrate or hybridize that quickly. It used to take generations, and that was with very small numbers. Furthermore, now when you have the Internet and other fast means of communication, you're never away from home; you never feel you've really left. This slows any process of integration even further. I'll give you a very simple example, which really struck me when I first came across it. This was thirty to forty years ago, when refugees were coming out of Vietnam. It didn't click in my head what it actually meant on the ground. I met a young person who was making little discs and talking Laotian Hmong into a disc, and sending it back to his relatives who lived in the middle of Laos. He was a refugee and had no way of going back, and there was no way his relatives could come visit him. But sending discs home was fine; it was permitted. So he made this little disc and bought a machine for playing it and sent it all back to his relatives. He had been doing it for a long time. He put it to me very bluntly: "This way, I'm never away from home. I may be thousands of miles away, but my relatives and I are communicating every other week. I just pay the postage both ways. I send them the money for postage as well because they have no money. I provide everything, but that keeps me close to them. I'm never away from them."

And this was before the Internet. So you see, nobody is really far from home today. Now, my wife and my daughters communicate with each other every day through the Internet. They're all ICT literate now, and there are so many ways to get in touch with each other. They tell each other what they're doing every day. In that way it doesn't matter where you live. So, if you have many more millions of Chinese newly living overseas, they will remain Chinese for a very long time.

Why should they integrate, unless business requires it, or their survival requires it, or there is intermarriage? And if you are living in big cities — which is what the Chinese prefer — you're more anonymous anyway. You can be Chinese forever in the city. In the countryside that becomes harder. The urbanization of the world makes it even easier to not be integrated. In this context, "anonymous" means "Chinese".

The word "anonymous" is very interesting here. Anonymity is what preserves your thing, your uniqueness. If you want to join in and socialize, you lose it. If you remain anonymous, you get to keep that sense of uniqueness. In the past, if you left home, that was it. You probably never went home again. You wrote a letter home now and then.

Imagine the people who left in the days of the *Ming* Dynasty, or the early *Qing* — it must have felt that it was forever.

OKB: Yes. For example, when Irish men and women left for America in the old days, it was for good, and the farewells expressed the finality of those partings.

WGW: It was for good. And that was why the Chinese family never left. It was always some young boy going off: "Good luck to you. And if you make something, send some money back. We'll hear from you when we hear from you. If you disappear, we'll write in the family genealogy: 'Went abroad, not heard of again'." And thousands of them did disappear completely. There were, of course, those who survived, and became some kind of king — in southern Thailand, or Ipoh or West Kalimantan, or such like.

OKB: For every one of them, quite a few disappeared.

WGW: Absolutely. Apart from being eaten by tigers, killed by the Dusuns or the Ibans. This went on for over a thousand years until the mid-nineteenth century — and then the world changed. Millions of Chinese came out, and the politics changed. China changed. Now we're meeting the second phase. China rises and millions go out again, though in a different way. There has to be a total transformation again for the traditional Overseas Chinese, who will have to readjust their ways.

OKB: The present Peranakans, the localized Chinese, are fighting a losing battle in keeping their old identity.

WGW: Not only the Peranakans, even those after the Peranakans — the post-Peranakans — are going to face the next lot. So we're going to witness the Peranakans' struggle for cultural survival. I would tell Peranakans: "There was the Peranakan stage once, but now we're at the Anglo-Peranakan stage, which is going to contend with a new stage where the "Anglo" becomes diluted and vague. The Peranakan stage was actually Melayu-Peranakan, which was followed by people like you and me. We're Anglo-Peranakan. But the next stage is already arriving.

OKB: Typically, there has recently been an explosion of Peranakan museums.

WGW: That's an example of the end of the story. The Anglo-Peranakans don't admit it, but actually that's where they are. None of my Peranakan friends are anything but Anglo in this part of the world, in Malaya. In Indonesia it's different. They've become completely nationalized and naturalized. They're no longer Anglo or Dutch; they're no longer even Peranakan. They're now Indonesian; they're actually almost *pribumi* now. Some of them have become accepted as *pribumi*. The group as a whole is diminishing, and the remnants are trying to be Chinese.

Now the question is, how long can the Anglo-Peranakans last? That depends on U.S.-China relations, I think. As long as the United States is dominant, all the Chinese in Singapore will remain Anglo. To be sure, the American story is not just an Anglo one. "Anglo" is not just America — it is global. "Anglo" is no longer English or American. It's actually Global Anglo — we have developed into the Global-Anglo-Middle-Class.

That is in a way what Kishore Mahbubani is talking about — this "convergence" that he identifies; this global middle class that is going to set the standards for the whole world. And English is the one common language that this middle class will share. It will be harder and harder for people to avoid joining this middle class. You can have your own languages, but all of you will operate in one language at that middle-class level. That I think is quite likely. It's beyond America now. The Americans themselves are being challenged at home by the Latinos. Spanish is now very, very powerful, but it doesn't cross over. English does. In fact it's now almost impossible to hold an international conference without using English.

So the Anglo-Chinese in the region will last for a while yet. The Anglo-Peranakan will be the local boy. If you're born in Singapore, that means you're Anglo-Peranakan. The only question will be if you'll become Sino-Anglo instead, the mix being turned the other way around. It's an interesting thing — learning Chinese is not easy, but learning to speak it is not that hard. The same thing goes for the other end of the hyphenation. Being Global-Anglo doesn't require you to be that fluent in reading or writing, as long as you can communicate; and there are so many varieties of English in which you can do that. So the Global-Anglo is pretty adaptable.

And maybe a Global-Sino is also already coming into being. A lot of people are already learning to speak it. Speaking Chinese is not that difficult. Imagining that one should speak it absolutely correctly with the right accent and so on, is ridiculous anyway. The Chinese themselves don't do that. They all have their accent; everybody's got their accent. Like English. You don't have to worry about correct English in England. It's your own language then. So the Chinese can do the same. The number of people who can now speak fairly fluent Chinese, no matter how terrible their accent, is growing quite fast in many countries. Singapore doesn't have that much of an advantage now, in comparison.

But it's still a difficult language, so the desire to learn it is not great. In monolingual countries like the United States and Australia — the English-speaking world — you still find a lot of resistance. But the change is happening. Personally, I think the Europeans will probably learn Chinese faster.

OKB: Universities in the West are already encouraging that.

WGW: Even in America. It's quite amazing. Someone gave me some figures to show that, at one time, only about fifty universities taught Chinese. Now there's something like two thousand universities doing it. The standard may not be very high, but they will offer courses in Chinese. And another thing ... once upon a time only a handful of libraries had Chinese books in the United States. Today, all these two thousand have the beginnings of a Chinese library. And at least one to two hundred of them have excellent Chinese libraries. This is quite unbelievable.

OKB: And everything is going digital as well, making such developments much easier.

WGW: That's happening. The Americans have the wealth to do it. Some countries would like to do it but don't have the funds, and that's where the Confucian Institute comes in. The Chinese are helping, and this is part of their soft power. So now you have four to five hundred Confucian Institutes... I've lost count.

OKB: At Stockholm University where I was attached, the teaching of Chinese is now being done more and more by the Confucian Institute, which provides teachers for this.

WGW: They offer you native speakers. Of course, if you want to teach high-standard Classical Chinese then they can't do it. Again, it's the oral part which is the beginning. This is modernity now; nothing to do with classical learning. But even in the past, language transmission was oral. Anything literate is very hard.

The Chinese literary culture never advanced out of China, but its oral culture did. That's how it spread into Yunnan and all these other places; people just learned how to speak it. Even the Cantonese had to learn to speak Mandarin. You see, it's the oral skill that's important here.

I would say that English succeeded through trade, and the same thing goes for Bahasa Melayu. Economic power does have that soft-power element. For example, I was always fascinated by how Malay became the language of Indonesia. It was a minority language, with Malays making up less than four per cent of the regional population. So how did this language become *the* language? Very simple — it facilitated business. Some people will argue that it was religion, Islam. But I think that even *that* was because of business — Islam was following the trade. By the time the Chinese came in, by *Zheng He*'s time, whether you were trading in Java or Sumatra, Malay was already being used. When the Portuguese came, Malay was already dominant. You can see it in the Portuguese record. Malay was used right across the Java Sea, and to the Spice Islands. And when you get to the Dutch material, that phenomenon was very obvious. In every port they went to, Malay was being spoken. So it was commerce that was the vehicle for this dominance.

Among the Chinese in the region, Hokkien nearly became the lingua franca. For archipelagic Southeast Asia, Hokkien was most important, while Cantonese was prominent in the mainland part, as it also was in the United States, the whole of Oceania and in Australia. Hokkien dominated in the islands — and it was orally spread.

THE FAMILY AS SOCIETY'S BASE

OKB: If I push you to suggest what you think will come to

constitute *Ti* in the Chinese case, I suppose Confucian concepts will start turning up.

WGW: Yes, that has to be. In a way it's a pity to try to link it with Confucius. It's simply just being Chinese. And the root of it is the family. Confucius and Mencius, between the two of them, articulated that idea best. I like the way Mencius put it: the family is simply the most natural relationship of all; and everything about life is about relationships.

Have I told you this story before? When I was in primary school — it was a Chinese primary school — the Chinese school text tried to teach us about the West. It would tell us stories about Isaac Newton and the apple, or about how Washington never told a lie. And it would tell us the story of Robinson Crusoe. This is the interesting part. When we read the story in English, it was about Robinson Crusoe the hero, the man who survived in the middle of nowhere, on a deserted island. Now the Chinese text tells the same story, but the conclusion is just the opposite. Its lesson was, "There you see, man cannot be alone. To be civilized, you must be in a society and relate to other people. If you are alone, you lose your civilization, your culture. Crusoe had to work so hard to preserve it, but it was a losing battle." The consciousness was about sociality; society is the key. So the moral of the story was just the opposite of the Western one. I remembered that as a schoolboy! I remember telling my father, "This is a totally different story!" The difference was properly captured there.

Mencius reminds us that by yourself you're nothing. Who are you? You are your father's son, and your brother's brother, and your mother's son, and the father of your children — all that makes you somebody; gives you an identity. The family is the most natural unit. Branching out from family relations, you start relating to people from other families, and so on and so forth. In the end you have your society. It was not Confucius who invented that idea; he simply articulated it. Confucius himself always said he was not teaching anything new: "Everything I say is from tradition. I've simply put it down for you to learn." So that's deep, very deep.

The other profound influence is the *Yi Jing*, The Book of Change. Nobody seems to know when it started; it's been there all the time. Why did it survive all this time? The underlying thing is so important: that everything changes — that's why it is called The Book of Change. Nothing is universal and forever. Everything changes, everything is change*able*. Now, that is fundamental.

So, you live in a world in which your relationships provide you with the core, and your relationships provide you with a way of dealing with the changes. It is not about you, because you're nothing, but you're part of a group.

It's like the *Yin-Yang* symbol. You cannot have just one part of it; the two are inseparable. They're always related. That's not Confucianism. That's Chinese. And has that changed? Even through the period when Buddhism reigned supreme in China, that basic notion never disappeared! It's always been there. Buddhism never challenged it. It simply merged into that way of seeing things. You've got to perceive how all the parts fit. And when they fit, it works. When two people meet and there's something that they share and agree upon, it works. But by yourself, what can you do?

So the Chinese simply cannot understand the idea of individualism. Not because they don't like it — the Chinese are pretty individualistic — but they always fall back on family. You are a great individual because you have your family behind you. But to be an individual without anything makes no sense; it's not logical to the Chinese. So the idea that the individual is sacred is beyond comprehension — that comes really only from monotheistic religions.

When the Buddhist monks brought the idea to China of separation from the family, the Chinese didn't like it at all. So the Buddhists had to modify that. Chinese Buddhism today is different because they modified it to accommodate the family; otherwise the Chinese would not have accepted its teachings at all.

OKB: So a son can become a monk and yet come home to the family on occasion.

WGW: Sure, and still acknowledge his parents. But, in theory, you are not to do that. You're supposed to step away completely. The Christians have it the same way. Till this day, the problem with the Catholic Church is this business of "no family", and the Chinese thinks that makes no sense. The Church says it's about you and God, and yet what happens is you still have the gathering of bishops and cardinals. There is still a group; the family sits in the Vatican, and that's a *very powerful* family.

OKB: The insight I like most in Confucianism or Confucian thinking is the purported connection between *Li* (rituals) and *Ren* (compassion). Compassion does not come from nowhere; instead it grows out of the practicing of rituals. And the particular set of rituals, the particular set of *Li* created by a particular society over time, is the basis for its civilization, for its *pathos* and its *ethos*.

WGW: Again, the starting point is relational. Otherwise there's no *Li* at all, and no *Ren*. You have to be *with* something.

OKB: You work out how to get along with each other, and as you go through that process, ethics and piety are born.

WGW: The Chinese have this traditional debate about whether or not a newborn person is innately good.

OKB: The difference between the two Confucians *Xun Zi* and *Meng Zi* (Mencius) …

WGW: The difference does have certain ramifications in thinking, but in practice it does not matter much. If you're innately good, you spend your life protecting that goodness. In the face of all kinds of challenges, you protect and preserve that goodness throughout. In *Xun Zi*'s view that you're innately prone to wickedness, it is required that you be educated — civilized — through *Li*. His point of departure is much more real, in the sense that you assume the worst in you, and you correct yourself and become good. But the Chinese language is not very clear on that.

I was asking Roger Ames the other day about his interpretation of the word *Shan*, which basically means good, and he was trying to explain it in terms of inclination.[6] You have inclinations. You could go either way, and the Chinese are not dogmatic about it. Although Mencius says one thing and *Xun Zi* says another, the assumption is that you could go either way. How you go depends on your environment and your relations. Your relationship with your parents, your brothers and your sisters, can actually make you good or better, or make you worse, depending on the way they treat you. If your father beats you all the time, you become a nasty person too. If your mother loves you all the time, you become very gentle; and so on.

The environment nurtures, helps to guide nature, as it were. And you don't choose between the two — you don't argue whether it's more nature or more nurture. The Chinese don't accept that argument, which comes from the Western analytical mind — whether it's more nature or nurture; 50–50 or 40–60 or 20–80. The Chinese don't use it that much. In the end it's the *Yin-Yang* sign again, merging the two, so things can go either way. And once you allow that, then all these concepts become interdependent. Whether your *Ren* emanates, develops, or is lost is dependent on many different factors.

OKB: In both *Xun Zi* and *Meng Zi*, *Li* is needed, either to develop the *Ren* in the one case, or to protect it in the other.

WGW: For *Xun Zi*, you need the *Li* to make sure that your *Ren* heads towards good. The *Li* puts you on the straight and narrow. Without it, you could end up anywhere. So that's the application. *Meng Zi*, I think, is more optimistic. He thinks *Ren* will grow naturally and overcome challenges. Having said that, I don't think he was dogmatic about it either. Again, the terms are very un-analytical ones and can be interpreted one way or another.

The *Yin-Yang* is very basic to a lot of my own thinking and to the way my Chinese friends think. They don't care for these sharp divisions about things. I remember again, as a schoolboy, being very struck by something that *Hu Shi* said.[7] He said, "To the Chinese, everything is *chabuduo* (more or less; good enough). He coined the term Mr *Chabuduo*. He had been trained in the West, and he knew that what Western philosophy asks is, "Is it this, or is it that?" So he was exhorting his students: "How can you ever be a good scientist if you are so vague in your attitudes?"

There is truth in that. Mathematics and Science require you to be exact, and *Hu Shi* used that to explain why the Chinese did not develop science further. They had all the opportunities and all the potential to do that, but this philosophical lack of analytical thinking held them back from seeing the importance of sharp definitions. They always thought, "Well, I know there is a difference, but actually it's not very important."

OKB: In social relations you need that vagueness, don't you?

WGW: Exactly! If you're sharp, too sharp, things become very difficult. If it is always *chabuduo*, then we can be good friends! You can be *chabuduo* good, I can be *chabuduo* bad, and so there is room for agreement. Again, we see how a whole society, a whole world view is determined by certain assumptions and premises. This is the *Ti* part that has to be learnt. This is where twentieth century Chinese began to glide away. They said, "Yes, modern methodologies and technologies depend on exactness: two plus two equals four. This is absolute, unchangeable." Distinctions are vital; otherwise you can't go any further.

Those were major decisions. But can you adopt that without affecting the rest of your civilization? I think the Chinese are learning, as the Japanese had learnt, that you can. These two can coexist because your *Ti* goes back to the Chinese way of thinking, and the *Yong* part can help without necessarily changing the nature of your *Ti*. In fact your *Ti* gives you the confidence to deal with *any* particular part of the *Yong*. So you have this tremendous strength from retaining your *Ti*.

In the end, now that they have mastered the *Yong*, what do they do with it? And the question of what to do with it, brings back the question of how to be Chinese, how to do it the Chinese way, how to be — as I would put it — modern *and* Chinese at the same time. For a long time now, for the Chinese, to be modern was to be Western; to be modern was to copy the West — think like them and eat like them. Using chopsticks was not modern; using your hands, worse still. But now I think Chinese have come round to realizing that that was never the point.

BIG POWERS ARE MORE ALIKE THAN THEY THINK

OKB: China and the United States each signify the different ways of thinking you're talking about, but they have to live together.

Can these two ways of looking at existence and social life find common ground?

WGW: Actually they are merging in all sorts of way. The lines are not sharp. This partly confirms the Chinese way of looking at things. The lines are not sharp. It's the Americans who tried to make them sharp, but they are now giving in. The Americans are no longer so insistent. They've seen the Arab Spring. They can see that the insistence on clear definitions doesn't work. All the calls for democracy at Tahrir Square used the same words, but they didn't mean the same thing. The Americans are coming round to that; the language they use now is no longer so clear-cut. They have realized that the wish for exactness, precision or certainty is good in science and technology, for methodology. But for *Ti*, everybody's *Ti*, anybody's *Ti*, it doesn't really work.

After all, where did Fascism come from? From the West! Their own reality is not so clear-cut. Look at racism re-emerging — like anti-Semitism in Central Europe. It's all still there. It hasn't gone away. You can do what you like and say, "This is bad, this is good", but the people remain the same. When they don't like foreigners, they don't like foreigners. When they don't like Jews, when they don't like Chinese, they simply don't like them.

I think the Americans are realizing that. You can see it in President Barack Obama's language use. The language of their politicians is no longer confident. Even Nixon, Kissinger and Clinton didn't talk with the kind of confidence that Roosevelt, or Kennedy, obviously had. They had much stronger confidence then. They may use the same rhetoric now, but it is without the force and conviction of the past. They use it as a rough symbol of where they stand — it's all been converted to *chabuduo*.

Even Singapore may be a democracy in their eyes now. In other words, they're softening their lines. I remember when I was young the definition of democracy was very clear — Singapore was *not* a democracy. But now you can say, "It's a kind of authoritarian democracy", whatever that means. The fact that they're changing all these words goes to show that we are converging in another sense, because the reality is such that none of these absolute things can really stand the test of the real world. The Chinese have always known that.

The Americans don't have the power now to enforce their traditional attitude, so they have to live with it. Once you say you can live with it, the process begins; and you have to accept the fact that you can't win. Absolute statements, just like absolute relativism, cannot stand the test of time. Those are extreme positions. A scientist saying that everything must be quantitative, mathematical and calculated, and that if it cannot be quantified it's not worth anything, is in fact taking an extreme position.

What makes most practical sense is The Middle. Traditional Chinese thinking seeks The Middle. This means they allow for both, and the direction you push in depends on the circumstances. I would say that throughout Chinese history, the Chinese have simply not gone for extreme positions. When they picked out extreme positions, they used them as markers: "That's the extreme, that's where you don't want to go; stay away from there."

They were not pure relativists either. Pure relativists may say, "There is no God", for example. The traditional Chinese would never say "There's no God". He would say, "There may or there may not be, but does it matter? For me, it matters sometimes and it doesn't matter at other times. When it matters, I go and pray. When it doesn't matter, I forget about it."

Again, if you look at political science internationally today, going for the middle ground is the common approach. It's all about the middle now. If you want to win in democratic politics, you have to go for the middle ground. Be it the Tea Party or the absolute liberalism you find in New York, an extreme position cannot win the majority. So, in the end, how different are the Americans from the Chinese? Not that different, I believe.

Notes

1. Wang Gungwu, "Getting China to Play by the Rules", *Straits Times*, 12 February 2013.
2. See the Central Intelligence Agency, *World Fact Book* <https://www.cia.gov/library/publications/the-world-factbook/rankorder/2108rank.html>.
3. The Taiping Uprising was the most serious rebellion against the Qing. Led by the Hakka, *Hong Xiuquan*, it lasted from 1850 to 1864. The *Nian* Rebellion began in 1851 and ended in 1868. In Yunnan, a Muslim rebellion began in 1862 and was defeated in 1873. In the northwestern provinces, a Muslim rebellion also broke out in 1862 and lasted until 1873. See Jonathan D. Spence, *The Search for Modern China* (New York: Norton, 1990).
4. See Joseph S. Nye Jr., *Bound to Lead: The Changing Nature of American Power* (Basic Books, 1991); and *Soft Power: The Means to Success in World Politics* (Public Affairs, 2005).
5. *Yan Xuetong* is Dean of the Institute of Modern International Relations at Tsinghua University and Chief Editor of the *Chinese Journal of International Politics* (Oxford University Press). He received his PhD in political science from the University of California, Berkeley in 1992. In 2008 Yan was named by the American journal *Foreign Policy* among the world's top one hundred public intellectuals. One of his most recent books is *Ancient Chinese Philosophy, Modern Chinese Power* (Princeton University Press, 2010).
6. Roger T. Ames is Professor of Philosophy at the University of Hawai'i at Manoa and the National University of Singapore. This well-known Sinologist has written a range of noted books on Chinese philosophy, most of which have been translated into Chinese. He is the editor of *Philosophy East and West*.

7. *Hu Shi* (1891–1962) was a leader of China's *New Culture Movement*, an advocate for the use of written vernacular language, and a key contributor to Chinese liberalism. He was president of Beijing University, and was nominated for the Nobel Prize in Literature in 1939.

Chapter 5

COMBINING CONTINENTAL AND MARITIME POWER

DISTORTED IMAGES OF EACH OTHER

OKB: The western edge and the eastern edge of the Eurasian landmass historically viewed each other across a threatening cultural and geographical expanse, and would therefore have conjured in each of their minds a messy mix of diverse phenomena about the other. "The Other" would have been perceived by each through a highly distorting filter of in-between cultures.

WGW: It is very significant that both these edges — Western Europe and China — saw each other from afar, across a continental mass. "The Other", for both of them, was everything on the other side. Being fringes, they had not been in direct contact with each other. Now, in the global age, both sides still exhibit residual thinking from earlier times. We still talk about the East and the West, and the West still entertains notions of "The West versus the Rest".

But all this should also remind us about how important the core was to them. The core both filtered and coloured at the same time everything that was on the other side. Today, all that has changed; the world is now effectively round. The Americas have made all the difference. The Americas include Europe, but also East Asia. We have the North Atlantic world, and we have the APEC world, for example. The continental fringes have met each other, and perspectives have changed. The edges now hold the global initiative.

What I wanted to point out when I wrote my article about the Two-Ocean Mediterranean was that the Mediterranean expanded into the Atlantic, and made that the second Mediterranean. Europe and America controlled this Mediterranean, and this Mediterranean came to control the world, spreading into the Indian Ocean and then the Pacific Ocean. This expansion now lines all these up, until the other end of the continent is reached. A maritime linkage is made, bordering China, Russia ... and maybe India. India is not quite sure whether it is part of the maritime world or part of the continental world.

China is quite clearly continental in nature. To survive a maritime global world, it has to have a navy. But in knowing that it can never be what the United States can be, it is really a continental power acquiring enough maritime power to protect itself against the maritime global world. It has to depend on this world because trade is dependent on it.

In any case, an arc of power has been assembled around the continent. India can't quite join it, but Indonesia can, and that's why the Chinese are desperately trying to keep Indonesia on their side, so that the arc is not sealed completely. If the Straits of Malacca, the Sunda Strait, and Indonesia in general are kept neutral, then the Chinese have a chance. If the arc is closed, then China is really in trouble.

Whichever way you look at it, the Cold War was won by keeping the Soviet Union continental, by never allowing them out of their continent. In the end it suffocated. And that is how China came to recognize that they must have a navy.

OKB: Is the difficulty involved in breaking out of the historical maritime blockade a major reason for China's investment in space?

WGW: Yes, they were quite clear about that. But human life is still based on the globe and will remain maritime. The global is maritime. You can't get away from that. If you accept that, then everything falls into place; to my mind anyway.

OKB: Will the melting of the ice cap up north be relevant to what we are talking about?

WGW: That's a matter concerning the United States, Canada and Russia. For China, it is about being allowed passage in places like the Indian Ocean; nothing more than that.

OKB: What about Africa in all this?

WGW: They are never going to become one big continental power, so they won't be a threat to anyone else. And no African state has maritime power to speak of. They will continue to play a subordinate role because they cannot develop into a power that is both continental and maritime. They will continue playing some role between the two rivals, the big one, which is the United States, and the minor one, which is the Chinese response.

    The American arc connects the Atlantic to the Indian Ocean, and goes up the Persian Gulf. The Chinese are interested in the Middle East because it is an extension of the core. Iran is of great interest because if it is not part of the arc, it does give China some relief. If Iran — and Afghanistan — were part of this arc, it would make things even more impossible for China.

ISLAMIC CONTINENTAL POWER

OKB: Islam penetrated most successfully into Central Asia over a millennium ago. So a lot that came out of Central Asia in succeeding centuries would have been under the Islamic banner, would it not?

WGW: Islam became part of the continental core because of the Turko-Mongol conversion. They broke into Russia, into Eastern Europe, and into the Mediterranean to link up with the Arab world all along the southern coast of that sea. They broke into Iran and India as well. This was the most cohesive expression of continental power to reach out to the sea. The Russians really became a bastion against the Islamic world. Under Peter the Great, they wanted to reverse matters and take control over the core from the Islamic world. To some extent they did win the battle for the core. The core now certainly includes many Russian cultural traits.

Once upon a time, the Arabic-Islamic world stretched from North Africa all the way past Turkic regions into *Xinjiang*, and into large parts of Russia and along the coastline of the Indian Ocean. This Arabic consolidation of the core pushed the Europeans ever more to the fringe. The Europeans fought back, but failed. The Greek–Roman Empire had controlled the Mediterranean, but that was lost, and control over that sea was divided ... till today. Crusade after crusade failed to push the Muslims back. It was only when the problem became redefined by maritime power in modern times, that the Europeans could overcome this incessant pressure. With global economic development, they could finally confine this power from the

East. The last battle is over the Tigris-Euphrates Fertile Crescent, and over the last half a century we have been seeing this take place. The Anglo-Americans, through Israel, are still trying to control this part of the world. This contest will continue for a while yet.

OKB: I had always wondered why the BBC, in its international broadcasts, is always so concerned about the Middle East.

WGW: Very concerned! For the Europeans, the East starts there. The Greeks defined Asia, and the West has retained the perspective of the Orient beginning from the Bosphorus. The Greco-Roman civilization — and Christianity — was linked to this. Jerusalem is there, and that cannot be shaken off. So the main story for the West has always emanated from there.

That has been a very powerful core precisely because the Central Asian world was tied up with the Islamic world of the Mediterranean. In fact, deep down, it had always been the case; even in the days of the Babylonian and the Egyptian civilizations, the linkage between Central Asia, the North African coast and the Mediterranean was always there. The Mediterranean was one outlet for the Central Asian core to reach the sea. It was originally Greek and Roman, but Islam provided the link between the Middle East and Central Asia, between the Steppes and the desert. With that the Europeans were pushed further into being a fringe, cut off from the riches of the East.

Ever since then they had been trying to find an answer to the Muslim blockade. The crusades cost a lot of lives, and it was only when they went to sea that the Europeans finally had a chance to break through.

OKB: Along the coasts of northern Europe, the much-feared maritime movement southwards by the seafaring Vikings would have overlapped in historical impact with the Mediterranean legacy's movement northward. How did this influence later developments, if at all?

WGW: My own feeling about the Vikings is that they were on the fringe, more on the fringe than many others. And like other fringe peoples, they wanted to penetrate continental regions. But they had no real chance to do that. They did not have the numbers, and they were seafarers. And by the time they got going, they were too marginal. By land, they could do very little.

A handful of Swedes turned up in Rus, and in the Ukraine. They couldn't survive there. Quite frankly, there were just not enough of them. They tried to get to the Mediterranean but it was too far again — several bridges too far. Normandy was about the furthest they could go. They were trying to do what the Portuguese did hundreds of years later; which was to push out to sea. But they were too far north; they kept coming up against the coasts of Iceland, the Faroe Islands, Greenland and the Canadian coast. The seas were often blocked by ice, so their landings and travel were very much limited to the northern regions. They could still go quite far out to sea, no question about that. They were pioneers, but again it goes to show that the fringe can do very little.

The Japanese and the Chinese were also trying to reach out along the Pacific coastline, but there was nothing there worth risking their lives for.

OKB: Today the Vikings are generally remembered as just barbarians.

WGW: I know a couple of people who are great Viking scholars, digging up Viking graves and so on. They say these people were certainly not barbarians. They had their religions, their rituals, and a great social sense. They were in a way traders trying to trade, but because — and this was a kind of excuse — they never had the numbers, the further away they sailed, the more they had to just grab and run. Functioning in the Mediterranean was really too difficult, but they had to try to get there because that was where the centre of civilization was for them.

OKB: The settlements they managed to create functioned very often as stockades.

WGW: That was the best they could do. The Celts and the Anglo-Saxons were a bit too difficult for them. So until William the Conqueror (1028–87) defeated the newly crowned King Harold in 1066, all they could do was nibble at the edges. They would have loved to do more, but they just didn't have the numbers. Numbers count in history. Whether you are a democracy or a monarchy, numbers count.

OKB: In our region, Indonesia is always important because of that, if nothing else.

WGW: Well, you remember how Napoleon dismissed papal power by asking, "How many battalions does the Pope have?"

CONTINENTAL AMERICA

OKB: Can you comment on the American Civil War and the economic and ideological differences between the North and the South? Are these relevant to our discussion about the continental and the maritime? Was the South more a continental type of culture, while the North wasn't?

WGW: Well, both the Yankees and the Confederates became continental. They were in the middle of going continental back then. Once you go beyond the Appalachians, you are continental. For two hundred years, from the first settlement down to the Civil War, the Americans were coastal dwellers and maritime in nature. They were still Atlantic settlers. Going too far inland would require them to fight the natives all the time. But once the Industrial Revolution began and advanced guns were produced, the game changed.

The history of the Wild West can be measured through the advances of weaponry — by the next better gun, be it the six-shooter or the rifle. Each step of the way they stayed ahead of the natives, who were buying guns from the settlers. But soon the Yankees were producing guns on American soil.

Now, the Civil War was the first to be fought in a modern way, as a mixture of frontal battle and guerilla warfare. The classical thing to do in Europe, right down to the Napoleonic War, and even the Franco-German War, was to face off against each other. Two armies confronted each other, one trying to overwhelm the other. In World War I this led to a stalemate. The American Civil War was fought differently. When outnumbered, the Confederates carried out successful guerilla attacks against the Yankees, leading the Yankees to adopt similar tactics as well. All the confrontational battles resulted in a disastrous human toll. Both sides used the most modern equipment available. During this time the armament industry grew fantastically. The South had less, and had to buy from the British, who sympathized with them. They lost in the end because their arms were cruder and less efficient.

The Confederates' point of view was that the Yankees beat them with technologies, not because they were braver or better fighters: "The South fought for a cause while the North did it for money and greed." There is an element of truth in that. The

Yankees were the capitalists and the industrialists. Steel and iron were still the basis of industrial revolution, and all the steelworks were in Pittsburgh and Pennsylvania. The most sophisticated armoury works were in New York and New England from the very beginning. So in a way, the victory was a victory of industrial revolution technology over an agrarian world. But the war was very much a continental one, unlike the sea battles England had been fighting since William the Conqueror.

OKB: There is an American tradition, obvious in popular literature and in Hollywood road movies, about urbanites travelling into the rural wild and meeting weirdoes and getting into trouble. Is that connected to how the West was won?

WGW: The conquest of the West was in many ways achieved by defeated Confederate soldiers. After having lost their homes, they just went westward. Many so-called cowboys were southerners. The northerners provided the capital, built the railways, created the postal system, sailed around to San Francisco, and provided the lawyers and the politicians — all the guys in smart pants, as it were. In the meantime, the guys on horseback, killing and shooting their way westward like Billy the Kid, were southerners. They were the ones who went to Texas and threw the Mexicans out. And it was Texans who went into Oklahoma, and crossed the Rockies.

The northerners provided the brains and the money, but the brawn and the fighting — with the Indians especially — came from the southerners. This is one reason why to this day the U.S. Army is to a large extent comprised of southerners. They are more ready to join the army than the northerners, who tend to join the navy. Where there is a fight, the southerners don't mind being involved. Armed conflict was the norm, both in the development of the slavery system, and later in the occupation of Indian territories.[1]

The Yankees paid their way. They funded the infrastructure and financed the cowboys to fight each other and bring in the cattle to Chicago. Chicago was from where the beef was moved on to New York, and then to Europe. So, capitalism in the end was more dynamic than slavery. It destroyed the plantation economy of the South. Capitalism was by then a combination of the maritime and the continental. By the time of the Civil War, both sides had started moving into the continent. The northerners' combination of maritime and continental proved more effective, what with technologies emanating from the Industrial Revolution.

In a way technology beat the southerners, who were hard to defeat basically because they were more united than the northerners. The southern army had fantastic morale, and it was not at all certain that the North would triumph. The North fought on because in the end they could no longer afford to lose. They were not united the way the Confederate army was.

THE END OF THE CENTRAL ASIAN CORE

OKB: You have mentioned a few times that it was only in modern times that the Central Asian core was actually destroyed. I wonder about Stalin's project of ethnic classification when applied to that area. What role did that play in undermining the core's integrity?

WGW: My reading of Stalin is that he inherited a Russian empire that was already spread over the whole of Central Asia. Rulers like Peter the Great (1682–1725) and Catherine the Great (1762–96) sent Cossacks and Tartars into Siberia to reach the Pacific. They wished to consolidate the core as their core — a Russian core. This was in reaction to the fact that they had been victims when the Mongols and the Turks pushed into Russia — the Mongols in the north and the Turks further south. Moscow barely survived, so they understood that the core was strategically vital. They were practically part of the core, but had been dominated by peoples who were even more powerful. So now they wanted to expand their role. If they were the core, if Eurasia was totally Russian, then they could control the world. That's my understanding of Peter the Great. The Russians were absorbing technology from the West in order to overcome the core to make sure that it would be theirs and that they would never be the victims again.

Stalin just inherited that legacy. He wanted to make the region more securely Russian, and make the Central Asians junior partners to the Russians. He was not a Russian, and was also concerned about protecting the Georgians and the Caucasians. Recognizing minorities was of course a progressive idea, a part of Marx's and Lenin's thinking. It was modern, secular and inclusive and would enable the Soviet Union to be an even more powerful Russia. Tsarist Russia was fragile because these Turkic states could always turn aggressive. Incorporating them into the Soviet Union would minimize this threat. Stalin would then actually carry on the Tsarist legacy with the help of techniques that would make the core a clearly Russian one — a core for the whole world.

I think it was practically with that same understanding that the maritime nations fought the Cold War. It was about either victory for the core or victory for the maritime edges. The core was now communist, and in the hands of their worst enemy. The edges were under threat again, and from a core regime inspired by a universal doctrine.

Once China also turned communist in 1949, the fear grew even greater. Would China become a vassal state to the Soviet Union? Strategists in Britain and America in the 1950s argued over this. Those who understood China claimed that Mao Zedong would be another Tito, and China could never be a satellite state to the Russians, and therefore encouraged the West to prompt Mao in that direction. Others regarded the communist ideology too great a unifying force, and considered that, if anything, Mao would probably want to take Stalin's place after the latter's death. For these analysts, when Mao refused to accept Khruschev's leadership after Stalin passed away, it just showed that they were right and that the Comintern could come under the control of a Chinese instead of a Russian.

In the end Mao Zedong did become a Tito; but unlike the Yugoslavians, the Chinese could constitute a real threat to Russian dominance. Khruschev could not possibly exert any power over Mao the way Stalin could, and when he tried, the Sino-Soviet break became a reality. This was at the Twentieth Party Congress in 1958, at which Khruschev denounced Stalin.

Liu Shaoqi went to Moscow in 1960 for a crucial meeting with the Russians. Mao had refused to go. *Liu* reported back that close relations between the two were not possible, but argued that China should not break with the Russians for fear that the Americans would then begin bullying Beijing.

This, I think, constituted the background to the Cultural Revolution (1966–76). Mao thought *Liu* had gone too far, and that his supporters within the Chinese Communist Party were inclined to think that World Communism had to stay united. Now, Mao was not that much of a communist to be ideologically tied down by it. He was still a Chinese emperor, and the Chinese emperor part in him said this was not the way to go — China was still China, and China must be Number One. The Great Leap Forward (1958–60) marked the beginning of the disagreement with Khruschev, who had criticized Mao's backyard industrialization for being traditionalist and superstitious. In anger, Mao spoke out against Soviet theorizing and said China would do things her own way. This proved disastrous for the Chinese economy no doubt, but the break with the Russians was now painfully clear.

In the American literature from the 1960s, one sees the Americans wondering, "Is this for real?" One lot said, "Yes it is, and we must take advantage of it and pull the Chinese away from the Russians." Others distrusted the Chinese, and so there was some hesitation over what to do. Henry Kissinger's role was crucial at this point. He took China seriously and, when the opportunity came, as Secretary of State he managed to persuade President Nixon to approach Mao. Nixon was of course totally anti-communist, but it was because of that that he saw the need to make the split between the two communist giants permanent. The Americans were losing in Vietnam at that time, so this was a big opportunity for them to change the game. And Mao Zedong was also waiting for it.

OKB: Had the two communist giants managed to unite, then there would have been one big continental power having a chance also to become a maritime power, just like America.

WGW: What happened after the eighteenth century was the advent of a maritime global economy powered by the Industrial Revolution, which created completely different conditions for continental power. As I said, the global is maritime. A power that is only continental cannot exert global influence in the same way a power like America can.

This was the closing of a chapter in human history. In the last two centuries, after the Industrial Revolution began, pure continental power was just not enough.

Now, the Russians just couldn't break out of those constraints. Their sea was the Arctic Ocean. On all sides — the Baltic, the

Mediterranean, the Bosphorus, the Black Sea — they were blocked. They only had one little port, Vladivostok, to service their empire. How could they become global, if global was maritime? They needed China. They certainly wanted to hang on to Port Arthur — to Dalian. In fact, in the early 1950s the Chinese were relentless in forcing the Russians out of Port Arthur. The Russians were most unwilling to leave. So I would say that the Russian expansion to take the whole of Siberia was actually the last gasp of the Continental Story.

After that it was plain that global power had to be both maritime and continental at the same time. Britain's imperial history would soon show that a maritime power without continental power could not last. Russia's experience would show that continental power without a navy could not get very far.

What's left? Balancing the two forms of power seems the only way if you are to exercise global authority. This is the basis of American power. And the only other country in the world today that can have such a range is China. However, while America has no potential enemy sharing its continental borders, China does. This is America's fantastic historical advantage; *and that advantage is forever*. China cannot have that, because it is forever held back by an eight-thousand-mile land border with Russia, other Central Asian states, India, and ASEAN as well. That entire land border is not secure.

China's power at sea will always be constrained by its vulnerability on land. America is not constrained that way. This advantage is not only geographical — it is a formula whereby your continent is secure, your maritime reach is secure, and you have cyber and air power besides. Together, that makes you quite unbeatable. The Chinese are vulnerable on all these fronts.

OKB: And American oceanic power stretches out in more than one direction.

WGW: Yes, it reaches out eastward and westward. And on the continent itself, they are not threatened. They may self-destruct, but that won't be due to the Chinese.

Note

1. Of related interest is the book by James Webb, *Born Fighting: How the Scots-Irish Shaped America* (New York: Broadway Books, 2004). It attempts — perhaps in parts too eagerly — to explain Southern culture and its attitudes and values through reference to the Scots-Irish and their age-old resistance to the English.

EPILOGUE

REVISITING THE PRESENT

A history of the world, when cogent, holds substantive significance for how the reader is to revisit the present. Furthermore, while a good approach to describing the past may seek to avoid outright predictions, it cannot help but insinuate lines of development into the future.

The discussions I had with Professor Wang Gungwu generally did not go into details specific to each of the regions we touched on. The originality of his ideas certainly reignited my childhood interest in humanity's past. In the months following the completion of the manuscript, I found myself searching red-eyed for history books to deepen my understanding of the issues he brought to my attention and to satisfy the curiosity he so recently reawakened. I now appreciate more than ever how great an impact the past — when properly explained — has on our take on current circumstances.

To summarize, the dialogues revolved around several key points of knowledge. The main argument is that a major actor has often been missing from most understandings of world history, whose impact on human history this side of the Ice Age has been enormous. This is Central Asia, of course, with its particular type of dynamism found in its sustained steppe-based societies.

Civilizational histories have most often been written separately, by largely unconnected peoples found at the Eurasian peripheries, and so it is not strange that they do not always complement each other as narratives. It is through bold perspectives like Professor Wang's, that younger scholars like me are reminded that the parts are not unrelated at all. In fact they are dynamically linked, even if not always in a direct and obvious fashion. Before the global age, global histories were not really possible for want of an empirically global perspective. Even in recent times, most attempts at a global history have been either ideologically or ethnocentrically constructed. By revolving mankind's political history around Central Asian innovativeness and expansionism, Professor Wang weaves a dynamic tapestry upon which events over millennia are easily followed. The didactic power of this approach, to my mind, is simply stunning. The principle of Occam's razor — which prefers the scientific approach that assumes the least complexity — has been well applied by him.

When Francis Fukuyama proclaimed the end of history following the fall of the Berlin Wall, he was misinterpreting what was merely the end of a phase — no doubt an extended one — in human history.[1] The continuation of history since the 1990s testifies to that. History has not ended, it is just entering a new phase following the final subjugation of Central Asia by the many civilizations arrayed against it from its peripheries.

THE AGE OF COLONIALISM

The successful turning of the tables by historically besieged European powers on the rest of the world over the last five hundred years ushered us into the age of global colonialism. This bred us two bloody world wars, one Cold War, numerous social and political revolutions, and reordered the world into nation states. It also developed the capitalist system of production that now pervades the world. Interestingly, as colonialism waned after World War II and huge ideological battles came to an end in the early 1990s, we began to see the rise of the other major Eurasian edges — China and India. Multipolarity in global political and economic power has quickly become the new imaginary of our age. This is in effect the second potent claim made in this book — humanity has entered a totally new phase. The victory of the western edge — and, over time, of the edges as a whole — appears to have been rather thorough in that sense.

While some scholars may argue that civilization was hampered by the Central Asian peoples, there is merit to the counterclaim that in some cases it was due to the need to resist them that settlements at the edges reached the civilizational heights they did. For example, Fernand Braudel recognized their key role in the history of the Far East, specifically India and China, although he classed these pastoral societies more as disturbances than as major protagonists in world history. It appears that his narrow definition of Central Asia did not lead him to recognize the incessant and transformative power these same peoples in various configurations also exerted over the Mediterranean and over Europe as a whole, and not only in East and South Asia.[2]

At the same time, the break from the old phase of human history cannot be expected to be a clean one. No doubt the imageries emanating from the millennia-old trauma of merciless hordes on horseback and in chariots, present in the minds of Europeans, Indians, Chinese, and many other peoples, will continue to infect international relations, poison human ties, and steer policymakers for decades to come. However, a richer understanding offered in this book, of the age-old continent-wide political dynamics that differentiated regions and perpetuated distrust and animosity between civilizations can lessen such harmful legacies.

With the advancement of maritime technologies, the Europeans managed to traverse the oceans, breaking the stranglehold that their ancient enemies to the east and south had exercised on them. The extensive power of Central Asia was no doubt felt in all directions, but the East and South Asians did not conceive of the traversing of the oceans as a solution to their perpetual security dilemmas. For millennia the Chinese rebuilt and repaired their Great Wall, keeping the political focus westward and northward, even as their economic base moved towards warmer and wetter climes. The long voyages of Admiral *Zheng He* during the early *Ming* period were an exception, and even they were cancelled in favour of expenditure on continental defence instead. Seeing how the next invasion of China did in fact come from within the continent in the form of the Manchus, this switch was justified.

The Indian subcontinent may have had the advantage of the Himalayas as a defensive wall, but this simply meant that invasions were compressed into coming from the narrow northwest passage instead, wave after wave, through today's Pakistan, Afghanistan and Iran. Those flows of invaders went easily westwards from there into Mesopotamia and Asia Minor towards Egypt and the Mediterranean Sea.

Interestingly, and this shows how cogent the perspective adopted in this book is, nationalists in China and India in the twentieth century blamed their last Central Asian conquerors for their civilizations' inability to resist the European colonialists. In India, the fact of the Mughal conquerors being Muslims was made a politically salient reason for resistance, as had been the case all along Europe's eastern and southern front. In the Far East, religion did not play a role in the discarding of the Manchus by the Chinese. Whatever the strategic content of this blame game, the phenomenon itself does act as a reminder to us of how powerful the Central Asian kings and khans actually were, and the effectiveness of their warrior classes.

Between the time that Kublai Khan extended the Mongol Empire to cover the whole of China in 1260 and the fall of the Manchu dynasty in 1911, the indigenous Chinese were in charge only during the *Ming*, which reigned from 1368 to 1644, i.e., 276 out of 650 years. As the Manchus were crushing the last of the *Ming* resistance to their invasion — finalized in 1683 with the defeat of rebels holed out in Taiwan — the Moghul Empire in India, which had been consolidated under Akbar the Great (reigned 1556–1605), was being turned into an Islamic state under his great-grandson Aurangzeb (reigned 1658–1707). Decay and chaos followed his long reign, leaving a power vacuum that the English East India Company would fill by the end of the eighteenth century.[3]

Direct English military power was felt in China only a half century later, when modern gunboats forced the *Qing* Emperor to open up key trading ports to Europeans traders following the First Opium War (1839–42).

Where the western Eurasian edge was concerned, the fall of Constantinople in 1453 secured a new foothold for the Muslim Turks from which effective military campaigns against Europe could be launched. The line between Christian Europe and the Muslim world was to be decided only in 1580 after decades of sea battles in the Mediterranean. That line remains today.

The Muslim Moor presence in Spain ended in 1492, the same year Christopher Columbus reached America by sea and signalled the conquest of the New World — and soon also much of the Old World.

GOING MARITIME

The third point poignantly made in the dialogues is that the global — the modern age — is maritime. Though a recent development, the conquest of the seas was an amazingly effective solution to a problem as old as human civilization itself. Maritime adventurism and technological innovation happened in response to the relentless forces of a Central Asia that had expanded over time to threaten civilizations situated at the fringes. And this innovation coalesced in Europe for various reasons.

It has now been over half a millennium since Christopher Columbus crossed the Atlantic, and much has changed in the way of political thought and human organization. Sea power has admirably managed to counteract the power of continentally based armies, aided by the many innovations coming out of the European Renaissance, the Reformation and the Enlightenment.

Today the global balance of power still favours the western edge, which now includes the Americas. The United States — and this is the fourth key point to take away from this discussion — is in principle unassailable, if its power base is understood from Professor Wang's standpoint. Not only does this big power have a navy that is peerless, its land borders are totally secure. This cannot be said of any other potential competitor today.

EQUESTRIAN POWER

Two areas that I am personally drawn to do more research on after working on this book are, first, the role of horses in Central Asian development, and second, the flows of people and culture out of the Central Asian Steppes, especially in prehistoric times.

Possessing effective and reliable means for traversing great — especially barren — distances is necessary for any army dreaming of long-distance surprise conquests. At sea, having steady ships, state support and navigational skills was what allowed the

Iberian kingdoms to be the first to circumnavigate the globe, and to loot and colonize the New World. In losing superiority at sea by the start of the seventeenth century, the Spaniards and the Portuguese also lost the ability to maintain their empires, enabling latecomers like the Dutch and the English instead to achieve wealth and power beyond what their size alone should allow. On land, the ability to mobilize warriors over long bleak expanses for swift plunder and sudden conquests required the domestication of the horse. The impact Central Asia had on the world would not have been possible without their early success in domesticating a huge number of animals — and none of these was as important as the horse. Warriors on horseback were an unbeatable innovation. And once armed with a powerful bow, they became the stuff of nightmares for their enemies.

Chariots seemed to have appeared in Eurasia over three thousand years ago, and soon reached the Indian subcontinent with the migration of the Indo-Aryans. Chariots turned up in China by 1200 BC, at the end of the *Shang* period. This ties in with the phenomenon of the royal hunt, apparently centred around the Iranian plateau, and covering adjacent regions such as "Mesopotamia, Asia Minor, North India and Transcaucasia". Such hunting was also noted in the western regions of China, where there was "a fascination with hunting dogs, fine horses, and falconry".[4] Weapons of war and hunting tools were of course closely related, enhanced by early advances in metallurgy.

> In the Old World there are two principal types [of bows]: the composite or reflex bow of eastern Eurasia and the single piece or "self-bow" of northwestern Eurasia. Both were widely employed in hunting and in warfare.[5]

Interestingly, although the *Equus* species is believed to have evolved in the Americas, it had become extinct there about nine thousand years ago despite having survived the Ice Age. It was in Central Asia that the horse was tamed, and once tamed it had the greatest bearing on the development of human history.

Horses are believed to have been domesticated in what is today's Ukraine as early as 4000 BC, and they were being ridden by 3700 BC. Pastoral nomads had appeared by 2000 BC, maintaining huge herds in the Steppes, and engaging in seasonal migration. It was just one small step for these horsemen to take from herding and hunting to marauding and pillaging.[6]

> The nomads, masters of horse-borne mobility (and possessing a large amount of the world's horsepower), became fearsome warriors whose lightning-like raids and clouds of arrows terrified their victims. Their modes of warfare changed little over millennia.[7]

In Karen Armstrong's *The Great Transformation*, she argues that the Axial Age, during which universalist ethics appeared in dispersed regions of the world, was a reaction to the cruel and endless warfare waged by Eurasian peoples using technologies learned from northern India and Mesopotamia. Armed with bronze weapons from the Armenians, riding horses they had tamed, and shooting arrows from their powerful bows, they set forth to enjoy "the fruits of mobility".

> Violence escalated in the steppes as never before. Even the more traditional tribes, who simply wanted to be left alone, had to learn the new military techniques in order to defend themselves. A heroic age had begun. Might was right; chieftains sought gain and glory; and bards celebrated aggression, reckless courage, and military prowess.[8]

As understood in Professor Wang's narrative, the core is not only limited to societies based in Central Asia proper. Along the eastern Eurasian edge, in China, the divide between agriculturalists and pastoralists was a most obvious representation, and the geographical divide was also apparent. But given geographical, political and historical differences, and the length of time we are dealing with, an array of mixes between city dwellers and nomads came into being in all directions, and have to be acknowledged.

The affinity of peoples who had migrated out of Central Asia to the attitudes and cultures of the core region is something that requires more looking into. As recently as the late seventeenth century, after the largely Sinicized Jurchen state had conquered China and changed its name to the Great *Qing*, it decided to ban all Chinese from Manchuria itself. This was to keep it pristine for the use of the Manchus to satisfy their increasing need to keep their members as closely acquainted with the pastoral lifestyle as possible. Examples of such an attachment to the culture-sustaining wide-open pastoral spaces and horseback and hunting lifestyle of Central Asia have been witnessed in all the directions in which migratory waves and military campaigns have ventured.

One final, and perhaps the most important, factor to contemplate in Professor Wang's history of the world, is the difference between imperialist politics and localized politics. What also defines the modern age, apart from nation states, maritime power and science and technology, is the notion of power coming from below, broadly understood by us as democracy. This was something that existed in ancient Athens and in German tribal customs, among others. It was also a consciousness that trading towns also tended to inculcate.

The new phase in human history, following the overshadowing of continental forces by maritime power, is characterized by the decentralization of political legitimacy. Power now comes as much from the bottom as it does from the top, and the need to balance these two forces informs all varieties of political organization in modern times. Theocracies and aristocracies no longer hold sway, and all political power today has to at least state that it is of and for the people, if not by the people.

These are just some of the thoughts immediately inspired by my dialogues with Professor Wang. More will come to mind as I contemplate further the many lines of thought he has provided me. I look forward to exploring them.

Notes

1. Francis Fukuyama, *The End of History and the Last Man* (Simon & Schuster, 1992).
2. Fernand Braudel, *A History of Civilizations*, translated by Richard Mayne (1987; repr., Penguin Books, 1993).
3. See Francis Watson, *India: A Concise History* (1974; repr., Singapore: Thames & Hudson, 1979); and Jacques Gernet, *A History of Chinese Civilization*, translated by J.R. Forster (Cambridge University Press, 1982).
4. Thomas T. Allsen, *The Royal Hunt in Eurasian History* (Singapore: Institute of Southeast Asian Studies, 2013), pp. 14–15.
5. Ibid., p. 21.
6. For a thorough discussion on the history of the domestication of the horse and the migratory expansion out of the Steppes, see Pita Kelekna, *The Horse in Human History* (Cambridge University Press, 2009).
7. Peter B. Golden, *Central Asia in World History* (Oxford University Press, 2011), p. 12.
8. Karen Armstrong, *The Great Transformation: The World in the Time of Buddha, Socrates, Confucius and Jeremiah* (London: Atlantic Books, 2006), pp. 6–7.

LIST OF PUBLICATIONS BY WANG GUNGWU SINCE 2008

(As compiled by the East Asia Institute, National University of Singapore, 2 April 2013)

Books

Another China Cycle: Committing to Reform. Singapore: World Scientific, 2014. 264 pages.

Renewal: The Chinese State and the New Global History. Hong Kong: Chinese University Press, 2013. 172 pages.

《华人与中国：王赓武自选集》. 上海：人民出版社, 2013. 376 pages.

Renewal: The Chinese State and the New Global History. Hong Kong: Chinese University Press, 2013. 172 pages.

Another China Cycle: Committing to Reform. Singapore: World Scientific, 2013.

Wang Gungwu: Educator and Scholar. Edited by Zheng Yongnian and Phua Kok Khoo. Singapore: World Scientific, 2013. 411 pages.

Wang Gungwu, Junzi, Scholar-gentleman, in Conversation with Asad-ul Iqbal Latif. Singapore: Institute of Southeast Asian Studies, 2010, 261 pages.

中国的'主义'之争 — 从'五四运动'到当代 (郑永年合编). 新加坡：八方文化创作室. Singapore: World Scientific, 2009. 381 pages.

Voice of Malayan Revolution: The CPM Radio War against Singapore and Malaysia, 1960–1981 (Editor, with Ong Weichong). Singapore: S. Rajaratnam School of International Studies, 2009. 350 pages.

Hong Kong Challenge: Leaning In and Facing Out. Hong Kong: University of Hong Kong Centre of Asian Studies Hong Kong Culture & Society Occasional Paper Series, 2009. 12 pages.

China and the New International Order (Editor, with Zheng Yongnian). London: Routledge, 2008. 316 pages.

Articles/Papers

"Student Movements: Malaya as Outlier in Southeast Asia". Review Article, *Journal of Southeast Asian Studies* 44, no. 3 (2013): 511–18.

"Continental Power". *Global ARC Quarterly* [Geopolitics: Our interview with Wang Gungwu] (Spring 2013): 10–19.

"Chineseness: The Dilemmas of Place and Practice". In *Sinophone Studies: A Critical Reader*, edited by Sih Shu-mei, Chien-hsin Tsai and Brian Bernards. New York: Columbia University Press, 2013, pp. 131–44.

"新移民：何以新？为何新？". In 赵红英、张春旺主编《世界视野：走出国门的中国新移民》，北京：中国华侨出版社, 2013, pp. 3–17.

"Thoughts on Four Subversive Words". *Asia-Pacific Journal of Anthropology* 13, no. 2 (April 2012): 192–202.

"王赓武访谈录——在全球化时代反思中国历史"，《中国人类学评论》, vol. 22, 2012年, pp. 138–52.

"China's Historical Place Reclaimed". Review article in *Australian Journal of International Affairs* 66, no. 4 (2012): 486–92.

"A Two-Ocean Mediterranean". In *Anthony Reid and the Study of the Southeast Asian Past*, edited by Geoff Wade and Li Tana. Singapore: Institute of Southeast Asian Studies, 2011, pp. 69–84.

"Post-Imperial Knowledge and Pre-Social Science in Southeast Asia". In *Decentring and Diversifying Southeast Asian Studies: Perspectives from the Region*, edited by Goh Beng-Lan. Singapore: Institute of Southeast Asian Studies, 2011, pp. 93–124.

"Sun Yat-sen and the Origins of Modern Chinese Politics". In *Sun Yat-sen: Nanyang and the 1911 Revolution*, edited by Lee Lai To and Lee Hock Guan. Singapore: Institute of Southeast Asian Studies and Chinese Heritage Centre, 2011, pp. 1–14.

"Link-points in a Half-Ocean: Introduction to the Worlds of East and Southeast Asian Seas". In *Connecting Seas and Connected Ocean Rims: Indian, Atlantic, and Pacific Oceans and China Seas Migrations from the*

1830s to the 1930s, edited by Donna R. Gabaccia and Dirk Hoerder. Leiden: Brill, 2011, pp. 169–71.

"孙中山与现代中国政治的起源". 收入廖建裕主编。《再读孙中山、南洋与辛亥革命》。新加坡：华裔馆，东南亚研究院，2011, pp. 3–17.

"中国情结：华化、同化与异化"，《北京大学学报》，no. 5, 2011, pp. 145–52.

"黨國民主：三代海外華人的進與退"，《中央研究院近代史研究所集刊》，Bulletin no. 67, 2010, pp. 1–15.

"Party and Nation in Southeast Asia". *Millennial Asia: An International Journal of Asian Studies* 1, no. 1 (2010): 41–57.

"The Peranakan Phenomenon: Pre-national, Marginal, and Transnational". In *Peranakan Chinese in a Globalizing Southeast Asia*, edited by Leo Suryadinata. Singapore: Chinese Heritage Centre and National University of Singapore Museum Baba House, 2010, pp. 14–26.

"Family and Friends: China in Changing Asia". In *Negotiating Asymmetry: China's Place in Asia*, edited by Anthony Reid and Zheng Yangwen. Singapore and Honolulu: NUS & University of Hawai'i Press, 2009, pp. 214–31.

"The Fifty Years Before". In *1959–2009: Chronicle of Singapore: Fifty Years of Headline News*, edited by Peter H.L. Lim. Singapore: Editions Didier Millet and National Library Board, 2009, pp. 15–27.

"One Country, Two Cultures: An Alternative View of Hong Kong". In *Rethinking Hong Kong: New Paradigms, New Perspectives*, edited by Elizabeth Sinn, Wong Siu-lun and Chan Wing-hoi. Hong Kong: Centre of Asian Studies, University of Hong Kong, 2009, pp. 1–24.

"Chinese History Paradigms". *Asian Ethnicity* 10, no. 3 (2009): 201–16.

"越洋寻求空间：中国的移民"，《华人研究国际学报》1, no. 1 (2009): 1–49.

"Southeast Asia: Imperial Themes". *New Zealand Journal of Asian Studies* (June 2009): 36–48.

"The China Seas: Becoming an Enlarged Mediterranean". In *The East Asian "Mediterranean": Maritime Crossroads of Culture, Commerce and Human Migration*, edited by Angela Schottenhammer. Wiesbaden: Harrassowitz Verlag, 2008, pp. 7–22.

"Flag, Flame and Embers: Diaspora Cultures". In *The Cambridge Companion to Modern Chinese Cultures*, edited by Kam Louie. Cambridge: Cambridge University Press, 2008, pp. 115–34.

"China and the International Order: Some Historical Perspectives". In *China and the New International Order*, edited by Wang Gungwu and Zheng Yongnian. London: Routledge, 2008, pp. 21–31.

"南侨求学记：不同的时代，走不同的路". 收入李元瑾，《跨越疆界与文化调适》. 南洋理工大学中华语言文化中心；八方文化创作室，2008, pp. 13–28.

"内与外的解析－论海外华人作家",《世界华侨华人研究》. 第一辑，2008, pp. 1–10.

Book Reviews

Review of *Religion and Chinese Society*, edited by John Lagerway. Hong Kong: Chinese University Press and Ecole francaise d'Extreme-Orient, 2006. Two volumes. *International Sociology* 24, no. 2 (2009): 191–94.

Review of *Sources of East Asian Tradition. Vol. 1; Premodern Asia; Vol. 2, The Modern Period*, edited by Wm. Theodore de Bary. New York: Columbia University Press, 2008. I: 909 pages; II: 1,152 pages. *East Asia: An International Quarterly* 26, no. 3 (2009): 259–61.

INDEX

A
Africa, 82–83, 215–16
age of colonialism, 229–32
age-old continent-wide political dynamics, 230
agrarian structure, collapse of, 145
Akbar the Great, 232
Alexander, 3, 59–60
America, 226
    Britain and, 135
    defence services in, 183
American arc, 215
American Civil War, 219, 220
American Revolution, 108
American system, 142
Ames, Roger T., 211n6
Anderson, Ben, 194
Anglo-Americans, 10–11, 188, 217
    imperial system, 17
Anglo-Dutch relationship, 111
Anglo-Dutch Treaty, 99
Anglo-French powers, 82–83
Anglo-Japanese alliance, 98
Anglo-Peranakan stage, 199, 200
Anglo-Portuguese ties, 86
anonymity, 197
anti-colonialism, 123–24
anti-imperialism, 123–24
Appalachians, 220
Arabic consolidation of core, 216
Arabic-Islamic world, 216
Arab-Persian shipping, 73
armed conflict, 221–22
Armstrong, Karen, 235
Association of Southeast Asian Nations (ASEAN), 57, 90
    vs. EU, 137–38
Austronesian migration, 119
authenticity, concept of, 194
authoritarian democracy, 210
Axial Age, 235

B
Babylonians, 3–4
Balkanization, 90
Battle of Salamis, 92n2
Battle of Talas, 20
Beiyang, 97

Book of Change, The (Yi Jing), 204
bows, principal types of, 234
Braudel, Fernand, 230
British Commonwealth, 136–37
British democracy, 115
British Empire, 125
British Isles, 112–13
British Parliament, 157
British scholarship, 116
Buddhism, 39–41
   in India, 176
bureaucratic system, 143
Burmese naval power, 66
Byzantines, 25

C

capitalism, 144–45, 222
   China, 146
Caribbean, 77
Catherine the Great, 222
Catholic Church, 178
Catholicism in the Philippines, 78
Central Asia, extensive power of, 231
Central Asian core, 222–27
Central Asian development, 233
Central Asian Steppes, 233
Chams, 64, 65
chariots, 234
Chiang Kai-shek, 144–46
China, 214
   bureaucracy, 4

Cold War, 83
communism, 142, 145
communist party, 151, 156–57
Confucian order, 27–41
continental front, 167–73
continental power, 165–66
decolonization, 135
democracy, 43, 126–27
economic development, 127–28
economic growth, 130–31
education, 5
entry into global age, 1–6
vs. India, 129–39
navies, 164
Opium War in, 141, 164, 172
political-economic structure of, 138–39
religion's capture of politics, 19–25
second-largest economy, 142
and soft power concept, 173–91
in world history, 6–19
Chinese agrarian system, 145
Chinese Buddhists, 152, 205
Chinese capitalism, 146
Chinese Communist Party, 101, 224
Chinese historiography, 101
Chinese imperial state, 142–43
Chinese labour, 196
Chinese library, 201
Chinese literary culture, 202
Chinese Muslims, 152

Chinese nationalists, first
    generation of, 144
Chinese school, 203
Chinese territory, 100
Chinese universities, 191
Chola Empire, 67
Christian, 21–22
    vs. Muslim conflict, 82–83
Christian Europe and Muslim
    world, line between, 232
Christianity, 217
Church, 24
Churchill, Winston, 82
civilizational centre, Eurasia as, 6
Civil War, 220, 222
Clive, Robert, 14, 55n3
Cold War, 83, 90–91, 135, 149,
    165, 214
colonialism, age of, 229–32
Columbus, Christopher, 69,
    83–84, 232–33
communism, 142, 145
Communist China, 94
Communist Party, 100–101, 144,
    151, 156–57
Confederates, 220
Confucian, 5, 142–43, 151, 179
    heritage, 142
    order, 27–41
    system, 18
    thinking, 142
Confucian Institute, 201
Confucianism, 28, 34–38, 43, 45,
    142, 150–51, 205

Confucian literati, 143
Conservative Party, 115
conservatives, 116
constitutionalism, 116
Continental America, 219–22
continental and maritime power,
    combining, 213–16
    Central Asian core, 222–27
    Continental America, 219–22
    Islamic continental power,
        216–19
continental fringes, 214
continental holiday idea, 81
Continental Phase, Chinese
    history, 8
continental power system, 118
cultural imperialism, 175
Cultural Revolution, 224

D
decolonization, 94, 135, 136
defensive mechanism, 121–22
Deng Xiaoping, 156, 158
    reforms, 141
Dong Xi Yang, 96, 97
Dongyang, 97
Dutch case, 107
Dutch, defensive mechanism,
    121–22
Dutch East India Company, 112

E
East Asia in modern times,
    94–106

East Asian cultures, 160
Eastern edge of Europe-Asia landmass, 141
East India Company, 15–16, 122
economic power, 174
  multipolarity in, 230
Elliot, Charles, 87
English-Dutch relationship, 111
English East India Company, 232
Equestrian power, 233–37
Equus species, 234
Eurasian continent, 121
Eurasian continental model, 119
Eurasian globality, 162
Eurasian peripheries, 229
Eurasian power structure, 118
Eurasian power system, 134
Europeans, 24–25
European Union (EU), ASEAN vs., 137–38
Europe-Asia landmass, eastern edge of, 141
Europe, local politics in, 25–27
examination system, 36

F
Fa concept, 45
Fa laws, 155
fall of Constantinople, 232
Falun Gong, 55n7
farming in China, 12
fascism, 149
Fei Xiaotong, 102
First Opium War, 232
foreign capitalism, 146
"forward defence", 80, 91
France of Napoleon, 114
Franco-German War, 220
Franco-Prussian War, 108
French colonialism, 64
French Revolution, 107–8
Fujian province, 96
Fukuyama, Francis, 229
Fuzhou, 97

G
Germanic tribal systems, 25
German-Viking tradition, 62
GIC. *See* Government Investment Corporation (GIC)
global age, China entry into, 1–6
Global-Anglo, 200
global economic development, 216
global political power, multipolarity in, 230
Global-Sino, 200
Government Investment Corporation (GIC), 181
Great Leap Forward, 131, 224
Great Transformation, The (Armstrong), 235
Great Wall, 231
Greco-Roman civilization, 217
Greco-Roman tradition, 5, 59–61, 182
Greek Christian, 61

Greek–Roman Empire, 216
Greeks, urban civilization development, 59–60
Guangxi, 103

H
Hainanese Association, 193
Han Chinese, 53–55, 102, 129
Han dynasty, 34, 143
Han Feizi, 31
Han Hui, 104
Han Muslims, 104
Han Wudi, 32
Hastings, Warren, 14
Hebei province, 147
Hindu-Buddhist Malay Archipelago, 21
Hindu-Buddhist tradition, 117–19
Hobbes, Thomas, 46
Ho Chi Minh, 189
horse-borne mobility, 235
Hu Shi, 211n7

I
imperial system, 141
India
  British entry into, 15–16
  Buddhism destroyed in, 176
  vs. China, 129–39
  Columbus, 83–84
  trade with, 72
Indian Civil Service, 132
Indian Ocean, 58, 73

Indochine, 95
Indonesian communist party, 91
industrialization, Soviet Model of, 131
Industrial Revolution, 220, 222, 225
Inner Asian Frontiers (Lattimore), 13
International Law, 154–55
Internet communication, 196–97
Iran, 215
Iranian Revolution, 177
Irish peoples, 81–82
Islam, 22, 24
Islamic continental power, 216–19

J
Japanese modelling of West, 144
Japanese navy, 184
Japanese territories, 100
Japanese war, 146
Java, 62
Javanese style, 117
Jews, 4
Jia, 45
Jiafa, 45–46
Jiang Zemin, 158
Judeo-Christian tradition, 5
Junjichu, 53

K
Kangxi, 18
Kang Youwei, 54–55

Khan, Kublai, 232
Khmers, 63–64
Kissinger, Henry, 225
Koxinga, 93n14
Kuomintang of China, 100, 141, 144
  nationalism, 145

L
labour, China, 196
Labour Party, 115, 116
Laos, 64–65
League of National Empires, 124
Liang dynasty, 39
liberalism, 146
Li concept, 44–45, 155
Li Keqiang, 158
Liu Shaoqi, 91, 224
Locke, John, 116
long-distance ocean trade, 74
loyalties, 115
Luguoqiao incident, 147
Luther, Martin, 26

M
Macedonians, 59–60
Mahbubani, Kishore, 199
Malacca Strait, 170
Malay Archipelago, 106
Malay Peninsula, 105
Malays, 119–21
Malay style, 117
Manchu dynasty, 232
Manchus, 52–54
  use of, 236

Mandala system, 133
Mandala Theory, 119
Mao Zedong, 28–29, 83, 102, 131–32, 145, 156, 224–25
Marco Polo Bridge Incident, 147
maritime, 232–33
  culture, 119–21
  technologies, advancement of, 231
maritime power
  combining continental and. *See* continental and maritime power, combining
  overshadowing of continental forces by, 236–37
Marx, Karl, 108
Mauritius Campaign, 92n5
Mediterranean, 217
  Christianity, 61
  conquering oceans, 73–86
  small islands, big empire, 86–92
  Southeast Asia, 57–73
Meiji's imperialistic view, 144
Melayu-Peranakan stage, 199
Mencius, 34, 43, 46
military power, 174
Ming dynasty, 48–49, 164, 198, 231–32
minzu zhengce, 102
Mongol Empire, 232
Mongols, 223
Mon-Khmers, 63, 65
monotheistic system, 4

Mountbatten Command, 94
Mo Yan, 41
Mughal conquerors, 231
Mughal Empire, 67–68
Muslim Moor, 232
Muslim Rebellion, 211n3
Muslims, 65–66
   Christian conflict vs., 82–83
   war in Xinjiang, 172
   world, line between Christian Europe and, 232
Myanmar
   government, 169
   Indians in, 168

N
Nanhai Trade, 96
Nanyang, 96–98
Napoleon, defeat of, 86–87
Napoleonic War, 87, 220
nationalism, Kuomintang, 145
Natural Law, concept of, 154
naval power, 64, 74, 166
Nazism, 149
Neo-Confucian philosophy, 151
Nian Rebellion, 211n3
non-State Confucians, 35–36
Normandy, 218
Nye, Joseph, 175, 181

O
Obama, Barack, 166
Occam's razor, principle of, 229
one-god scheme, 4

Opium War, 97, 141, 164, 172
orthodox interpretation, 101
Ottoman Empire, 70–71

P
Palestine, 72–73
pastoral nomads, 235
Penang, 15
People's Liberation Army (PLA), 99, 164, 185
Peranakans, 198–99
Peter the Great, 216, 222–23
Philippines, trade in, 84–85
PLA. *See* People's Liberation Army (PLA)
political legitimacy, decentralization of, 237
politics
   in China, 19–25
   in Europe, 25–27
Port Arthur, 226
Port of Singapore Authority (PSA), 171
port systems, 14–15
Portuguese case, 107
Portuguese engineers, skills of, 68
Portuguese, Malacca under, 78–79
power, global balance of, 233
pragmatic *vs.* pious laws, 154–58
Protestant movement, 26
PSA. *See* Port of Singapore Authority (PSA)

Q

Qianlong, 18–19
Qing dynasty, 18, 104, 164
Qing emperor, 18, 232
Qing Empire, 125
Qing map, 101
Quanzhou, 96

R

Reformation, 26
Renaissance, 26
Ren concept, 44–45
republicanism, 108
revolutionary movements, 145
riverine civilization, 58, 59
Roman Empire, 122
    Christianity, 61
Rousseau, Jean-Jacques, 46–47

S

Sabah, 99
Sarawak, 99
Scandinavians, 59, 62
scholars, 54
School of Oriental and African Studies (SOAS), 96
sea power, 233
SEATO. See Southeast Asia Treaty Organization (SEATO)
secularism, 5
secularization, 28
Security Council, 120–21
Shandong province, 147

Shang dynasty, 12, 22–23
Shen Buhai tradition, 30–31
Singapore, 88–89, 192
    Government Investment Corporation (GIC), 181
Sino-Japanese military conflict, 171
Sino-Japanese War in 1894, 172
Sino-Soviet, 224
    agreement, 101
"Socialism with Chinese Characteristics", 151
Socialist Harmonious Society, 152–53
"soft power", concept of, 173–91
Solomon Islands, 87–88
Song dynasty, 37, 48–49, 180
Southeast Asia, 57–73, 77–78, 85, 88, 95
    in modern times, 94–106
Silk Road, 134
South East Asia Command, 94
Southeast Asia Treaty Organization (SEATO), 90
Soviet Communism, 149
Soviet Model, 131
Soviet Russian Communist model, 149
Soviet Union, 147
Spain, enterprises in, 75–76
Spanish Civil War, 149
Spanish Lake, The (Spate), 84
Spanish Netherlands Empire, 106

Sri Lankan civil war, 171
Standing Committee of the Political Bureau, 158
state-backed private enterprise, 74
State Confucianism, 35–38, 43, 143
Sub-Saharan Africa, 72
Sun Yatsen, 55, 145
Suu Kyi, Aung San, 168–69
systematic government-sponsored massacres, 93n12

T
Taiping Rebellion, 172, 211n3
Tang dynasty, 19–20
Taoists, 32–33
Thais, 65
Tian, 4, 23
Tianxia, 4, 101, 113
Tianzhu, 4–5
Tian Zi, 29
Tibetan independence, idea for, 125
Tigris-Euphrates Fertile Crescent, 217
tortoise shells, 23
Treaty of Tordesillas, 76
Treaty of Westphalia, 107, 113
tribal groups in Eurasia, 20
Tsarist legacy, 223
Tsarist Russia, 223
Turko-Mongol conversion, 216
Two-Ocean Mediterranean, 214

U
Universal Law, 154
urban civilization, Greeks development of, 59–60
urbanity, 59

V
Venetians, 71–72
Vietnam War, 189
Viking scholars, 218
Vladivostok port, 226

W
Wang Anshi, 48–49
Wang Jingwei, 147
Washington Naval Treaty, 98
Weightman, George H., 93n12
Wen, 33–34
Western Eurasian edge, 232
Western model in China, 148
Western societies, Confucian role in, 41
Wild West, 220
William the Conqueror, 219, 221
Wolters, Oliver, 133
World Communism, 224
Wu, 33–34

X
"xia Nanyang", 97
"xia Xiyang", 97
Xi Jinping, 158, 163

Xinjiang, 216
    Muslim war in, 172
Xun Zi, 206–7

Y
Yamamoto, Isoroku, 184
Yankees, 220–22
Yan Xuetong, 187, 188, 211n5
Yin-Yang, 207
Yongle, 51
Yongzheng, 18

Yunnan province
    Muslim rebellion, 211n3
    for oil, 169

Z
Zhang Juzheng, 52
Zheng Chenggong, 88, 93n14
Zheng He, 65, 66, 231
zhonghua minzu, 102
Zhou dynasty, 12, 22–23
Zhou Enlai, 83
Zhuang, 103, 104
Zhu Yuanzhang, 49–51

ABOUT THE AUTHOR

OOI KEE BENG was born and raised in Penang, and is presently the Deputy Director of the Institute of Southeast Asian Studies (ISEAS), Singapore.

He is also Editor of the Penang Institute's *Penang Monthly* (www.penangmonthly.com). He was Visiting Associate Professor at City University of Hong Kong and Adjunct Associate Professor at the Department of Southeast Asian Studies at the National University of Singapore. His PhD thesis is titled *The State and its Changdao: Sufficient Discursive Commonality in National Renewal, with Malaysia as Case Study*. This was completed at Stockholm University's Department of Chinese Studies, where he was a lecturer for several years.

His books include *The Right to Differ: A Biographical Sketch of Lim Kit Siang* (2011); *In Lieu of Ideology: An Intellectual Biography of Goh Keng Swee* (2010); *Between Umno and a Hard Place: The Najib Razak Era Begins* (2010); *Arrested Reform: The Undoing of Abdullah Badawi* (2009); *Malaya's First Year at the United Nations* (2009); *March 8: Eclipsing May 13* (2008); *Lost in Transition: Malaysia under Abdullah* (2008); *Chinese Strategists: Beyond Sun Zi's Art of War* (2007); *Continent, Coast and Ocean: Dynamics of Regionalism in Eastern Asia* (2007, co-edited with Ding Choo Ming); and *The Reluctant Politician: Tun Dr Ismail and His Time* (2006).

The Reluctant Politician won the "Award of Excellence for Best Writing Published in Book Form on Any Aspect of Asia (Non-Fiction)" at the Asian Publishing Convention Awards 2008, while *Continent, Coast, Ocean: Dynamics of Regionalism in Eastern Asia* was named "Top Academic Work" in 2008 by the ASEAN Book Publishers Association (ABPA). He has also translated several Chinese classics on strategy into Swedish and English. These are collected into *Sunzis krigskonst och sju andra kinesiska mästerverk* (with Bengt Pettersson and Henrik Friman, Santérus 2010) and *Chinese Strategists* (2007).

He writes opinion pieces regularly for regional and global mass media on Malaysian matters (see wikibeng.com), including in *The Edge Malaysia*. His most recent books are *Done Making Do: 1Party Rule Ends in Malaysia* (2013) and *ISEAS Perspective: Selections 2012–13* (editor, 2014).

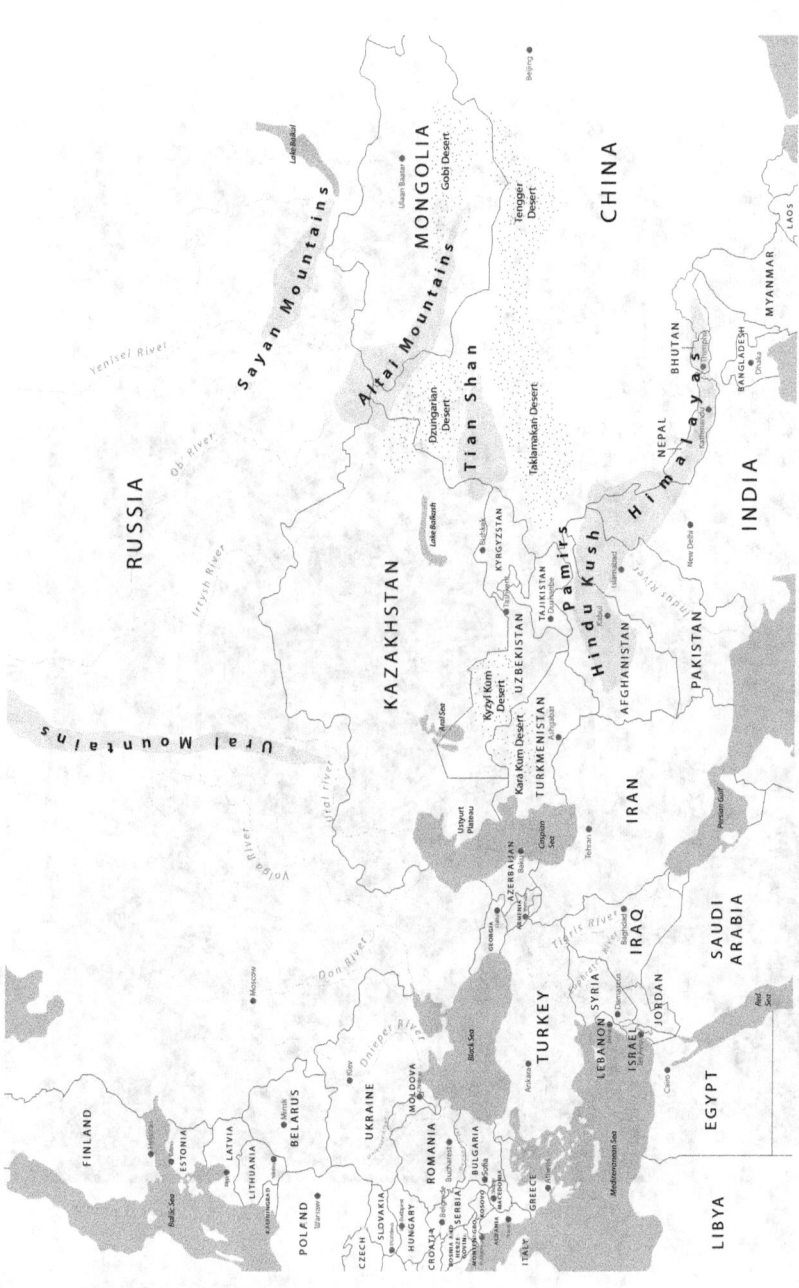

1. Map of Central Asia. Courtesy of Aaron Kao Jiun Feng.

2. The Portuguese are defeated by the Dutch at Jaffnapatnam, 1658.

3. The Great Wall of China today.

4. *The Fall of Constantinople.* Lithograph from *Hutchinson's History of the Nations*, 1915, Dudley, Ambrose (fl. 1920s), Private Collection, The Bridgeman Art Library.

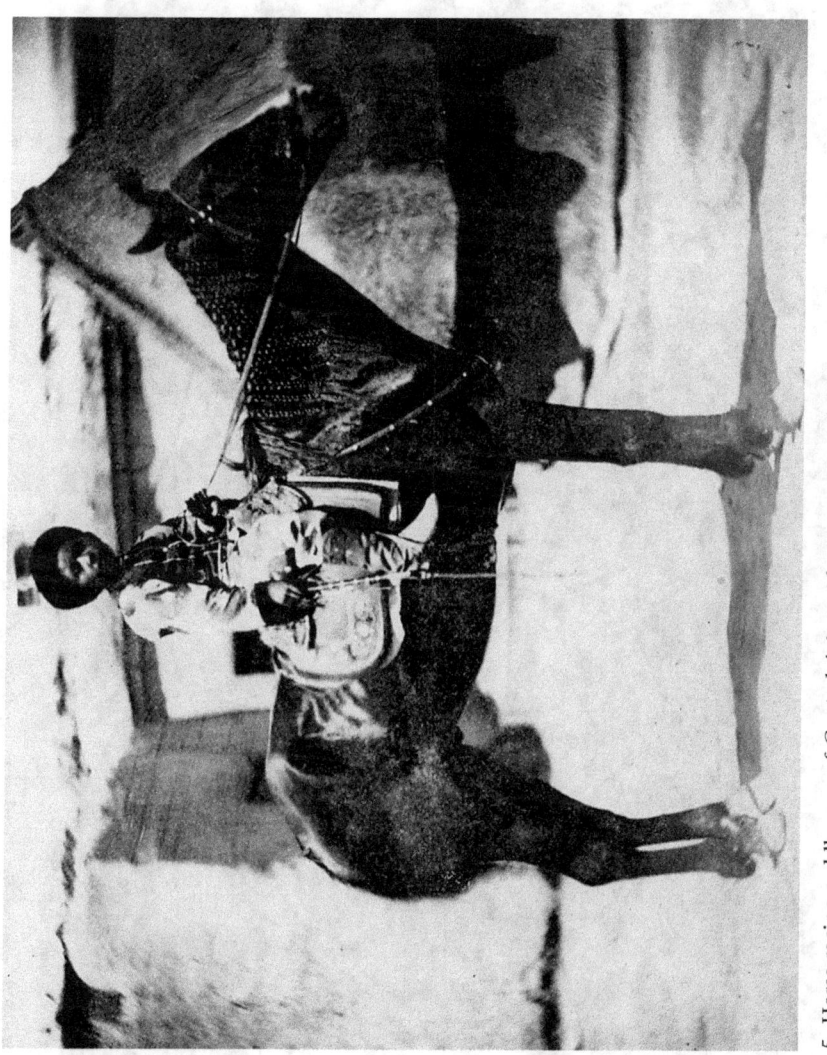

5. Horse racing saddle gear of Central Asia, mid-nineteenth century.

6. *The Charge of the Persian Scythe Chariots at the Battle of Gaugamela.* Engraving by Andre Castaigne (1898–99).

7. *Shah Jahan and Dara Shikoh*, c.1638. Victoria and Albert Museum, London.

8. *Attila, the Scourge of God.* Illustration by Ulpiano Checa.

www.ingramcontent.com/pod-product-compliance
Lightning Source LLC
Chambersburg PA
CBHW071348290426
44108CB00014B/1472